MILLINGTON SAVINGS BANK

Millington Savings Bank is proud to sponsor *Schoolhouses of Early Bernards Township: A Photographic History of Schools.*

Ours is an area rich in history, from the revolutionary beginnings of our country to the present day, positioned squarely in the center of the busy Northeast corridor. For over 95 years, Millington Savings Bank has been privileged to play a part in the growth of this area.

As we say in our slogan, we are *Community-Minded.* It is in this spirit that we proudly sponsor this look back at the wonder and charm of schoolhouses from the early years of Bernards Township. We invite you to enjoy this treasured book today and for years to come.

Gary T. Jolliffe
President & CEO

The Olcott School, Bernardsville, New Jersey, ca. 1905

SCHOOLHOUSES
of Early Bernards Township

—◆—

A Photographic History of Schools

Josephine M. Waltz

THE
DONNING COMPANY
PUBLISHERS

Dedication

———•·—

For June O. Kennedy, who for the past 17 years dedicated
countless hours to teach children and adults the history
of Bernards Township

For the early settlers of the region whose vision was to improve
the quality of life for their children through education

For the children of the past, present, and future

For all the dedicated teachers who enlighten, inspire, and educate hundreds of children each year

Net proceeds from the sale of this book will benefit local school media centers.

The Donning Company Publishers
184 Business Park Drive, Suite 206
Virginia Beach, VA 23462

Steve Mull, General Manager
Barbara Buchanan, Office Manager
Kathleen Sheridan, Senior Editor
Amy Thomann, Graphic Designer
Derek Eley, Imaging Artist
Scott Rule, Director of Marketing
Tonya Hannink, Marketing Coordinator
Susan Adams, Project Research Coordinator

Mary Taylor, Project Director

Library of Congress Cataloging-in-Publication Data

Waltz, Josephine M.
  Schoolhouses of early Bernards Township : a photographic history of schools / by Josephine M. Waltz.
      p. cm.
  Includes bibliographical references and index.
  ISBN–13: 978–1–57864–434–6
  1. School buildings—New Jersey—Bernards (Township)—History. 2. School buildings—New Jersey—Bernards (Township)—Pictorial works. 3. Bernards (N.J.
: Township)—Buildings, structures, etc.—Pictorial works. I. Title.
  LB3218.N5W35 2007
  371.609749'44—dc22
                        2007016085

Printed in the United States of America by Walsworth Publishing Company

Contents

Foreword

Schoolhouses of Early Bernards Township truly is a gift to everyone interested in the story of children's education in the Somerset Hills.

It is a one-of-a-kind book, for it is the only single and complete reference that contains the earliest attempts of parents, clergy, and educators to provide a better future for children.

Mindful that the youth had been denied formal learning, mothers and fathers contributed monetarily and physically to do what was necessary—be it helping to dig, travel via basic transportation, or conduct fundraisers for the education of their children.

New Jersey did not have formal education until the State Legislature enacted a law about 1851. That did not stop the operation of small one-room schoolhouses prior to that time. Primitive at best, these structures were attended by children from the farmhouses of Bernards Township and Bernardsville, and these students persevered—sometimes missing lessons because they were needed on the family farm.

Until the early part of the 20th century, high school was not an option; there wasn't one. Can you imagine centers of learning without electricity, heating, or plumbing with four classes taught by the same teacher in the same room? Some pupils were fortunate after graduation from eighth grade to travel by train to a business school to "round out" their education. Others stayed in school for another year or two, then sought employment locally.

Whatever their choice, they were the generation that supported these early schools and encouraged further enrichment—all evidenced in today's superb school system in Bernards Township and Bernardsville. It must be noted that until 1924, Bernardsville was part of Bernards Township. Although it became a separate municipality, Bernardsville was administered by the Bernards Township Board of Education until 1956, when it established its own school administration.

Schoolhouses of Early Bernards Township is the culmination of an intense two-year project that involved sixth-grade students of the William Annin Middle School in Basking Ridge, their research, and letters to former faculty and former students, all now senior citizens.

Josephine Waltz is to be commended for bringing this noteworthy project to fruition. It is an enjoyable and enlightening read and an invaluable reference that every library, school, educator, and parent should own.

Ms. Waltz's search extended from the ivied walls of Princeton and Rutgers University Libraries to New England and throughout the Middle Atlantic states.

Now, finally, we have before us a book that defines the spirit, courage, and dedication of those who fostered the education that resulted in the school systems of today.

Bravo!

—June O. Kennedy
Bernards Township Historian

Preface

———————◆·◆·◆———————

From the earliest days of Bernards Township, the residents of this small farming community valued education. Although formal elementary education was not required, the Township had eleven one-room schoolhouses in operation by 1844. The outstanding school system that today exists in Bernards Township and Bernardsville has its roots in these simple arrangements—and in the vision and commitment of the parents, educators, and citizens who established this legacy of learning. How did this educational legacy begin? Who was responsible for these schools? Where are these one-room schoolhouses today?

Schoolhouses of Early Bernards Township: A Photographic History of Schools traces the educational structures that served the area's children from the 1700s through the 1960s. This book is a product of a community's efforts to capture the past through treasured photographs and to celebrate its commitment to educate all its children. The project began during the summer of 2005 when I contacted June Kennedy. She provided more than twenty addresses of senior citizens who were residents of the town or were school alumni.

In fall of 2005, my students wrote letters to these local residents seeking vintage photos and related information. A few months later, some replies trickled in, and student research began in earnest. Meanwhile, I began to scan images archived at the Brick Academy in Basking Ridge, including those loaned to me by area residents and some I later obtained from university libraries and the Library of Congress.

June Kennedy was instrumental in leading us to valuable resources, while a few students discovered sources unknown even to her!

At first, students relied on computer search engines but soon discovered their limitations. I found myself saying, "We have to look to other sources."

But much to my delight, toward the end of the summer of 2006, I stumbled upon a wonderful Website, freepages.genealogy.rootsweb.com/~kennedychronicle. "The Kennedy Chronicle" was written and designed by Katharine McCarthy Young. She was none other than the great-great-great-great-great-great-granddaughter of Reverend Samuel Kennedy, the founder of the first school in Bernards Township, the Classical School. What a discovery! The modern age of technology did, in fact, pay off.

During the following weeks, the students' efforts to find primary sources about early education in the 1700s in Bernards Township met with limited success. We speculated that the early residents may have been more interested in planting and harvesting crops, chopping wood, and building sturdy homes than in recording the educational accomplishments of the young village.

However, we found some interesting references, including: *Among the Blue Hills . . . Bernardsville . . . a History* (1974) by the Bernardsville History Book Committee; *Look to Your Schools* (1973) by Melvina M. Oehlers; and *Education in Bernards Township* (1960) by Louise M. Flint. We also found an invaluable newspaper article, "Early Schools in Bernards Township" (1948) by Anna W. Lines.

Undoubtedly, these historians conducted painstaking research while they gathered snippets of information from deeds, memoirs, vintage photographs, old maps, newspapers, and stories from longtime residents who remembered the area's one-room schoolhouses.

Yet, we were not completely justified in assuming no early records existed; one historical account noted that a pastor from the Township did indeed see value in the preservation of church activities, though perhaps not in the most conventional manner. Around the handle of a broomstick, he fastened records of the marriages he presided over; the broomstick was later found in his attic!

A few enthusiastic students managed to locate sources from several newspaper clippings, from visits to local history rooms, and from long-forgotten newspapers stored at our school's media center. They began to see that the recording and tracing of history is quite complex. Were the facts correct? Was the information reliable?

At one point, there were more questions than answers, and those who could provide the answers were no longer living. How I wished for a time machine to see the children seated in the one-room schoolhouses and follow them throughout their day!

And what about the teachers, we wondered?

One useful account was *The Old Rural School As I Remember It,* by Velma Fowler Matson, who attended a one-room schoolhouse in 1916 and later taught in a country school. Matson describes a teacher's typical day: She rose early, ate breakfast, packed her lunch, and walked the distance to the schoolhouse. Once there, the teacher faced countless chores and had little time in which to do them:

> Upon arriving, she carried wood and kindling from the woodshed and built the fire. As the building was warming, she carried in the day's water for drinking and washing hands. The room was tidied, lessons for the day were reviewed, plans were made, questions and instructions were written on the blackboard. Time was always too short, as pupils soon began to arrive with things to share, questions to be answered, quarrels to be settled, etc. etc.

Matson further notes that the teacher "was almost always a single woman who had to be a 'paragon of virtue.'" She explains that teachers often boarded with families, sharing a room with a child. Their duties kept them busy from sun-up until sun-down:

> From 9:00 a.m. until school was dismissed at 4:00 p.m., not one moment could she call her own. During the day, she "wore the hats" of superintendent, principal, counselor, teacher, coach, nurse, janitor, referee, baby-sitter and others. Decisions to be made were her own—there was no one to help or advise and no telephone to call for help should she need it.
>
> When 4:00 p.m. came and the last child had left, she drew a sigh of relief, picked up the broom, did the sweeping, checked the buildings and grounds, began her planning for the next day's lessons and on and on. Finally, as the sun was getting low in the sky, she trudged her weary way toward her boarding home, loaded down with a big pile of papers to correct.

It took a special individual to be a teacher in a one-room schoolhouse. These professionals undoubtedly received a great deal of satisfaction from their work. Though the teaching conditions in the 21st century unquestionably are different from those of previous centuries, one ideal remains unchanged: love for children and a passion to inspire them.

Armed with newly discovered facts, my students pressed on. They wondered: What was the rationale for the placement of schools? Together, we learned that schools were erected on the basis of availability of land and population needs. Families did not want their children to travel great distances. In some instances, existing buildings were converted to schoolhouses to reduce overcrowding.

But where exactly were our one-room schoolhouses?

We turned to old maps, some of which June Kennedy provided. The maps showed crossroads that led to the schools' locations. My students were filled with pride and excitement each time they located a schoolhouse a group was researching. We used a large laminated map to mark the schools' sites.

As research continued, they faced another challenge—discrepancies in dates, facts, and spellings. Despite the setbacks, sixth-grade students made reasonable assumptions and worked diligently to piece together the school-house puzzle of long ago.

By then, I had gathered a collection of images of schoolchildren who had attended the area's one-room structures a century earlier. Clearly, these photos told their own stories.

Teachers, male and female, young and old, sweet and stern, stand resolutely beside their students. The children appear well groomed; you see little girls holding bonnets and wearing white pinafore dresses. The boys wear jackets, knickers, and sturdy shoes. The children display steadfastness and a sense of pride.

Included are exterior images of schoolhouses; in a few cases, the interior is shown. Some are modest white-frame structures, with separate entrances for boys and girls. Others are more elaborate red brick and stone buildings.

Most photographs show white children—immigrants from Western European countries and their descendants. At first, I wondered: Were there no minority children who attended our schools during the 19th century? But I did discover some standing proudly in a few school photographs.

Life was a struggle in those years, and families worked hard to eke out a living from their farms. Yet, most of the images portray a community that was vibrant, prosperous, and growing.

Seeing these images for the first time, my students were surprised. Some giggled and exclaimed, "They look funny" or "Nobody smiled!"

I mused—What will people say about us 100 years from now?

Mindful that photography was a new technology in the 1830s, I suggested that the serious expressions were due to the children's curiosity as to what was going on behind the tent of the camera. I sent an inquiry to the American Museum of Photography. William B. Becker, director of the museum, replied with an e-mail. Below is an excerpt of his correspondence:

Dear Ms. Waltz:

Thanks for your message.

It is inaccurate to say that people did not smile in early photographs. Smiles are certainly less common than in photographs made in the late twentieth century, but people can be seen smiling in photographs dating back to the 1850s.

I can offer a couple of suggestions that people have made regarding the paucity of smiles and pleasant expressions in early photographs:

- Smiling for no reason was considered the sign of a simpleton
- People were hesitant to smile because it might reveal their ill-formed or missing teeth.

We also need to remember that when the first portrait photographs were made in 1840. . . . People were conscious that they were passing their image to their descendants. . . . They appear strong, resolute, upright, hard working, sober, and prosperous—not because they never let down their hair, but because these were the qualities they admired and the self-image they wished to present.

In the case of children . . . a wriggling child could be an economic threat, because parents would not pay if the picture turned out blurry from the child's movements. You can rightly assume that many children did not react well to a stranger ordering them sternly to SIT STILL.

I took another look at the images, and indeed in the front row were a few young boys with grins ready to burst into wide smiles!

But beyond these observations, I challenged my classes to study the images and draw their own conclusions about what life held for these early schoolchildren.

In addition, students learned that Bernards Township was settled in 1717 and was known by many names: Baskinridge, Baskenridge, Baskeridge, and Baskingridge. Its name was born from a record in the annals of the Basking Ridge Presbyterian Church in 1733. "According to legend the name originated with the early settlers who saw wild animals come up from the swamps to 'bask on the ridge,'" reported Dorothy L. McFadden. "Today the wild animals of the adjacent lowlands were accustomed to bask in the warm sun of this beautiful ridge" was the true entry in the church records.

As early as the 1750s, one-room schoolhouses that contained all grades began to emerge throughout the then 29-square-mile area of Bernards Township. For a small fee, those who could afford the expense sent their children to neighborhood schoolhouses.

A fact that resonated with all student researchers was the early settlers' high regard for education, as proved by the numerous one-room schoolhouses that existed in the Township. In these buildings, children learned to read the Bible. The structures also served as places to hold prayer meetings; perhaps that was why many one-room schoolhouses resembled churches.

As school came to a close, I continued to research during the summer months, scan more images and reshape the text. June Kennedy became my mentor, and was very willing to tell me about the historical significance of the area and its schools.

This book is presented as a photo journal narrative, a memoir with oral histories initially researched by sixth-grade children and their teacher, coupled with tremendous support and encouragement from the Township's historian.

The purposes in writing this book are to stimulate interest in the early history of Bernards Township schools; to instill a love of history in our young children; to provide students with a first hand opportunity to write historical accounts; to encourage dialogue with seniors; to broaden students' understanding of education in the 19th and 20th centuries; and to understand and appreciate Bernards Township's rich and colorful past.

Students who participated in the initial chapter work have been noted at the end of each passage.

The information in parentheses beneath the images indicates the source of the photo, not the source of information.

We welcome any additional information that may shed light on this complex and intriguing research project. Please feel free to contact me at William Annin Middle School or June Kennedy at The Historical Society of the Somerset Hills.

—Josephine M. Waltz, Teacher of the Gifted and Talented

Acknowledgments

———•◦•———

It is with deep gratitude and appreciation that I thank Bernards Township historian June Kennedy for making this venture possible. She arranged for me to scan more than 200 images and to speak to local history room librarians and residents of the Township. She gave freely of her time to talk to my gifted and talented students on the early schools of Bernards Township and provided an opportunity for me to search the archives at the Brick Academy, headquarters of The Historical Society of the Somerset Hills, and was most gracious in sharing her personal information and expertise on the subject. Without her continued reassurance, this book simply would not have been possible. Her efforts helped me establish a springboard for my sixth-graders' initial research efforts. She kindly suggested tidbits of unique, interesting information for our manuscript and reviewed and edited the content several times.

There was never an instance in which she did not follow through on a request, even when I suggested she donate the last of the Maple Avenue School assembly hall benches to William Annin Middle School. The bench now sits proudly in the front office as a reminder of those who came before us.

My deepest gratitude and respect to Shannon Hitchcock, a fellow writer and mentor, for her honest, sincere guidance in my writing ventures, and especially for her advice on *Schoolhouses of Early Bernards Township*. I offer my humble thanks.

My sincere gratitude goes to Cheryl Dyer, former district curriculum director, who saw value in the project and encouraged me to pursue it. A very special thank you to Principal Nick Markarian of William Annin Middle School for his steadfast patience and kindness in guiding me through many logistical stages and recognizing the project's potential merit; to Vice Principal Karen Hudock and Ridge High School Principal Francis Howlett for continued support and understanding of my varied school projects; to Marge Bradley, former school secretary, for her kind words of encouragement and attention to details; to Principal Dr. Kathleen Pecoraro at Liberty Corner School for sharing school history files, to Principals Dr. Jane Costa at Oak Street School and Judith Slutzky at Mount Prospect School for giving of their time to answer questions; to Principal Joseph Mollica at Cedar Hill School for responding to my inquiries and conversations over the years; to school media specialists: Connie Rose for her generosity in sharing her archived materials about Cedar Hill School, Elaine Porac at WAMS for all her continued hard work in maintaining files, documents, and books for staff and students, and Susan Philhower at Oak Street School, who found a scrapbook filled with old news articles, a window to the past!

My appreciation goes to: Jean Hill and Marion Kennedy, Bernardsville Library Local History Room staff volunteers, who assisted me in scanning images, shared their recollections of the Borough, and helped me find many additional sources; the reference staff at the Bernards

Township Library for their help in locating research and photographs; Betty King Sisto, lifelong resident, and Nancy Childs Knobloch, a sixth-generation resident and former music teacher at Cedar Hill School, who both provided me with images and conversations about their school days at Liberty Corner School, Maple Avenue School, and Bernards High School; to Pauline Hilmer Merrill and Connie Malisky, former district schoolteachers, who sat with me one December afternoon at Fellowship Village and reminisced about "those good times"; to Janet Haas McGahey, who met with me at the Bernards Township Library to discuss her recollections of the Township and shared that her father was a graduate of Pleasant Valley School, a one-room schoolhouse that today houses the restaurant Café Rustica; to Bill Allen for generously sharing information and a 1911 photograph, and to Dorothy Agans Stratford at the Somerset County Historical Society.

I gratefully acknowledge the Frelinghuysen family whose members have contributed their time, resources, energy and devotion to shape our American way of life for the past three centuries.

My appreciation to Ted Kooser, for his gracious conversations about poetry and permission to include his poem "Country School."

I also wish to express gratitude to Gordon Jolliffe, who met with June Kennedy and me for an afternoon of reminiscing. His candid remarks and sharp wit were delightful.

My gratitude goes to Charles Green and Annalee Pauls, special collections assistants for general manuscripts in the Manuscripts Division, Department of Rare Books and Special Collections, at Princeton University Library, for assisting me in locating and deciphering archival letters written by the Reverend Robert Finley.

Additional gratitude goes to Kate Young, who generously allowed me to use passages and photos from her Website on the Kennedy archives; and to Katherine Kearns Connolly, whose attempt to return a long-forgotten safety patrol badge she wore at Oak Street School led her to write of her early school experience at Maple Avenue and Oak Street Schools. With her permission, wonderful excerpted passages have been included in this book.

I gratefully acknowledge Mary Taylor, the project director from the Donning Company Publishers, for her friendship and positive spirit; Kathy Sheridan, Amy Thomann, and Tonya Hannink for professional guidance in the making of this book; and Peter Miller, a former resident of Bernards Township, for his support and detailed account of his school days at Cedar Hill School.

To Alexis McCormack, current resident and owner of the converted Franklin Academy Schoolhouse, for graciously showing me the refurbished interior of the one-room schoolhouse and allowing me to photograph the exterior of her home.

To the sixth-graders for their enthusiasm; and especially to Lisa Wooldridge.

My gratitude goes to my daughters: Casey, for reviewing the manuscript and providing me with recommendations; Chelsea, for taking the household reins, enabling me to work on the manuscript; and to my son, Jeffrey, for maintaining a great sense of humor through it all.

My appreciation goes to my husband, Charlie, who encouraged me to pursue my school writing ventures.

I also extend my admiration and appreciation to all the dedicated historians who researched and read land deeds, diaries, municipal documents, and newspaper articles and recorded the information in their wonderful books and articles. And to the volunteers at The Historical Society of the

Somerset Hills who maintained meticulous records and postcard collections in countless albums. Their commitment paved the way for those of us who would later seek historical information.

And finally, to the Millington Savings Bank for sponsoring the publication of this book, thank you for your generosity.

—J. M. W.

Country School

The Apple Valley School has closed its books,
wiped off its blackboard, put away its chalk;
the valley children with their parents' looks
ride busses down the road their parents walked.

The Apple Valley School is full of bales,
and the bell was auctioned off a year ago.
Under the teeter-totter, spotted quail
have nested where the grass would never grow.

The well is dry where boys caught garter snakes
and chased the girls into their memories.
High on the hill, nobody climbs to shake
the few ripe apples from the broken tree.

—Ted Kooser, Official Entry Blank, 1969
Thirteenth poet laureate of the United States

Introduction

Early education in Bernards Township did not occur in traditional schoolhouses. Children were educated on a farm, in the basement of a stone house, in an old church, and in a converted ice-house. As the population grew, and more people settled in the hamlets and villages of Bernards Township, schoolhouses were constructed.

Often, a farmer donated a corner of his land for the schoolhouse, ensuring that his own children did not have to walk a long distance to school. Then local residents supplied the materials to build the schoolhouse and hired the teacher. The earliest instructors were parents, then clergymen; but once schoolhouses began to appear, male and female teachers were employed.

An account of January 24, 1861, reports Bernards Township tuition as an amount of 3 1/3 cents for 55 days, equaling $1.83, paid for a single pupil.

This was not uncommon, but the number of pupils varied and, with it, so did the teacher's salary. Tuition was not always paid in cash; sometimes it was paid in goods, such as potatoes, eggs, firewood, or cloth.

By 1844, schoolhouses constructed of logs, wood, brick, or stone dotted the area. Children were taught by one teacher who may have had as many as 30 students, ranging from grades one through eight, in a single schoolroom. Large or important schoolhouses that offered a wide course of study were referred to as academies or seminaries.

Schoolteachers usually were provided with room and board. They tended the schools' wood-burning stoves and served as the schools' custodians. During the winter, keeping the schoolhouse warm was a challenge. By most accounts, it was not until the end of the school day that the classroom had lost the last of its chill.

Children attended school to learn the four R's: reading, writing, arithmetic, and recitation. They walked to school in all sorts of weather, and at times their trek was more than two miles to reach the closest schoolhouse.

In front of the teacher's desk was a long seat called the recitation bench. There the students sat to recite lessons they had memorized. A daily schedule of instruction might include reading, arithmetic, and history during the morning hours. Afternoon subjects might consist of writing, grammar, geography, and spelling. The school day ended by mid-afternoon, usually around three or four o'clock. During the summer months, most schools were not in session.

There was no free public education in the 1700s, nor was there a single school system that served all the children of the Township, at least, not for a while. Most parents paid a fee to send their children to school.

In *Early Schools in Bernards Township* (1948), Anna W. Lines writes:

> In 1820, the legislature authorized townships to levy a tax for the education of "such poor children as are paupers, belonging to the said township, and the children of such poor parents, residents in said township as are or shall be, in the judgment of said committee, unable to pay for schooling the same." This law was the origin of the so-called "pauper schools" and was in force for some years.

By the mid-1850s, schools were assigned a number and were known as district schools; a particular school served a certain area of the Township. Teachers who were hired by a school district received a contract for their terms of employment.

In the same article, Lines provides the details of such a document:

> An 1822 contract between Stephen Rush, teacher, and subscribers whose children he taught gives a list of parents who paid for the tuition of their offspring. The appropriate term "pauper" did not apply to them....In the contract note the responsibility of keeping the school building is taken by the subscribers. The contract reads as follows:
>
> "We the undersigned Subcribers doth Agree to Imploy Stephen Rush to teach Inglish School in the Schoolhouse near Samuel Woodards Mill, and doth Ingage to put the Schoolhouse in good Repair, on or before the 16th day of this Month, Decr. 1822, when the school is to Commence and the said Stephen Rush doth promise and Ingage to keep a Regular Inglish School In the Various Branches Vis. to teach the Alphabet, Spelling, Redding, Wrighting, Arrethmetic, Geography, and Inglish Grammar, for the term of three Months and we the undersigned Subscribers doth promise to pay to the said Stephen Rush for teaching Each Scholar Sent or Subscribed for, one Dollar and twenty-five Cents, at the Expiration of said term, and to furnish him with decent Board, washing and Lodging, and fewel for the use of said School an Equal proportion to each Scholar, as witness our hand this 6th Day of Decr. 1822—"

Lines concludes with this statement:

> In closing, we shall go back to the state convention assembled in Trenton in 1838 which appointed a committee with Bishop Doane as chairman and Theodore Frelinghuysen a member to issue an address to the people. "Every free state must provide for the education of her children," the address proclaimed:
>
> "Tax yourselves for the support of common schools and you will never be in danger of taxation from a foreign power. You will need less taxation for the support of pauperism and the punishment of crime. Look to your schoolhouses. See that they are convenient of access; that they are comfortable; that they are neat and tasteful. Look to the teachers. See that they are taught themselves and apt to teach- men that fear God and love their country. See that they are well accommodated, well treated, and well remunerated. Respect them, and they will respect themselves, and your children will respect them. Look well to the scholars. Remember you are to grow old among them. Remember, you are to die and leave your country in their hands."

—Max Rogers, Tejus Pradeep, and Lisa Wooldridge

The rural nature of Basking Ridge, ca. 1900, included unpaved roads, and transportation by horse and buggy. (Special Collections and University Archives, Rutgers University Library)

Early Beginnings

Sir, my mind is made up on the subject: you know my wish: I have no objection to you as a teacher on any subject or any other ground: but if you don't comply immediately on this point, prepare your accounts, and collect your money: for you sha'nt be here a week.

—Rev. Robert Finley

In the early 1700s, settlers began moving to the northern part of Somerset County from areas known as Woodbridge, Elizabethtown, and Piscataway, New Jersey. Many people emigrated from Northern Ireland, Scotland and England; among them were Scotch Presbyterians. Collectively, they settled in small hamlets around Basking Ridge, and Liberty Corner and throughout the surrounding area. The first pioneers, like the American Indians, found the County to be a favorable location. The hilly woodlands had an abundance of wild game and fertile farming soil.

In 1717, John Harrison, an agent for King George I of England, bought 3,000 acres from Chief Nowenoik of the Lenni Lenape Indians for $50. William Penn purchased 7,000 acres.

Over time, these landholdings were subdivided and sold, giving way to legal land titles. Agricultural settlements soon dotted the vicinity. The rural nature of the area fostered a prosperous community complete with farms, mills, tanneries, shops, churches, and eventually schoolhouses.

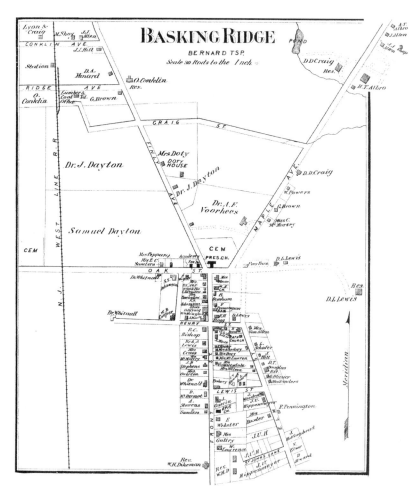

The center of Basking Ridge Village, 1873, from the Atlas of Somerset County, New Jersey. Map shows the location of residents and the Brick Academy on the center upper left side of Finley Avenue, and to its right, the cemetery and Presbyterian Church. (The Historical Society of the Somerset Hills)

The area population grew, and in 1760 King George II issued a charter to Bernardston Township. The name was in honor of Francis Bernard, who was royal governor of New Jersey from 1758 to 1760.

By 1730, 29 families lived on farms surrounding the village of Basking Ridge. Families generally were quite large, and it was not uncommon for a household to have as many as ten children.

Resident ministers from the Basking Ridge Presbyterian Church, established in about 1717, took the lead in educating the growing number of children. Fourth pastor, Reverend Samuel Kennedy, began a classical school in 1764; it continued operating until 1787.

Kennedy taught in a schoolhouse located within the boundaries of his 300-acre plantation on King George Road, about four miles from the church.

On August 27, 1764, Reverend Kennedy advertised his school in the *New York Mercury*:

The Rev. Samuel Kennedy, of Baskinridge, or Bernard's Town, in the County of Somerset, and Province of New Jersey, designs to have the learned languages and Liberal Arts and Sciences, taught under his Inspection, in a School-House built on his own plantation: where Persons may be fitted to enter any class in College. Any convenient Lodgings may be had near the said School House. N. B. There are Scholars now learning the Latin and Greek Languages in said School.

Two years later, a public notice announced the sale of Kennedy's property in the *New York Mercury*. After relocating closer to the church, he continued teaching young men at the parsonage. His students were young men from New York, Philadelphia, and other faraway cities who boarded with local residents. Students under his direction were qualified to enter the College of New Jersey, today known as Princeton University.

His great-granddaughter, Sarah Elizabeth Kennedy, writes in the *Kennedy Chronicle*, published in 1891:

The labors of Mr. Kennedy among the people of his charge were very extensive and successful. . . . He contributed extensively by his prudent counsels and faithful labors. . . .

The efforts toward educating area children earned Bernards Township a distinct reputation for its intellect and Christian character. The Basking Ridge Classical School, regarded as a seminary, was unsurpassed by any other in its popularity, usefulness, and excellence.

In 1751 Reverend Samuel Kennedy, a native Scotsman born in 1720 and educated at the University of Edinburgh, became the fourth pastor of the Basking Ridge Presbyterian Church. He married Sarah Allen, and they had seven children.

Along with his pastoral duties, he was a practicing physician, and in 1768 became a member of the New Jersey Medical Society. He received an honorary degree from the College of New Jersey.

The establishment of Reverend Kennedy's classical school provided a unique opportunity to educate the surrounding area's young men during the mid-1700s.

———— ◆ ————

Reverend Robert Finley's father, James Finley, a native of Glasgow, Scotland, was a yarn merchant. He immigrated to the United States in 1769 with his wife, Miss Angres, at the invitation of a friend, Reverend John Witherspoon, then president of the College of New Jersey.

Once the Finleys had settled in Princeton, New Jersey, a son, Robert, was born in 1772. He entered Princeton University at age eleven and in 1787 graduated at the age of fifteen.

Robert Finley was master of Nassau Hall Grammar School in Princeton in 1787–88 and again in 1792–93. He held several positions at Princeton: clerk of the faculty, librarian, and tutor (1793–95), and a trustee of the college (1807–17). From 1812 to 1817, Finley was the director of Princeton Seminary, where he once studied.

After a few teaching engagements in Allentown, New Jersey, and Charleston, South Carolina, Finley returned to Princeton at age 22 to study theology. He was ordained on June 16, 1795. Three years after his appointment to the Presbyterian Church, Finley married Esther Caldwell, daughter of the famous Revolutionary War patriot, Reverend James Caldwell. The Finleys had

nine children, all born in Basking Ridge. The family farm stood near what today is South Finley Avenue.

Finley's interests extended beyond the ministry and education. His publication, "Thoughts on the Colonization of Free Blacks," which he printed and distributed to members of the U.S. Congress, earned him much attention. Some believe his personal experience with minorities in his own congregation heightened his desire to help improve the welfare of black Americans. He was one of the key organizers of the American Colonization Society, whose goal was to set aside a territory on the southwest coast of Africa for freed black Americans. The result of the society's efforts was the formation of the country of Liberia. Its capital, Monrovia, was named to honor President James Monroe.

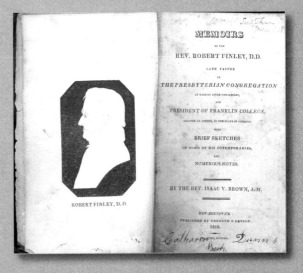

The only known image of Dr. Robert Finley is a silhouette found in the book "Memories of the Rev. Robert Finley," written two years after his death by Reverend Isaac V. Brown, pastor of the Presbyterian Church of Maidenhead, New Jersey. (The Historical Society of the Somerset Hills)

After serving the community for 22 years, in 1817 Reverend Finley became president of Franklin College, known today as the University of Georgia at Athens. U.S. Congressman Henry Southard delivered a farewell sermon at the Basking Ridge Presbyterian Church. However, Finley did not serve as president of the college for very long. Just three months after arriving there, he died. College trustees offered his wife college-owned property for a residence.

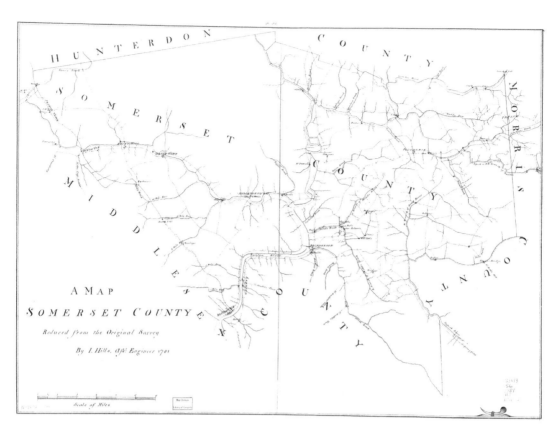

Somerset County map from 1871 by I. Hills, Afs: Engineer, shows surrounding county names, distances of brooks, rivers, and established towns and villages. (Courtesy of The Library of Congress)

The Brick Academy, ca. 1900. (The Historical Society of the Somerset Hills)

Main Street in Basking Ridge, ca. 1910, with a cornfield to the left. The street later was renamed Finley Avenue in 1912 to honor Reverend Robert Finley. The Brick Academy stood to the left of this scene. Dayton's Hall is to the right, where dances and graduation ceremonies were held. In addition, this view was across the street from where the Basking Ridge library was located. (Betty King Sisto)

She also includes details about her grandfather's salary:

> He, Mr. Kennedy, established a classical school at Baskingridge, which was of a high order, and extensively patronized. . . . There was a parsonage farm, which was rented for nine pounds, for some years, and afterward for twelve pounds, which swelled the salary to about £120. The last of my grandfather's life salary was retained to £120, with the benefit of the parsonage free, the house and land kept in repair, and firewood cut and delivered without any of his expenses.

Kennedy died on August 31, 1787, after serving the village for 36 years as pastor, doctor, and teacher. He is buried along with his wife, Sarah, and youngest son, Ebenezer, in the churchyard of the Basking Ridge Presbyterian Church.

After Kennedy's death, the pulpit of the Basking Ridge Presbyterian Church remained vacant and the classical school inactive. It wasn't until 1795, under Reverend Robert Finley, the fifth pastor, that the classical school was reinstated.

Finley began teaching in his own home, and in 1802 his first class of four students graduated. Soon, he was teaching a class of ten pupils in the church parsonage, until the school outgrew that space, also. A small schoolhouse was erected in the center of the village to accommodate the growing numbers of pupils.

As the school's reputation increased, so did the enrollment. At one point, it had more than 40 students, although it originally was intended for 25. In a letter dated March 15, 1809, Finley discussed his plan to build a new schoolhouse. Well-to-do New York City men helped finance the new building with contributions including $700 of Dr. Finley's funds, and that same year, the doors of the new academy opened.

Finley had many plans for the future.

In another letter, dated June 19, 1809, he writes Ashbel Green, a theologian and future president of the College of New Jersey (1812–22), about his idea for a Greek vocabulary book:

> In my teaching I have often thought that a Radical Vocabulary of the Greek Language would be a very desirable thing and have often inquired if there be any such thing in existence. If you know of nothing now prepared

Right: The transcribed "for sale" real estate notice and a photo of Reverend Kennedy's original homestead, the parsonage. Photo taken in 2002. (Katharine McCarthy Young)

"For sale" notice, dated 1767, advertises Reverend Samuel Kennedy's plantation. (Katharine McCarthy Young)

To be sold at publick Venue on Wednesday the 17th Day of June next, by the Revd. SAMUEL KENNEDY of Bernard's Town in the County of Somerset, and Province of New-Jersey; his Plantation on which he now lives, containing 300 Acres of Land, more or less, well watered and timbered, bounded on one Side by Dead-River, & on the other by the River Passaick, having the publick Road that leads to the City of Perth-Amboy going through it; it is 20 Miles from said City, 8 from Bound-Brook, 5 from New-Brunswick, 3 from Lord Sterling's Buildings, not quite four along a publick Road to Baskinridge Meeting-House, and about 1 Mile and a half of Mr. Solomon Boyle's Mill, on which Plantation there is a Dwelling-House with three Rooms and two fire-places on the lower floor, situate at a small Distance from the brink of said Passaick-River, and a good Quarry for building may be opened at the Distance of a few Poles from said House: There is also on the said Plantation, a good Barn, and a Stable at each End of it, and an Orchard containing 57 old Apple Trees, and 136 young Ones, some of which are grafted; there is about 72 Acres of plough Land cleared, and in good Fence, and about 27 Acres of Meadow cleared, 12 and half of which have been mowed for a considerable Number of Years, and about 2 Acres of it has been mowed for two Years past, and about 11 Acres sowed with Timothy Seed, together with one and half Acre more, are expected to be mowed this Summer, 100 Acres more of good Meadow may be made on a very rich Bottom, being the Plantation whereon Mr. Moses Doty formerly lived. On said Day Samuel Kennedy proposes to sell Horses, Cattle, Sheep, and Utensils of Husbandry, &c &c. when good Attendance will be given, and the Conditions of Sale made known. — The New York Mercury, No. 807, April 20, 1767.

The Basking Ridge Presbyterian Church, built in 1839, rests on the site of two former structures, a log cabin and a wooden building, which date to about 1717. The Reverend Samuel Kennedy was pastor of the church from 1751 until his death in 1787. Schooling was held on this site when the church was a wooden structure. Photo taken in 1871. (The Historical Society of the Somerset Hills)

do you know anyone willing and competent to the undertaking? An edition would soon sell and in my opinion answer a good purpose. I have often thought of the business myself. But I am so sensible that my constitution and habits are more active than accurate and that it would be improper for me to attempt it. . . .

(General Manuscripts [Misc.] Manuscripts Division, Department of Rare Books and Special Collections, Princeton University Library)

It is unknown whether Finley's book on Greek vocabulary ever materialized. We do know, however, that the Bible was one of the academy's main texts. In fact, when one of the schoolteachers protested this practice, the pastor won over the naysayer—by threatening his job. [*See quote at the start of this chapter.*]

Finley's classical school thrived as a private institution for many years. Students through age seventeen were taught subjects such as science, liberal arts, languages, and debate. The school prepared many young men for college and business.

Reverend Isaac Van Arsdale Brown writes in *Memoirs of the Reverend Robert Finley, D.D.* (1819):

Tombstone of Reverend Samuel Kennedy,
August 31, 1787.
Inscription reads:

God's holy law thy mouth proclaimed,
Pure gospel flowed through every vein;
To dying men thy lips proclaimed
The glory of thy Savior's name.
Sleep, then, beneath this earthly clod–
Thy flesh shall see its Saviour-God–
Till the bright morning shall appear,
And thou thy Saviour's image bear.

(Katharine Young)

Plaque commemorating Reverend Samuel Kennedy's pastoral
service is located at Basking Ridge Presbyterian Church.
(Katharine Young)

Reverend Kennedy's son, Ebenezer, is buried beside the
oak tree at Basking Ridge Presbyterian Church Cemetery.
(Katharine Young)

Right: Reverend Finley's letter written in 1809 to Ashbel Green. (General Manuscripts [Misc.] Manuscripts Division, Department of Rare Books and Special Collections, Princeton University Library)

Below: Reverend Finley's letter, second paragraph, shows his inquiry about the possibility of a book on a radical vocabulary of the Greek language, 1809. (General Manuscripts [Misc.] Manuscripts Division, Department of Rare Books and Special Collections, Princeton University Library)

Image shows envelope/letter and address of letter. Entire contents served as a letter, 1809. (General Manuscripts [Misc.] Manuscripts Division, Department of Rare Books and Special Collections, Princeton University Library)

Several circumstances conduced to the success of this institution. It was put in operation at a time when grammar schools were less numerous in the state of New Jersey than at present. Mr. Finley admitted a considerable number of the youth into his own family, near his person, and under his constant observation. From Mr. Kennedy's having superintended a similar institution, in the same place, the people had become sensible of the advantages of such an establishment to the neighbourhood, and disposed to encourage the seminary, and to facilitate all its operations. The situation was esteemed healthful, and the terms of accommodations were made reasonable. In addition to these circumstances, Mr. Finley's thorough experience and established reputation as a teacher and disciplinarian strongly attracted the public attention and confidence. The impression which he had recently made in Charleston, South Carolina, while teaching there, induced many wealthy and respectable citizens in that region to entrust their children to his able instruction and faithful guardianship.

Finley, founder of the Brick Academy, is remembered for his commitment to the ministry and education. His school's reputation for excellence continued well after his death. Abraham Messler writes in *Centennial History of Somerset County* (1878), "Somerville's Academy flourished extensively. It had no rival except Baskingridge."

—*Elena Baurkot, Sara Jones, Ryan Rogers, and Kevin Zhao*

Students pictured on the east side of the Brick Academy, 1883, with teacher, Mr. Dewey Wheat. Note the varied ages of the children and the girls' stylish button-down jackets and fashionable hats. Students include: Catherine Moffett, Lizzie Terry, Dela Wolfe, Ella Fort, Lidia Bird, Minnie Allen Craig, Kitty Allen, Carrie Dayton Faukner. Laura Rickey, Laura Van Lesin, Susie Simpson, Lottie Jones, Allie Ricky Ballentine, John Harner, Clare Boye, Henry Arthur Lewis, Bessie DeCoster, Annie Sanders, Joe Shaffer Van Dorn, and others are unknown. (The Historical Society of the Somerset Hills)

The Academy and Prominent Graduates

—————◆—————

Every child furnished his own books, pencil, pen, and slate.

—Mary Conkling Ellis, Brick Academy alumna

Reverend Dr. William Craig Brownlee, a Scotsman, succeeded Reverend Finley as director of the classical school in 1818. Brownlee held the position as headmaster until 1825.

An ad from *Palladium of Liberty*, April 1818, provides information about the academy under Brownlee for the prospective student:

Basking-Ridge
ACADEMY

Under the care of the Rev. W. C. Brownlee, A.M.

The summer session will commence on Monday 4th May.

Branches taught—Latin, Greek, French, English Grammar, Geography, with the use of the Globes, the principles of mathematics, &c.

Terms.—Tuition, $25 per ann. And $5 at entrance; board in respectable families, at the rate of $50 per session, or $100 dollars per annum.

Mr. B. is a graduate of the University of Glasgow, and has taught with reputation in Europe and in this country. For further particulars, gentlemen are referred to Dr. President Green; to Vice President Lindly, Princeton; to the Faculty of Queen's College; to Dr. Janeway and James Houston, Esq. Assistant Cashier, U.S. Bank, Philadelphia; and to Dr. Wilson, Columbia College, New-York.

April 20.

Vintage postcard of Basking Ridge village, ca. 1900. (Special Collections and University Archives, Rutgers University Library)

The Old Schoolhouse, the academy, ca. early 1900s. Note the little boy wearing a big bowtie and knickers. (The Historical Society of the Somerset Hills)

In 1825 Brownlee accepted a post at Rutgers College as professor of languages. Brownlee Place in Basking Ridge was named in his honor. In 1826 a new minister, Reverend John Coe Van Dervoort, was appointed to the directorship of the academy. On October 27, 1827, he placed advertisements in the *New York Observer* and the *Religious Chronicle*:

BASKING RIDGE CLASSICAL SCHOOL

This institution is located in the village of Basking Ridge, Somerset County, New Jersey, about 22 miles from Elizabethtown Point, and 37 from the city of New York; with which there is communication regularly twice a week by stage. The village is delightfully situated being high and healthful, and affords peculiar advantages to youth in the pursuit of an education for mercantile business, or for college.

Board—$1.50 PER WEEK

Its inhabitants are distinguished for their exemplary morals, hospitality, and intelligence, and it is believed that there are fewer temptations to vice here than in most places. The terms of tuition for an English education are from 5 to 8 dollars per Session and for language $12.50 per Session. There are two Sessions in the year, one commencing on the first Monday in May, and the other on the first Monday in November. Board may be obtained in the village at moderate price of $1.50 per week. On timely application, several young gentlemen can be accommodated in the family of the Principal. The greatest attention will be paid to the morals of the youth, and a system of government affectionately and impartially administered.

Despite its advertising and excellent reputation, the academy lost the status of its former years. The church also experienced a decline in membership, and by 1838 the academy closed its doors, and the building remained unused until 1851.

THE ACADEMY AS A PUBLIC SCHOOL

In the 1850s, the New Jersey legislature allocated a portion of State taxes to public school funds. Thus, the Basking Ridge School District was incorporated on May 7, 1851, and the academy was purchased by the school district on December 1, 1853. The Brick Academy opened as School District Number 12, a public school serving both boys and girls until they reached the age of seventeen. The academy served as a public school from 1853 to 1903.

The upper floor of the brick building was now rented for private education, and for a time it was leased to a private school. Professor Walter Rankin, son of Dr. John C. Rankin, pastor of the Basking Ridge Presbyterian Church, held daily instruction in the first-floor classroom.

To keep students warm while in school, huge "jug" stoves were placed in the center of the two upper-floor classrooms, replacing the old, drafty fireplaces. Mary Conkling Ellis, former student (1870), writes:

> The downstairs classroom was divided, with boys and girls seated on opposite sides. I picture again, the two rooms of equal size, one on the upper floor wherein we made our scholastic debut, the one below where in due course of time we eventually found ourselves, there to finish the course prescribed in those days. These rooms were furnished alike, with a huge stove in the center, scarred seats and desks built for two, a huge blackboard against the wall and the teacher's desk. In the hallway on each floor stood the water pail, new each year with a large dipper from which we all drank with relish and satisfaction.

Brick Academy schoolchildren in front of the Basking Ridge Presbyterian Church, 1898. The academy served as a public school, District 12. Teacher stands in rear. (The Historical Society of the Somerset Hills)

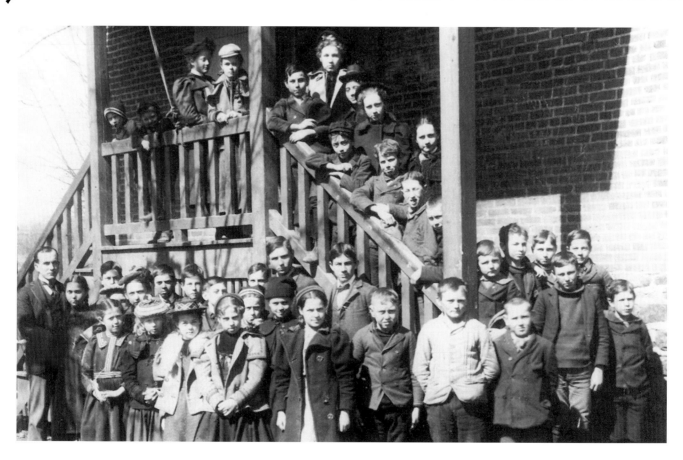

Students at the Brick Academy, 1895, stand on the front steps of the school, located on West Oak Street in Basking Ridge. Schoolmaster stands on the far left. The structure was a public schoolhouse until a much larger facility, the Maple Avenue School, was built. (The Historical Society of the Somerset Hills)

The original high fireplace, 1809, in the Brick Academy was restored to its former appearance by the removal of sheetrock and plaster. Photo taken in 1976. (The Historical Society of the Somerset Hills)

Initials and dates carved with students' jackknives on an upstairs closet door of the Brick Academy, ca. 1890s. (The Historical Society of the Somerset Hills)

Brick Academy as a public school, ca. 1900, with younger students holding their sunbonnets sitting in the front row and higher grades in second and third rows. Teacher, Miss Rich, barely taller than her charges, is standing in the back middle to right side. Students include: Marion Van Dorn, Sarah Dobbs, Ethel Craig, Katherine Rippert, Anna Kubish, Gladys Bird, Elizabeth Kubish, Alma Richardson, Gladys Dayton, Margaret Happe, Agnes Dupay, Dorothy Craig, Harold Peterson, Daniel Craig, Harold Crane, Gordon Happe, Willshaw, John Pope, Margaret Bergen Dunham, others unknown. (The Historical Society of the Somerset Hills)

Andrew Gulliford describes potbellied stoves in *America's Country Schools* as being located in the middle of the classroom, with a long stove pipe connected at a 90-degree angle to a brick chimney. The stoves were heated with an assortment of kindling, including cow chips and twists of hay. Most of the stoves were made of cast iron and sat on legs or on a metal pad that helped to distribute heat throughout the room. The stoves were eventually replaced by steam heaters. Coal and firewood were stored in the utility room on the ground floor.

Beyond the potbellies, the other prominent features in the schoolhouses were their bells, used to call students to class. The academy held a large metal bell and clapper on its roof. In the 1830s, a storekeeper, William Van Deren, mentions repairs to the building, including references to its steeple.

It is believed that this two-foot bell once hung in the bell tower of the Brick Academy, ca. 1809. It now temporarily rests on the third floor. The bell was made by a company called Rumsey, located in a New York town with the word "Falls" inscribed in it. (The Historical Society of the Somerset Hills)

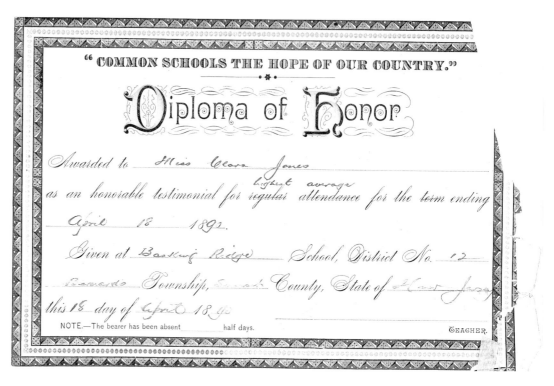

Pupil Clara Jones received a diploma of honor for attaining the highest average during the month of April 1890, awarded by Kenneth Mathieson, teacher/principal. (The Historical Society of the Somerset Hills)

Dan is the dog.
Dan is John's dog.
John likes Dan.
Dan likes John.
Baby likes the dog.
Dan, see Baby John.

Kenneth A. Turner Sr., a former student of the academy (1903), recalled a related schoolboys' prank—played on Principal Willett Neer, who called the boys by ringing the bell. Turner said that one afternoon when Neer stepped away, students cut the bell rope until it hung by a thread. When Neer returned and gave the rope a tug, it came down around his neck.

Turner recalled, "I can still see it, the rope around his neck and feet. Neer gave us a stern look, and that stopped the laughing. He spent the rest of the afternoon trying to figure out who did it, but he never did find out."

The infamous bell vanished from 1975 to 1990. It was discovered in the attic of the Bernards Township Municipal Building on Collyer Lane in Basking Ridge. The chief surveyor remembered seeing a bell hidden behind the eaves and delivered it to the school. According to the town historian, June Kennedy, "it had a fine, clear tone."

Many students recalled their time at the academy with fond anecdotes like the bell story. When, for instance, the first gradua-

Pages from Step by Step Primer *written by Susie C. Peabody, 1902, shows engravings of cats, dogs, and children, making for a child-based reader. (Archival books from The Historical Society of the Somerset Hills)*

tion ceremony with diplomas was held, tickets were in short supply. Programs for the event, held in the old Methodist Episcopal Church across from the school, were used as admission tickets, and there weren't enough to go around. To remedy the situation, graduates entered the gallery of the church and threw their programs out the windows to others who waited outside.

The golden days of the academy came to an end in 1903 because the outdated schoolhouse was no longer needed. In 1904 the building was sold to the American Order of Union Workers and used by the local chapter of this organization. Between 1925 and 1948, it was owned and used by the Junior Order of United American Mechanics as a meeting hall. Township meetings were held in the first-floor room. The former schoolhouse later was sold to Bernards Township and preserved for its historic value.

Today, the Brick Academy stands in the center of Basking Ridge. It has changed very little since its original construction. The brick exterior has remained untouched except for the rebuilding of one eastern wall. The ground floor is now used for research and serves as a storage place for archival books and historical documents. Plans are now underway to restore the upper floor to the original one-room structure, including a commemorative museum of related school artifacts.

The Brick Academy has stood strong since 1809 and is one of the oldest and most revered landmarks in the area. It is the only Federal-style public building in the Township. It currently is the headquarters of The Historical Society of the Somerset Hills. This organization welcomes school groups and scouts throughout the year, and so its educational legacy continues.

PROMINENT GRADUATES

During the academy's early days, as its reputation spread, enrollment at the classical school, the academy, and then the Red Brick Academy, as it was now called, grew. Students from as far away as Virginia, Maryland, New York, Philadelphia, and other parts of New Jersey matriculated and boarded with local residents. Many of Reverend Finley's students went on to enroll in the College of New Jersey. Their pursuits varied; some chose the ministry, while others turned to law, and indeed many achieved acclaim in foreign and national affairs.

NOTICE.

To the legal Voters of the School District of the Township of Bernards:—

Notice is hereby given that the Board of Education of the School District of the Township of Bernards has called a special meeting of the legal voters of the district, to be held at Basking Ridge School House to sell the old School Building, Furnace and Fixtures and apply the proceeds to the new school building—things not mentioned in contracts by architect, on

Friday, the 18th day of Sept., 1903,

at three o'clock in the afternon, to consider and vote upon the following resolution, which will be offered at the said meeting.

"Whereas, the new schoolhouse will be ready for occupation at the beginning of the coming school year; and

Whereas, the old school property located at Basking Ridge will no longer be required; and

"Whereas, the desks, fixtures, furniture and other furnishings in the old schoolhouse cannot be used to advantage in the new schoolhouse; and

"Whereas, it is to the interest of the inhabitants of the District that the old school property, together with the desks, fixtures, furniture and other furnishings therein, should be sold for the best price obtainable:

"Be It Resolved, that the Board of Education of this District be and it hereby is authorized and directed to sell the old school house property, together with the desks, fixtures, furniture and other furnishings therein, either at public or private sale, for the best price obtainable for the same."

Dated, Sept. 4, 1903.

J. E. BALLENTINE,
District Clerk.

Notice of September 4, 1903, informing Basking Ridge residents of the intended sale of the Brick Academy, its interior furnishings, and use of proceeds. Due to increasing student population, the sale of this structure gave rise to another school, Maple Avenue School. (The Historical Society of the Somerset Hills)

The Brick Academy was sold to Bernards Township in 1948. The municipal government was located in the structure for twenty-four years. The white sign hanging from beneath the porch reads: "Court, Township of Bernards." (The Historical Society of the Somerset Hills)

In 1956, Archibald Carswell, president of the Basking Ridge Historical Society, commemorates the unveiling of a historical bronze plaque before a number of Brick Academy alumni who last attended it as a public school. (The Historical Society of the Somerset Hills)

Anna W. Lines unveils the bronze dedication plaque on the exterior front wall of the Brick Academy. The inscription reads: "The building was erected in 1809 by Reverend Robert Finley, to house a classical school founded by him in 1797. Statesmen, professional men and business leaders were among its graduates. The Academy served as a public school from 1853 to 1903. Owned by: AOUW [American Order Union Workers] 1904–25, JOUAM [Junior Order United American Mechanics] 1925–48. Became Township Hall 1924. Purchased by Township of Bernards 1948." (The Historical Society of the Somerset Hills)

Arched fanlight, exposed after the porch from the Brick Academy was removed, shows details on the left side (west). Note the three charred wooden nailers, and a bent-over iron hanger to the upper left of arch. Photo taken on May 5, 1980. (The Historical Society of the Somerset Hills)

Brick Academy, ca. 1980, with fanlight and arched wood trim adorning the entrance. Native stone was used for the foundation. Iron "S" rods in the upper front and back of the gabled wall were used to attach the interior wooden frame to the exterior brick walls. (The Historical Society of the Somerset Hills)

Artifacts discovered in the Brick Academy's attic include a schoolmaster's adjustable eyeglasses, containers for black ink, and a pen with a nib. (Josephine M. Waltz)

The Honorable Theodore Frelinghuysen (1787–1862) attended the classical school. He was valedictorian of his graduating class at the College of New Jersey and held the position of chancellor at New York University. (The Historical Society of the Somerset Hills)

Samuel Lewis Southard was born in Basking Ridge (1787–1842). His reputation was rich with accomplishments, and he was known as New Jersey's "favorite son." (The Historical Society of the Somerset Hills)

William L. Dayton (1807–64) was born in Basking Ridge and attended the Brick Academy. (The Historical Society of the Somerset Hills)

Dr. Jacob Kirkpatrick (1785–1866) attended the classical school at the age of fourteen. He graduated from the College of New Jersey in 1804. (The Historical Society of the Somerset Hills)

Graduates included the renowned Theodore Frelinghuysen, who went on to attend the College of New Jersey. Frelinghuysen later served as a U.S. senator and in 1844 ran for vice president as a Whig candidate on a ticket with Henry Clay. Frelinghuysen later became president of Rutgers College, and one of the college's student dormitories was named in his behalf.

Another graduate was Dr. Jacob Kirkpatrick. In 1810, Kirkpatrick was ordained a minister. He served as a pastor of churches for 56 years in central New Jersey and also founded Hunterdon County Bible Society.

Samuel Lewis Southard also attended the classical school and graduated from the College of New Jersey in 1804, where he was best friend and roommate to Frelinghuysen. Southard was chosen a trustee of his college and a charter trustee of Princeton Theological Seminary. He was named a chief justice of the New Jersey Supreme Court and was elected to the U.S. Senate. In 1823 he was appointed Secretary of the Navy. Southard was New Jersey's governor from 1832 to 1833. He was re-elected to the Senate, serving as its president pro tempore during President John Tyler's term. Southard and his father, Henry Southard, were the first father-son team to serve in the U.S. Congress. Southard resigned from the Senate because of poor health and was succeeded by his cousin, William Lewis Dayton, who attended the Brick Academy.

Dayton was a U.S. senator from 1842 to 1851. In 1856 he was the first Republican candidate for vice president, as the running mate of John C. Fremont of the newly formed Republican Party. President Abraham Lincoln appointed Dayton minister to France in 1861. Lincoln wanted Dayton as his running mate for reelection in 1864, but the GOP preferred a Southerner to better balance the ticket, with Andrew Johnson selected instead. Had the GOP listened to Lincoln, there would have been a New Jersey president in 1865!

Robert Field Stockton, who became a hero of the Mexican War, also attended the academy. Known not for his exemplary decorum but, rather, his mischievous conduct, he was expelled from school. In 1850, Stockton played a dominant role in bringing California into the Union. He also was elected a U.S. senator from New Jersey.

Other graduates who achieved national reputation and represented early families of Bernards Township include: Alward, Annin, Ayers, Boylan, Breese, Conklin, Cross, Dayton, Doty, Guerin, Hall, Heath, Hill, Lewis, Pennington, Rickey, Vail, Whitaker, Winne, and others.

Abraham Messler acknowledges the outstanding contributions from the Township in *Centennial History of Somerset County* (1878):

> The region has always been distinguished by the intelligence and the decided Christian character of its institutions. For intelligence, culture, and refinement its inhabitants are excelled nowhere. It has given the State and the nation some of their noblest men. At the bar, on the bench, and in the pulpit. Society is nowhere better organized, property more secure, or comfort and happiness more generally infused.

The principles for excellence were set long before by dedicated ministers who sought to educate their charges at the academy. These teachers provided an exemplary model for educators and concerned citizens in future generations.

—Zoe Petitt, Kaity Vermillion, and Brian Woolford

The old Anderson Road schoolhouse on Mendham Road in Bernardsville, 1887. The structure was originally the Methodist Episcopal Church, built in 1846, and converted into a one-room schoolhouse during the 1880s. Left to right (first row) includes: Mamie Stinson, Ella Rundio, Lulu Wright, Bessie Taylor, Ella Conway, others unknown. Second row includes: Fred Ballentine, Joseph Lowery, Stephen Riel, Willard Smith, Bert Apar, Theron Smith, J. Rooney. In the center of the photograph are three gentlemen: on the left is George Thorpe, teacher, Charles Quimby, and James Allen. Children include: Amy Riel, Bertha Rundio, Minnie Wolf, Mamie Thompson, Stella Abel, Ada Allen, Mary Liddy, and May Apgar. Third row includes: John Rogers, John Fitzpatrick, Will Lowery, Earl Bunn, Leland Mitchell, Frank Blazure, Bently Amerman, others unknown. Edwin Spinning is one of the youngsters sitting on the fence. (Bernardsville Public Library Local History Room)

Bernardsville's Early Schoolhouses

In those days you got to school the best you could. Fortunately, we had a family pet, a Shetland pony, and I drove him, accompanied by Miss Agatha Greulock. In 1906 a horse-drawn "state" picked up high school children in Liberty Corner and along the road as far as the Basking Ridge Presbyterian Church. From that point on you still had to transport yourself.

—Mary Louise Henry, history teacher at Bernards High School

By the 1800s a number of schools were built throughout the vicinity. Bernards Township originally included the village of Vealtown, later renamed Bernardsville. The Vealtown schools were built by local residents and managed by elected or appointed individuals. In 1844 the trustee of the Vealtown School District was William Ballentine. He received an annual salary of $14.30 from the school fund to oversee the budget for school maintenance and the teacher's salary.

In *Old-Time Schools and School-Books* (1963), Clifton Johnson explains that, surprisingly, in order to be a trustee, one did not have to meet rigorous educational standards. The position offered no monetary compensation, nor did it have much status in the community. A trustee's duties included school repairs. Furthermore, he added, "The district system resulted in many a tea-pot tempest, for every person had decided ideas as to how affairs in his or her own neighborhood should be managed, and whatever action the committeeman took, he had to run a gauntlet of criticism that was often far from judicial or gentle."

39

BERNARDSVILLE
BERNARD TWP.
Scale 30 Rods to the Inch

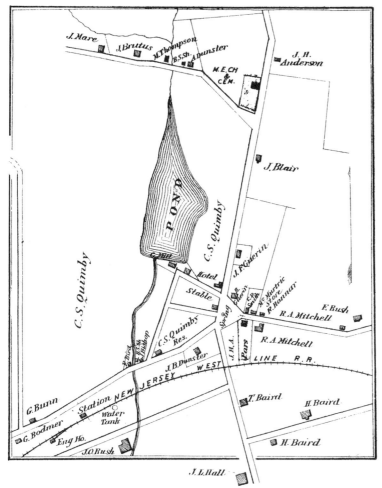

Bernardsville, from the Atlas of Somerset County, New Jersey, published by Beers, Comstock, and Cline, New York, 1873. (The Somerset Historical Society)

The first significant one-room schoolhouse in Vealtown was built in 1824. The Vealtown Schoolhouse was a square stone structure that was located on the corner of Anderson Road. A large potbellied stove stood in the center of the schoolroom. Older boys chopped wood to keep the stove burning. The desks had backless benches and were arranged around three sides of the room. Furthermore, the seats were uncomfortable. More often than not, the children's feet did not reach the floor. While students generally faced the walls, they turned around for recitation. Under each desktop was a storage place where two or three students kept their belongings. This schoolhouse served the village until 1840.

A second, larger schoolhouse was built in 1840 on a small plot more than a mile from the center of the village. This school was located slightly farther north on the same road at the crest of Anderson Hill. It was built on land belonging to Judge William Anderson, and it operated until 1880.

In 1880 a new Methodist church was erected on Church Street. The old church, which was constructed in 1846 at the corners of Mine Mount and Anderson Roads, was moved a short distance north and converted into a schoolhouse. The school property was adjacent to the original Methodist cemetery and replaced the Vealtown schoolhouse that had been in use since 1840.

Edwin Spinning writes in "One Room Schoolhouse Was Standard in the Old Days" (1964):

> The remodeled Methodist Church schoolhouse was a great improvement. The room was large, but a big pot stove in the center provided too much heat for those sitting nearest and too little for the ones farther away. There were four rows of double seats and desks, two long rows at the sides and two shorter ones in the center facing the rear, or west end, of the room. The teacher's desk was on a platform. Two long recitation benches faced his desk, the girls being on the south side of the room, the boys on the north.

Separate Entrances

> In about 1889 or 1890 the original church entrance at the front of the building was replaced with a window. Separate entrances were made for the girls on the south and the boys on the north. A small room at the rear was also partitioned off.

A standard school wagon, called a "state," was horse-drawn. It was manufactured to transport students to consolidated schools. These are Liberty Corner pupils on their way to Bernards High School in Bernardsville, ca. 1910. (The Historical Society of the Somerset Hills)

Landscape view of Bernardsville, ca. 1900. (Special Collections and University Archives, Rutgers University Library)

Old Methodist Church Schoolhouse, ca. 1891–92. Pupils from classes A and B are pictured. Some of the girls are wearing bracelets and rings, while a few of the boys have pocket watches. From left to right are: (front row) Edith Bowman, Ada Martin, Cecilia Gartz, Anna Ten Eick, and Edna Kinsey. Second row: teacher Kenneth Mathiesen, Earl Bunn, Eliza Faust, Lulu Wright, Mabel Guerin, Nellie Thorpe, and Will Douglas. Third row: Will Lowery, Henry Ten Eick, David Wright, Will Riddle, and Edwin Spinning. (The Historical Society of the Somerset Hills)

The Old Union one-room schoolhouse, 1851, located at the corner of Mosle and Roxiticus Road in Bernardsville stands in the area of Schiff Boy Scout Reservation at Mendham. (The Historical Society of the Somerset Hills)

Today the refurbished Old Union Schoolhouse is a residence in Bernardsville. (The Historical Society of the Somerset Hills)

One teacher taught all classes. There were no grades. One class was known as the fifth reader, the two highest being the A and B classes. The boys carried the coal and often tended to the fire. The windows were high and heavy, and as there were no sash weights, they had to be raised and held up with a window stick. Lighting was by kerosene bracket lamps, but when the separate entrances were made, a large lamp was suspended on a cable in the center of the room.

Drinking water was carried in pails from either the town pump or from a spring at the watering trough a short distance below the Anderson house. We have carried it many times from both places. Before the separate entrances were made, all dipped water from the same pail, and used the same dipper. They all survived!

Everyone had to walk to school, some for two miles or more and many lingered and played along the way home. The largest attendance was naturally during winter months, but if there was any work to be done on the farm, the older boys had to remain at home and help with it. During corn planting time, some of the boys would also fail to show up, temptation to earn a few cents being too great.

Excuses Approved

Corn was all planted by hand, the boys dropping it, men with hoes following to cover it, and like many of the other boys, this was my first job, the teacher always excusing us wither before or afterwards.

School kept until four o'clock and remained in session until the last of June. . . . When Kenneth Mathieson was the teacher during the early 1890s Algebra, Physics, Physiology, and German were introduced. As far as we have ever known, Mr. Mathieson was the first to have a public commencement exercise and award diplomas, and we in all probability, have one of the three that was awarded at that time, June 1894. There were few, if any, presented up to June 20, 1898.

Somerset Inn Schoolhouse in Bernardsville was a former icehouse, ca. 1895. (The Historical Society of the Somerset Hills)

Another notable school, the Somerset Inn Schoolhouse, was established in 1895. After the death of George Seney, owner of the Somerset Inn, the Somerset Land Company acquired his property. Evander Schley operated the old Somerset Inn. His employees requested that he provide a school for their children within walking distance, and Schley converted an existing icehouse on the grounds into a schoolhouse.

What must the children have thought, attending school in an icehouse? After all, schools were known for their drafty conditions, but being sent to an icehouse must have caused some concern. However, the icehouse was transformed into a warm and welcoming school, complete with a pot-belly iron stove that heated the room, warmed the pupils' metal lunch pails, and kept the ink in the inkwells from freezing overnight.

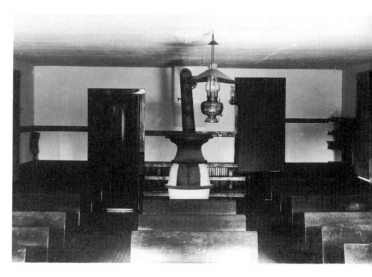

From the children's perspective, an interior rear view of Somerset Inn Schoolhouse (icehouse), ca. 1895, shows double desks and inkwells located in the front center of desktops. The teacher's desk traditionally was situated on a raised platform. (Bernardsville Public Library Local History Room)

From the teacher's perspective, an interior view of Somerset Inn Schoolhouse (icehouse) shows a large potbelly iron stove, recitation bench in the rear, and ceiling bracket light fixture, ca. 1895. (Bernardsville Public Library Local History Room)

Somerset Inn Schoolhouse (icehouse) in the distance. The small brown structure to the right of it is an outhouse with a brook running past it in the foreground, ca. 1890s. (Bernardsville Public Library Local History Room)

The lavish Somerset Inn at Bernardsville, New Jersey, is where guests vacationed in style, ca. 1890. It employed many workers to manage its golf course and casino where musical and theatrical productions took place. The inn included eight- and nine-room cottages. (The Historical Society of the Somerset Hills)

The first teacher was Miss Gent, whose salary Schley provided during the first year. The Township eventually took over the schoolhouse, which was moved to a site on Lloyd Road, just below the first bridge. The school operated until 1910. Teachers included: Margaret Bergen Dunham, Rachel Folsom, and Martha Dobbs Frost. It later was demolished, and some of the lumber was used in Bert McGee's home on Oak Stump Road, now West Oak Street, Basking Ridge.

Another early school, the Washington Corner School, was located in the estate area of Bernardsville. The area also was known as the Bernardsville Mountain Colony. The schoolhouse was situated in the vicinity of the present Lloyd Road.

Most schoolhouses in the village consisted of one or two small rooms, but that changed in 1905 when Fredrick P. Olcott, a philanthropist and resident of Bernardsville, purchased twenty-seven acres of land known as the Wolf Tract for $10,000. He erected a stone building there at a cost of $100,000.

At its dedication, Olcott presented the deed as a gift to the Bernards Township School District. The building, known

SOMERSET INN

THE SOMERSET INN, near Bernardsville, on the Delaware, Lackawanna and Western Railroad, is located among the highlands of New Jersey, in Somerset County (and in addition to the Inn there are for rent eight (8) handsome cottages, which cost to build $6,000 to $9,000 each, and are beautifully furnished.) Appreciation of the healthfulness and charms of this section is shown in the many beautiful homes with which the hills are dotted.

Hard wood floors and trim, handsome new furnishings throughout, the best of beds, large, well-ventilated bed rooms and bath rooms, hot and cold water, gas, steam heat, open fireplaces, spacious parlors, reading rooms, foyer hall and wide piazzas, make one's surroundings at Somerset Inn homelike and comfortable to a degree rarely found abroad.

Every convenience is maintained looking to the comfort of our guests: telephone, telegraph, post-office, good livery service, best accommodations for private turnouts, laundry, bowling alley, tennis court, golf links, billiard room, etc., while comfortable stages, meeting the eight trains daily, make the Inn easy of access.

Where else, so easily reached, can such accommodations and environments be found ? The Inn will open for guests May 1st and remain open until November 1st Should further information be desired, Mr. GEO. W. TUTTLE, the manager, may be found at the Inn, and will gladly afford every courtesy and attention to inquirers, either personally or by mail.

P. O. Address, SOMERSET INN, - BERNARDSVILLE, SOMERSET COUNTY, N. J.

Ad for the Somerset Inn boasts convenience for the well-to-do, ca. 1890. (Bernardsville Public Library Local History Room)

45

Washington Corner School, where Margaret B. Dunham taught in 1908–09 and traveled to and from school by horse and buggy. (The Historical Society of the Somerset Hills)

Schoolchildren, ca. 1908. (The Historical Society of the Somerset Hills)

Pupils Oscar Smith and Pearl Pickle, ca. 1908. (The Historical Society of the Somerset Hills)

Elementary school pupils at Olcott School, located in Bernardsville. Built in 1905, it initially served high school students who came from Bernards Township and the surrounding area from 1915 to 1927. (Bernardsville Public Library Local History Room)

as the Olcott School, became the first high school for Bernards Township. In the years that followed, it served alternately as a high school and an elementary school, its use determined by the needs of the growing community.

Mary Louise Henry highlights her freshmen year (1905):

> The high school consisted of two classes on the second floor and had two teachers, one of whom was Mr. James Shock, principal. The grammar school had the four first-floor rooms. By the time I graduated in 1909, the grammar school was crowded here and there, in the Methodist Church basement, the old railroad depot (where the *Bernardsville News* office is now located), and the high school was using as classrooms the little rooms on the third floor. A chicken-wire cage in the basement served as a chemistry laboratory. Physics was not taught.

In 1912 a stucco building was built to alleviate overcrowded conditions. The new building became the high school, while the elementary students remained at the Olcott School. When the need arose, however, the stucco building served as a grammar school for lower-grade students.

As a convenience, a tunnel was built from the basement of the grammar school to the lowest floor of the high school. Grammar school students used it in inclement weather, as it allowed them

The Olcott School, ca. 1905, was Bernardsville's new high school designed by Henry Janeway Hardenbergh, who was a Bernardsville resident and well-known New York architect. Hardenbergh was known for designing the Plaza Hotel and the Dakota apartment building on Central Park West in New York City. (Bernardsville Public Library Local History Room)

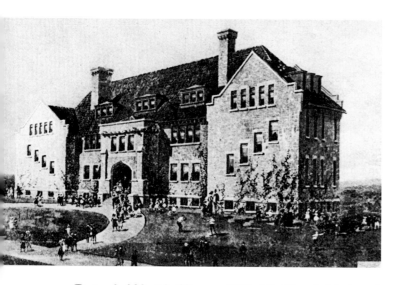

Postcard of Olcott building, ca. 1905. (The Historical Society of the Somerset Hills)

Bernards High School dedication ceremony. Patriotic citizens drape the American flag across the steps of the newly built structure, ca. 1905. More than 100 students, teachers, and townspeople attended the dedication, while others watched from the windows. Men in the foreground wear skimmer hats, while the girl in the lower right-hand corner sports a wide-brim sun bonnet. (Bernards Township Public Library Local History Room)

The Olcott School served pupils from Bernards Township and the neighboring areas, ca. 1906. (Bernardsville Public Library Local History Room)

Eventually, students were transported by windowless motorized buses, which replaced horse-drawn school wagons. (Bernardsville Public Library Local History Room)

Horse-drawn school wagons in front of the Olcott School. The U.S. Bureau of Education stated, "The best wagons are built so that drivers sit inside with the children." (From Andrew Gulliford's **America's Country Schools***) George L. Frost, a local freelance photographer, took the original photograph ca. 1907–10. The building consisted of four large classrooms on the first and second floors, along with a third-floor playroom for female pupils, and a gymnasium in the basement for male pupils. (Bernardsville Public Library Local History Room)*

Bernards High School pupils attend class in the Olcott building, ca. 1911. Seated in the front, wearing a plaid suit, is James Douglas Allen, a longtime resident of Bernards Township whose ancestors include the Holmes family. Seated in the same row and directly behind is John Kearns. The second pupil in the second row, diagonally behind James Allen, is Harold Starin, Peter Palmer's grand-uncle; the remaining pupils are unidentified. The photograph also shows the dark wainscoting approximately four and one-half feet from the floor and below the classroom windows—a common feature in schools around the late 19th century. (William W. Allen)

Bernards High School football team, the Crimson, ca. 1912. The team members include: fullback, Meany; right halfback, Bush; left halfback, Rausbury; quarterback, McGuirk; right end, Chrismon, Hurlburg. Right tackle, Bertram; right guard, Lisk, Brown; center, Everitt; left guard, Simmons; left tackle, Tompkins; left end, Weiss. (Bernardsville Public Library Local History Room)

Bernards High School girls' basketball team, ca. 1913. The "Bandana Girls" were so called for the bandanas they wore. The team competed against local athletic organizations. (Bernardsville Public Library Local History Room)

Graduating Class of 1915. It was not uncommon for young women to outnumber young men in graduating classes. Not all pupils were able to finish high school because some were needed to provide financial support for their families. (Bernardsville Public Library Local History Room)

to quickly get to art, shop, and music classes. The tunnel was lit by skylights that were at grade level on the school lawn.

In 1915, high school students were moved back to the Olcott School, and students from other grades were transferred to the stucco building. The Olcott School remained the Bernardsville High School until 1927.

On March 6, 1924, Bernardsville officially separated from Bernards Township. The Bernards Township Board of Education built a new high school in Bernardsville, which cost $275,000. It was "of the small type but which would meet the requirements of the Township."

The students were overjoyed with the new school's features, which included: a gymnasium complete with equipment; a cafeteria with all the necessary items to provide hot meals to the students; a shop for woodworking; a modern chemistry laboratory; a home economics room; and many classrooms for instructing those who were lucky enough to receive a four-year education.

Bernards High School, located in Bernardsville Borough, served students from Bernards Township, Far Hills, Peapack-Gladstone, Bedminster, and Passaic Township, now called Long Hill Township.

After 1948, Bernards Township experienced a larger surge in student population than did Bernardsville. Because of an imbalance in student numbers and operating costs, the Bernardsville

Bernards High School baseball team outside the Olcott building, ca. 1925. (Bernards Township Public Library Local History Room)

Bernards High auditorium had a seating capacity of 900. The stage, which had a red velvet curtain with the initials BHS inscribed in gold letters, was 40 feet wide and 20 feet deep and included dressing rooms. The side windows were cathedral style and ornate. (Bernards Township Public Library Local History Room)

Aerial view, ca. 1940, of the Olcott School on left side, Bernards High in center, and, in the background, the stucco school. It later became known as the "B" building; the building was razed in 1966. (Bernards Township Public Library Local History Room)

Peter S. Palmer, a 1954 graduate of Bernards High School, former Borough mayor, and now Somerset County freeholder, is well remembered for his fifty years as a band volunteer. In "He Still Loves a Parade," P.C. Robinson writes that Palmer played the clarinet in the Bernards High School band, and even while attending Cornell University, he volunteered to assist at Bernards High's annual band camp. He faced his biggest challenge in 1961, when many veteran band members left Bernards High School to attend the newly opened Ridge High School. "I was bound and determined to have the same size band, so we used a helluva lot of freshman." The end result was "a quality comparable to what they had the previous year."

Gordon Jolliffe, age ninety, born on August 9, 1917, is a native of Bernardsville. He attended the Olcott School, and in 1932 studied at Bernards High School for one year. During World War II, he was a volunteer spotter. (Josephine M. Waltz)

———————

Several years before the Bernards Township and Bernardsville School Districts were separated, the location of Bernards High School was an important site for volunteer spotters. During the early months of World War II, local citizens climbed an observation tower erected on the roof of the school. It was here that Gordon Jolliffe remembers climbing Bernards High School to report suspicious planes.

W. Jacob Perry writes in the *Bernardsville News* "When America was on Alert 60 Years Ago" (2001):

> The tower was a direct result of the Japanese bombing of Pearl Harbor on Dec. 7, 1941. Shortly afterward, Bernards American Legion Post 277 sponsored the erection of a tower at the Percy Pyne estate in the borough's mountain section.
>
> But getting spotters to the site on a 4-hour basis became a problem due to a rubber and gasoline shortage. That led the community leaders to eye Bernards High School, which was within walking distance for most residents.
>
> Builder Joseph Dobbs went on to construct the tower on the school roof at a cost of about $500, with the Board of Education providing $235 and the balance raised by the local Rotary Club. The structure was accepted and put into operation on Saturday, May 16, 1942. Jolliffe's father, Reginald James Jolliffe, volunteered as a spotter. The elder Jolliffe was a member of the Independent Organization of Odd Fellows, which met near Olcott Square and sent several volunteers. Ultimately, the father was joined by the son.
>
> The younger Jolliffe, who then worked at the old Dean Sage estate in the mountain section, would man the tower several times.

"It was always after my father got back from work, around 7 p.m.," he said. "We always hit (the tower) when it was fairly light."

"You were given certain hours of the day' in shifts of two or three hours," Jolliffe recalled. "You came until the next man came to relieve you. It was never left empty. There was always someone spotting a plane, and it was amazing how many planes you'd see."

The tower was glass-enclosed and had a heater, but "it wasn't anything permanent about it." As for computers or something else that might track a plane, "they weren't even invented then."

Ultimately, the tower was shut down without much fanfare. A single sentence in the *News* said it was discontinued on October 5, 1943—nearly two years before the war ended.

To Our Flag

Watching "Old Glory"
Waving in the breeze
Should make you
Get down on your knees
And thank the Good Lord
For being able to say
I belong to the Good Old
U.S.A.

—Gordon Jolliffe, Bernardsville
volunteer aircraft spotter, 1942

Mary Louise Henry, ca. 1922, a history teacher at Bernards High School. (Bernardsville Public Library Local History Room)

and Bernards Township school districts were separated. The impact on Bernards Township is discussed in Chapter Twelve, "Ridge High School."

This action solved one problem but created another: Who was the rightful owner of Bernards High? Was it Bernardsville or Bernards Township? The answer was not clear. Donated parcels of land and gifts of money clouded the issues.

The Superior Court determined that Bernardsville would own the building since the Bernardsville Board of Education had assumed responsibility for its operation.

Conflicts are not unique to the 21st century; they existed 100 years ago. The following article, excerpted from the *Bernardsville News*, "School Question to Date," written by Dr. W. B. Judd in 1900, bears witness to disagreements about expenditures, budgets, and management of funds between communities and school boards.

> I yield to no one in my admiration for the public school system. It is the training ground
> for citizenship, and the kindergarten of patriotism. The proposition that was defeated at the
> last school meeting was eminently fair to the two villages and to the whole township. The
> rural brethren who refused to become a party to help the cause of education in our district
> advertised themselves as non-progressive. If the same narrow spirit had been shown in past
> years with reference to improving roads, money collected in this part of the township would

Young middle grade students outside the Olcott School, ca. 1900s. Teacher sits on stone wall at right. (Bernardsville Public Library Local History Room)

Bernards High School contained nine classrooms, a cafeteria, auditorium, and gymnasium. Student athletes are pictured outside the school, ca. 1928. (Bernardsville Public Library Local History Room)

Pupils seated on a long bench at the Olcott School, ca. 1900s. Girls in the front row wear traditional, buttoned up shoes and oversized hair bows. The teacher is standing in third row, far right. (Bernardsville Public Library Local History Room)

Bernards High School Orchestra, 1923–26. Standing left to right: Clifford Ludlow, Harry Stern, Ellsworth Dobbs, Herman Phadenhauer, Jules Gardner, Charles Weymouth, Mr. Walter Crouse, Boyden Vlomerfelt, Sidney Jones, Henry Tiger, William Acken, and Raymond Ludlow. Sitting: May Bailey, Gladys Cavanaugh, Martha Shefcik, Ruth Van Dorn, Erma Goldsmith, Eleanor Bowers, and Ailene Allen (Liddy). (Bernardsville Public Library Local History Room)

Pupils from the Senior Class of 1912 stand outside the Olcott building. By 1914, class size had grown to 21 students. Left to right: (front row) Molly Price, Lila Nolan, Leona Bockoven, Adah Meeker, Edith Bolmer, Minnie Tewes, Madeline Sutpher, Beatrice Sharpe; back row: Lewis Baldwin, Robert Brown, David Neill, and Elmer Tiger. (Bernardsville Public Library Local History Room)

WITH THE APPROVAL OF THE BOARD OF EDUCATION

The Bernards School Savings Bank

operated for the pupils, by the pupils, will open for business in September
... in the ...

High School Building

| 5 CENTS | will open an account, when your account has grown to | 5 DOLLARS |

the Bernards School Savings Bank will open an account for you in the Savings Department of the BERNARDSVILLE NATIONAL BANK, where you will receive THREE per cent interest, compounded quarterly

BEGIN TO SAVE NOW and be the FIRST to get one of our SAVINGS BOOKS

Bernardsville National Bank

Evidence of Bernards High School's innovative method of teaching savings and banking skills to high school students, ca. 1908. (The Historical Society of the Somerset Hills)

S. S. Childs Memorial Cafeteria, 1928, a gift presented by Mrs. Emma F. Childs in memory of her late husband, Samuel S. Childs, a former New Jersey state senator. The cafeteria was built to feed 235 people in approximately thirty-one minutes. In addition to the many appliances (ranges, iron sink, gas oven, Frigidaire), the cafeteria also contained 1,656 pieces of china and 788 pieces of silver. (Bernards Township Public Library Local History Room)

have been spent in the immediate vicinity where it was collected instead of being distributed with an impartial hand throughout the township. It is my deepest convictions that this last school meeting did this village a wrong. It wronged every child in this district. This wrong still continues and will remain until men value mind and morals more than a few paltry dollars.

If the voters of this township in this enlightened age stand on the threshold of a new century with the Township valuation growing at the rate of a quarter of a million dollars annually cannot get in line with progress, and devise a plan to spend a few thousand dollars in the interest of education, they simply announce to the world that they should have been born in the Middle Ages when there was no public school system, and when the masses were not annoyed by the necessity of reading or writing. Certainly their mental affinities are several centuries back.

The Francis G. Lloyd Memorial Gymnasium contained a basketball court, parallel bars, rings suspended from the ceiling, mats, and two sets of bleachers—one with three tiers and the other with eight tiers. The gymnasium also was a place for social functions such as dances and parties, ca. 1928. (Bernards Township Public Library Local History Room)

Former Principal Dr. Lynn Caravello served 18 years before retiring in 2007. Today Bernards High School is run by Dr. Scot Beckerman. The school serves 750 students in grades nine through twelve from Bernardsville, Far Hills, Peapack-Gladstone, and Bedminster. In 2007, 172 students graduated high school. Bernards High School has maintained a history of academic excellence for its students. A total of 89 percent of graduates attended four- and two-year colleges in 2006, and 90 percent in 2007. Its graduates have attended competitive institutions of higher learning.

Reverend Dr. W. B. Judd can rest assured that the efforts of this little village exceeded the expectations set in 1900.

—*Kristina Cheung, Sara Jones, Michael Shaw, Sam Schraer, Ria Talsania, and Emily Zaboski*

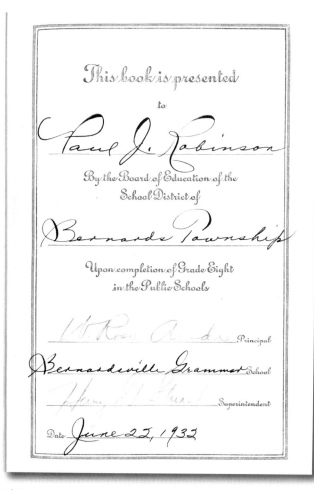

Title page from "Our Great State Papers," which eighth-grade graduating students received from Bernardsville Grammar School, 1932. Contents included: the Declaration of Independence, the Constitution of the United States, the Constitution of New Jersey, and the History of and Pledge to the United States Flag. (The Historical Society of the Somerset Hills)

The play, Li'l Abner, 1966, featured Phil Nardone as Abner and Meryl Streep as Daisy Mae. Nardone, a Bernards Township resident, is now assistant executive editor of the Bernardsville News. Meryl Streep, formerly of Bernards Township and Bernardsville, became a famous award-winning movie actress. (Bernardsville Public Library Local History Room)

Joined public school systems, Bernards Township and Borough of Bernardsville, communicate expenses for the month of October 1, 1929. (The Historical Society of the Somerset Hills)

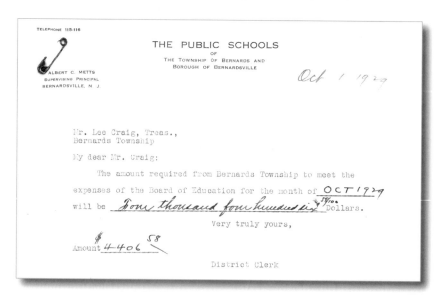

Second Section

The Bernardsville News.

BERNARDSVILLE. SOMERSET COUNTY, N. J.. THURSDAY. JUNE 18, 1953

112 Graduate in Bernards High School Class of 1953

Abbondanzo, John Anthony
Ansede, Carmen
Anstedt, Lilyan C.
Apgar, Janet K.
Bayless, Jane Cynthia
Beatty, William Henry
Beihl, William James
Berg, Gunnar Manuel
Bettler, Joan
Boardman, Edwin L.
Booth, Peter
Bowker, Elizabeth Mae
Bresee, Rienzi Augustus, 4th
Brown, Joan Beverly
Byrd, Leonard

Deutsch, Robert Carl
Downs, Sally H.
Dubus, Mary Anne
Eggling, Patricia Ann
Farese, Alice Ann
Field, Bensley H. L.
Fitzsimmons, Richard E.
Floden, Marie Ann
Frank, Elsie Agatha
Germuska, Thomas Andrew
Grimm, Jeannette P.
Hageman, Barbara Ann
Hanssen, George Parellus
Hill, John Edward
Hoffman, Harry Everett

Johnston, Ronald Linn
Kirby, Donald Dance
Kirchiro, Michael LeRoy
Kneser, Joseph Stanley
Knoke, Winfield Scott
Koenig, Marion Patricia
Kolb, Jon Frederic
Koppes, Donald Lee
Kunz, Mary Jane
Leuchter, Inge Christa
Liddy, Bernice
Mancuso, Amelia Marie
Martinot, Claude P.
Matthews, John Hall
McKee, Arthur Winston

Nervine, Frances Della
Niebel, Jeanne Ann
Nielsen, Elizabeth M.
Oberman, Donald Orr
Ortman, Mahlon Howard
Otten, Barbara
Parker, Gail Louise
Pearce, Robert Weldon
Pearson, Carol Ann
Pitman, Arnold Walter
Poindexter, James B., Jr.
Polacek, Sandra Ann
Pomeroy, Adrienne Joyce
Primavera, Mary Jo
Rebenstorff, Edna Anita

Russo, Rocco Lawrence
Ryan, Joyce Elizabeth
*Salegna, John
Sassi, Marian Margaret
Sawyer, Thomas I.
Sayer, Audrey Catharine
Scaff, Jack Hall, Jr.
Scheffler, Barbara Ann
Schoppe, William Craig
Seibert, Lynn Carol
Senkbeil, Robert I.
Sibilia, Mary
Simpson, Grace Ann
Skillman, Patricia Ann
Smith, Margaret Anne

Stewart, Barbara
Stinson, Margaret
Struthers, Elizabeth
Szarek, Albina Stella
Totten, Richard E.
Trebilcock, Benjamin
Trepiccione, Barbara
Trepiccione, Pasquale
Tuffnell, Glenn W.
Twichell, Jack Brown
Wack, Joyce Beverly
Weinhofer, John F.
Weining, Joan Marie
Weiss, Mary Anne
Wortman, Sherman

The Class of 1953 graduated 112 students from Bernards High School. Students from Bernardsville, Bernards Township, and other districts are pictured here. (Bernards Township Public Library Local History Room)

Tuition payment made out to Florence Jones, custodian of schools, for $6,000. (The Historical Society of the Somerset Hills)

Washington Valley one-room schoolhouse located on Washington Valley Road, Bridgewater, New Jersey, ca. 1850. (Somerset County Historical Society)

Lesser-Known Schools in Bernards Township

———◆———

The Board of Education of the Township of Bridgewater, will sell by Bargain and Sale Deeds, the following buildings and tracts of lands, situate, lying and being in the Township of Bridgewater:

1. WASHINGTON VALLEY SCHOOL, and land, located in the Washington Valley, on the north side of the road leading from Pluckemin to Martinsville. Being the same land deeded to the Trustees of the School District of the Township of Bridgewater, by William McBride, and Easter his wife, by deed dated October 26, 1850, which deed is recorded in the Somerset County Clerk's Office, in Book M. No. 2, of Deeds, page 78. Containing one acre of land more or less.

The area that is today West Millington, in the southeast corner of Bernards Township, was originally known as Pleasant Valley and described as a "mere hamlet" in 1840. It was the site of the Pleasant Valley School on the Stone House farm side of the road, referred to as "the Stonehouse School." In 1844 John Quick served as the school's trustee and received $15.17 for the school fund. This amount was slightly higher than the money allotted to the Vealtown School. That indicates that the Pleasant Valley School served a greater number of students in 1844 than did the Vealtown School, discussed in Chapter Three.

This lithograph, ca. 1874, hangs in the Brick Academy Museum. Fine print reads: "Entered according to act of Congress, in the year 1874 by Currier & Ives, in the office of the Librarian of Congress, at Washington." The lithograph is indicative of the times when American life and newsworthy events were depicted. The prints were drawn and lithographed by persons other than Currier & Ives. For nearly seventy-five years, the firm provided "Colored Engravings for People." Most Currier & Ives prints were hand-colored lithographs. Small folio prints originally sold for 20 cents and larger ones for $1 to $3. The date in which the lithograph was acquired by the academy is unknown. (The Historical Society of the Somerset Hills)

In 1867, William and Mary Smalley deeded property to trustees George Coddington, Isaac L. Runyon, and Simeon Mandy for the purposes of building a second schoolhouse. Melvina Oehlers, in "Look to Your Schools," provides details of its location in the following account. Deeds of the time were typically worded this way. Their obscure references, to stones that had disappeared and property lines that had moved through time, make it difficult to locate the original land tracts:

> Property for the second school described as beginning in the middle of the public road lead- ing from Stone House Village to Liberty Corner, at a corner of the land of Edward Vail's; thence running by the line of his land north to a stone therein; thence east to a stone; thence south to the middle of said road; thence west to the beginning.

The school's property covered half an acre, was valued at $150, and the site had access to a spring of water, according to Oehlers.

The spring provided the school with its drinking water. The teacher pumped water into a bucket twice a day, morning and noon. The bucket and dipper were left in the hallway.

Unlike the children of today who usually frequent the water fountain as they need to, Hilda Voss, who in 1922 attended a one-room schoolhouse in Butler County, Nebraska, explained that, "We only drank at noon and during recess, which was held twice a day, morning and afternoon. At first we used the dipper, but when we got older we brought our own cups and kept them at school."

The Pleasant Valley School structure outlasted many of the other schools of the day. It later was converted to a restaurant whose various names included the Carriage Inn, Bill's Corral, the One and Only, and Michael's. Today the restaurant that specializes in northern Italian cuisine is called Café Rustica. The building remains a historical landmark. Although no artifacts were found at the school site when the restaurant owners purchased the building, its charm is still evident.

As the Township continued to grow, so did the number of schoolhouses. At least three other schoolhouses were built on the outskirts of Bernards Township, including the White Bridge, Washington Valley, and Mount Vernon Schoolhouses. Some became well known, while others provided a shorter service until larger schools were built in the area.

Because there were no schools in the area of the former Lord Stirling manor site, the children who lived there attended the White Bridge Schoolhouse on the Pleasant Plains Road in Passaic Township, now known as Long Hill Township. The school was near a bridge that crossed the Passaic River about two miles from the Bernards Township line. In 1844 it received $5.17, from the State, which was the lowest amount given to any district. Christopher Barkalow was the district trustee.

School laws required children to attend the schools closest to their homes, so children in the vicinity of Liberty Corner attended the Washington Valley Schoolhouse on the north side of Washington Valley Road in Bridgewater Township. It was known as the "little red schoolhouse."

'Schoolmarm's house' in Liberty Corner part of a historic district

BERNARDS — A century-old home in the Liberty Corner section of the township is known locally as the "Schoolmarm's House."

The name was attached to the two-story stucco house because of its proximity to the Liberty Corner school and the fact that it was originally the home of the local teacher. Village records in the township library mention the "schoolmarm's wedding" in the home's front parlor.

The date of the home's construction is unknown but it is generally accepted that it was built about 1870. In the 1920s the owners added a 3-foot extension on the kitchen and bedroom and created a laundry room and pantry — and at the same time probably added indoor plumbing. In 1967 A fourth bedroom was created out of the crib room by decreasing the size of the master bedroom, and another addition was added to the rear of the house. In 1985 the bathrooms were renovated. In 1988, skylights, an atrium door and a deck were added to the conservatory.

In addition to the four bedrooms and two bathrooms, the house has a fireplace in the living room, pocket doors leading to the dining room — which has a china closet, a wraparound deck (balanced by a wraparound front porch in the front) and a two-car detached garage.

The house — part of the Liberty Corner Historic District — is listed at $295,000 by Walter Kearns of Weichert Realtors.

Courier-News photo by George R. Smith

The wedding of the local school teacher in this house is detailed in Bernards' recorded history.

Known as the "Schoolmarm's House," this century-old home was built in the 1870s and was said to be originally the home of a teacher whose wedding took place in the front parlor. Photographed 1990. (Bernards Township Public Library Local History Room)

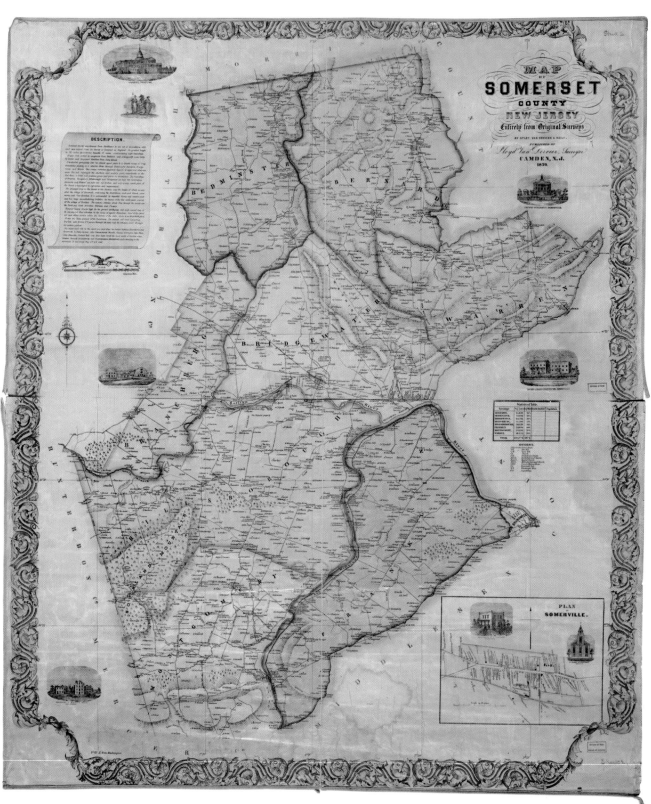

An 1850s map of Somerset County, New Jersey. Entirely from Original Surveys by Otley, Van Derveer and Keily. Published by Lloyd van Derveer, Surveyor. Camden, NJ. (Courtesy of The Library of Congress)

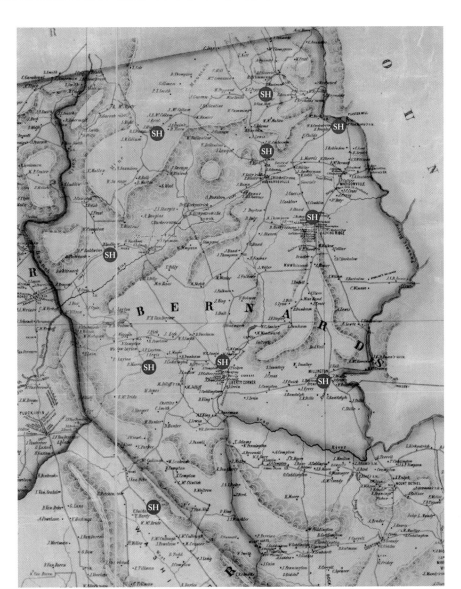

REFERENCE.

S.H indicates School House.
S.M. . . . . . Saw Mill.
G.M. . . . . . Grist Mill.
Ch. . . . . . . Church.
P.Ch. . . . . Presbyterian Church.
D.R.Ch. . . Dutch Reformed Church.
Bap.Ch. . . Baptist Church.
M.E.Ch. . . Methodist Episcopal Church.
F.M.H. . . . Friends Meeting House.
B.S. . . . . . Blacksmith Shop.
W.S. . . . . . Wheelwright Shop.
P.O. . . . . . Post Office

Above: Enlarged legend from 1850s map.

Left: A portion of the Somerset County map shows the Township of Bernards. The capital letters "SH" denote the location of schoolhouses in the Township in 1850. (Courtesy of The Library of Congress)

A view of Washington Valley from Washington Valley Road in Bridgewater, ca. 1900. (Somerset County Historical Society)

Side view of Washington Valley Schoolhouse in Bridgewater, New Jersey, shows the traditional gabled roof used by most country schools. (Somerset County Historical Society)

Margaret B. Dunham and students outside old Schley Hall on the fairgrounds in Far Hills, 1910. (The Historical Society of the Somerset Hills)

Students who lived two miles from the center of Liberty Corner traversed a cross-country route over a hill to the back door of the school. They walked through meadows and fields and past streams of the rural village, wearing a path to the schoolhouse. On these daily jaunts, the school-children carried gallon pails filled with their lunches. A typical meal consisted of a cold potato or hard-boiled egg, bread slathered with molasses or lard, and cold meat.

Washington Valley Schoolhouse was built in 1751 and stood opposite the origin of Mount Vernon Road. It was erected in the valley and was situated one mile east of Somerville Road. Bernards Township contributed tuition funds for students who attended. This school lasted until another stone school, known as Liberty Corner, was built on Church Street in 1905. Children named Frank Stetzer, Mamie Quimby, Jim Hunter, and Jesse Wilde attended Washington Valley School. Today, the building is a private home.

In *Historic Somerset* (1965), J. H. Van Horn includes an account by Wilde, who began attending the school in 1884, at age six. Wilde said that in order for students to save time during their three-mile journey to school each day, they often "cut cross country." Harsh winter weather was a challenge for the student; Wilde said that oftentimes, if he paused while walking, his "leather boots would freeze." Another obstacle was the outhouse's inconvenient location in the woods. "'But that was all right, too,'" Wilde said. "'It took us that much longer to get back to our work in the classroom.'"

Typical one-room schoolhouses provided a traditional outhouse for students. In *America's Country Schools* (1984), Andrew Gulliford notes that while most schoolhouses had only one outhouse, some had two—one designated for boys and the other for girls. One popular design had a coal or wood shed placed in the middle of the outhouse for added convenience and privacy. Some outhouses had two- or three-seat privies, where children could be sent as a group to use the facility. Of course, they were separated by gender. The teacher, however, had the benefit of using an outhouse a distance from that of her students. Gulliford further explains that outhouses not only served a practical function but also were used by the students "as safe bases for games of tag, convenient hideouts from other family members in school and fine places to conjure up plots."

The community of Far Hills was part of Bernards Township until 1921. An auxiliary building, Schley Hall, located at the fairgrounds in Far Hills, was used as an early elementary school for children living in the area until a public school was later built. Teachers at the Schley Hall in 1910 included Margaret B. Dunham and Miss Davis.

The northernmost school in the village of Bernardsville was Mount Vernon School, located on what is now Lloyd Road. Thomas Nutt, the trustee, lived close to the school in a residence on Nutt Road (now Washington Corner Road). In 1844 the school received $22.13 of the school fund. John Y. Marsh was the first schoolmaster of this one-room schoolhouse.

In *Look to Your Schools* (1973), Melvina M. Oehlers describes how, when Marsh was young, he rescued a man from drowning, and the grateful man subsequently funded Marsh's education as a minister of the Gospel. However, because of poor vision, Marsh traveled from New York to Bernards Township to become a schoolmaster instead. Oehlers adds, "It is said that, shortly after arriving, he fell in love with a local girl of the Sanders family, and immediately following their marriage they went to live in a little log cabin nearby."

Other locations such as the Pleasant Valley Pool and Pleasant Valley Park in Bernards Township were named in honor of the Pleasant Valley area.

Grant Barney Schley (1845–1917), brother of Evander H. Schley (who converted the ice house of the Somerset Inn), was a land developer and real estate broker from New York State. He visited the area of Bedminster and Bernards Township, where his brother had purchased thousands of acres of farmland, some sight unseen.

Old Schley Hall, 1910, school at Far Hills on Peapack end of fairgrounds, later served as the American Legion Post. (The Historical Society of the Somerset Hills)

Grant Schley's wife was pleased with the view and referred to it as the "far hills," thus giving the area its name. On lands set aside for community use, Schley paid for the cost of building a village school, a church, a firehouse, a social club, and a recreational area. He built stables, barns, and a grandstand to the fairgrounds.

The old Schley Hall in Far Hills was razed in July 1968. The building was a landmark in the Borough, the scene of many Visiting Nurse Association rummage sales and community meetings, and a one-time borough school. The building was located across from the Far Hills Fairgrounds.

With time off from school, children sleigh ride in Basking Ridge, New Jersey, ca. 1909. A common strategy was to link the sleds together and hook the sledders' feet to the runners located behind them. Highest school attendance was during the winter months, with a greater turnout of older boys. (The Historical Society of the Somerset Hills)

Margaret B. Dunham and class at the fairgrounds. Old Schley Hall stands in the background on far left of photo, 1910. (The Historical Society of the Somerset Hills)

Miss Davis, a teacher at Schley Hall, and a friend at the Far Hills station, 1909. (The Historical Society of the Somerset Hills)

By the mid-1800s, there was a shortage of male teachers like Marsh. Marian I. Doyle explains in "The Faithful Teacher Could Find Her Reward in Heaven" (1993), that as men headed West during the California gold rush, female teachers became the norm. A lack of male teachers prompted Congress to begin training young women for the profession. Women were paid less than men; it was generally believed that women did not hold much responsibility for the financial support of their families. In 1878 a man could earn $41.91 per month; a female teacher received $36.53.

Female teachers had to agree to a very strict lifestyle. Doyle cites an 1896 manual that advised the female teacher to "very much promote her own health by washing the surface of the body every morning in cold water."

"Schoolmarms" were not allowed to associate with men of "questionable morals" or to attend late night social functions during the school week. In addition, many female teachers were not allowed to marry. These restrictions remained in place for quite some time.

Not every aspect of schoolhouse history is charming. Many people think of the one-room schoolhouses as quaint, but in *America's Country Schools* (1984), Gulliford explains that the often romanticized "little red schoolhouse" was a myth. In reality, most country schools were white. They also were "crowded, dark and cold, and the interior arrangements and equipment did not lead particularly to attentiveness or order in the classroom."

Yet, towns and their historical societies readily recognized the importance of the "school-houses," as the first structures to educate children. These schoolhouses remain an important part of our American educational heritage.

—*Kristina Cheung, Jack Rogers, Michael Shaw, Emily McCormick, and Emily Zaboski*

The Franklin Schoolhouse originally stood forty feet in length and twenty-four feet wide with fifteen-foot posts and a ten-foot ceiling. In 1926 it became a private residence. (Josephine M. Waltz)

Franklin Corner Schoolhouses

I attended a prayer meeting in the schoolhouse for the first time.

—Nathaniel Douglas, resident of Franklin Corners
July 22, 1832

The Franklin School District was located on the northeastern side of Bernards Township in an area known as Franklin Corners. At different times in the 1800s, Franklin Corners was home to three one-room schoolhouses, which were located near the famous Van Dorn Mill, formerly known as Woodward's Mill. Parents privately managed the schools until a board assumed responsibility.

The first of the three schoolhouses was set in a locust grove behind the home of resident William Van Doren. This schoolhouse later was moved and converted into a private residence, known as the Gallagher house.

The second schoolhouse was built in the spring of 1832, but by 1849 it had become too small. The Board of Education proposed to move the school building, sell it, and build a larger one. Robert Rogers purchased it at an auction in 1851 for $75. He bought land on Hardscrabble Road and moved the structure there, later converting it into a residence. Today it bears no resemblance to a schoolhouse.

Built in 1851, the Franklin Schoolhouse is a rectangular clapboard building in simple Greek Revival style. The front gable faces the street, and flat columns flank the sides of the building. Windows on both stories are six-over-six with the majority having the old bubbly-glass panes. (Josephine M. Waltz)

The third schoolhouse, known as the Franklin Institute or the Franklin Academy, was built in 1851 on the same site as the second one. The school was built on Childs Road, across from and a short distance above the Van Dorn Mill.

The Board of Education held two fairs, which raised $803 to pay for the cost of building the school. This school was built without a bell tower; the teacher used a hand bell to call students to class. The Franklin Academy had the longest service of the three schools in the district. Most of its graduating students went into farming or mill life, but some pursued higher education.

In 1854, Nathaniel Douglass and Ferdinand Van Doren, neighbors of the schoolhouse, agreed to donate land on both sides of it to enlarge the play property. The local residents valued having spacious grounds for children's play. There is frequent mention of donated parcels of land surrounding the school properties for the betterment of the children who attended these early schools.

Three teachers alternately taught throughout the school year at the Franklin Academy. They earned 35¢ per day per student, or an average of $25 per month to teach 20 to 30 students. Parents paid for the number of days their children attended school. School sessions were for three 12-week periods, with one session extending into the summer. Summer sessions began at 8 a.m. and ended at 5 p.m., while the winter sessions began at 9 a.m. and ended at 4 p.m. Children had a one-hour lunch and recess period.

In a "Teacher Trustee Constitution," dated 1850, the trustees were held responsible for examining, hiring, or firing teachers. During such time, the trustees were directed to hear all grievances and to take appropriate action to settle them.

Clifton Johnson notes in *Old-Time Schools and School-Books* (1963) that a 1789 law in New England required supervision of the early schoolhouses, so regular inspections were conducted by ministers and select town officials. The inspectors were required to examine

The original Franklin School bell is typical of 19th-century bells. The ten-inch-high and six-inch-wide bell belonged to Margaret McMurtry, great-aunt to Nancy Childs Knobloch. (Josephine M. Waltz)

and visit the schools at least every six months. Their visits were very formal in nature. They inquired about the regulations, discipline, and aptitude of the students. "The whole delegation, comprised of the community's chief priests and elders—sometimes to the number of more than 20—went in stately procession to the schools in turn," said Johnson.

The visits to the Franklin Schools were conducted on a more frequent basis, once a month and probably with fewer attendees.

The Franklin School District held roll books or registers from the Franklin Academy dating as far back as 1809. These registers are privately owned now. The roll books reveal much information about school days at the Franklin Academy. A register dated 1871 records 53 children enrolled for the school year. However, for the January 1871-to-March 1871 session, only 17 children attended school—four girls and 13 boys. Of these students, the youngest was five and the oldest 18.

The 1871 register shows that all students were tardy at one time or another during the year. In addition, children from Passaic Township also attended this school, but their attendance was kept in a separate roll book. The register included disciplinary records as well. Apparently, five students were chastised or punished, but none was suspended or expelled during the 1871 January-March session.

Bobbie Kalman describes in *A One-Room School* (1994) the harsh punishments given to student pranksters. Both boys and girls were disciplined for arriving late, answering questions incorrectly, or falling asleep.

A deed dated March 1, 1854, and inscribed "Ferdinand Van Doren to the Franklin School District" for land adjoining the southeast corner of the schoolhouse lot for purposes of enlarging the school. It was signed by Van Doren and witnessed by Daniel McMurtry. This document was written on blue-gray paper and included a wax seal on the lower left corner. (Nancy Childs Knobloch)

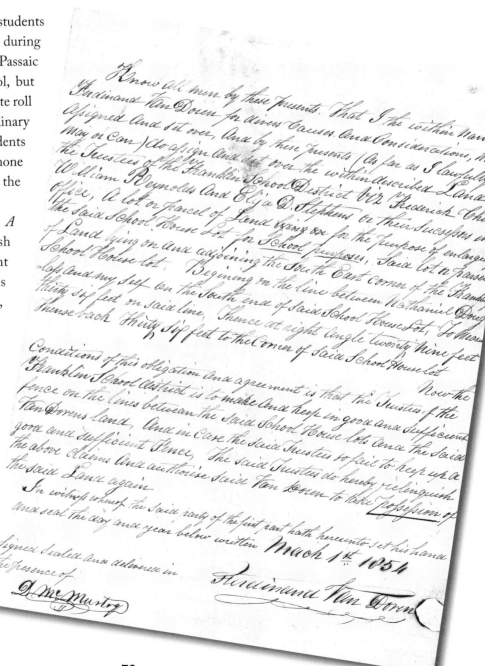

Kalman adds, "Besides being punished at school, children were usually punished again when they returned home."

Sometimes children were ordered to memorize long passages or write lines over and over. Teachers also shamed their students by making them wear a "dunce cap" or a sign around their neck. Students who enjoyed playing their pranks were not as happy with their punishments. "One boy was forced to balance on a block of wood, and the other was told to put on a bonnet and sit on the girls' side of the classroom." One of the most common punishments was getting a whipping with a hickory switch or a birch rod. Sometimes the strapping was so severe that students went home with red marks across their legs. The mere threat of "the peg" was enough to change any child's behavior. The guilty pupil's hair was fastened to a clip, which was pegged into a wall at a height that kept the child standing on tiptoes until the teacher thought the student had learned his or her lesson.

Not all punishments were as harsh as the peg. The schoolmaster sometimes ordered students to copy lines hundreds of times. "Writing lines was a gentle form of punishment, but it certainly wasn't any fun!" said Kalman.

However, the teacher was not the only one to hand out punishments to pranksters. In "Going Back to School Was Much Tougher in the Past," Marion I. Doyle details how students retaliated against *harsh teachers*:

Pupils, however, had found their own means of retaliation in the custom of "barring." At holiday time treats were expected, and woe to the schoolmaster who failed to provide them. The teacher who refused to cooperate would find that his pupils had arrived before him, barred him from his schoolroom, and were willing to do battle for days to keep him out. The standoff would only end after the schoolmaster had relented with a pledge to set out the cider and snacks.

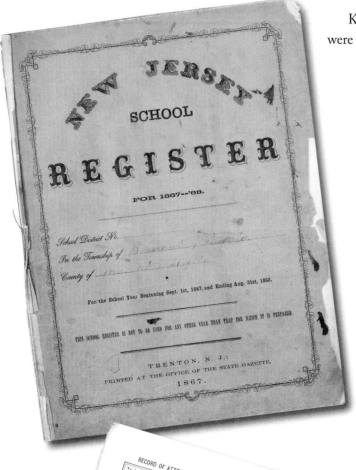

Top: Franklin School Register in Bernards Township for the 1867–68 school year. According to New Jersey law, teachers were required to maintain a school register in order to receive a salary. They turned in the registers to the district clerk. (Nancy Childs Knobloch)

Bottom: An inside look at the Franklin School Register, 1867. H. F. Robinson, teacher, marked and tallied attendance for a four-week interval or for each 20 school days. (Nancy Childs Knobloch)

Besides disciplinary records, the 1871 Franklin Academy Register also shows the number of students who studied specific subjects such as reading, writing, arithmetic, geography, and history. During the January session, 14 students studied spelling, reading, and writing, and only one student studied bookkeeping.

Along with such information about students' behavior and studies, the registers show the teacher's meticulous handwriting.

Penmanship was considered a valuable skill, and the teacher provided a stellar example for her students. People believed that neat handwriting was the sign of a cultured person. Knowing how to write, or cipher, was important for anyone wanting to be a storekeeper, craftsperson, or farmer.

Children who attended the Franklin Institute probably practiced writing by scratching a pencil on a slate, as many students did in those times. Both the pencil and the slate were made of hard rock. After many years of use, the slate was covered with hundreds of scratch marks. Other writing tools included goose-feather quills, which required a sharp nib. This was made with a knife, hence the name "penknife." After students or the teachers made a sharp nib, they dipped the pens into small glass inkwells. They then practiced writing in straight and slanted lines, making circles and swirls, while avoiding to press so hard as to make the pen squeak across the paper.

Eventually, the slates and penknives were put away. Having served the community well, the Franklin Academy School was sold at a public auction in 1906. James J. Lynch became the third owner when he bought the school and the surrounding 0.13 acres for $200.

The schoolhouse served multiple purposes over time. It was a learning center for its children; it also was a place where prayer meetings were held on Wednesdays; and it was a place for public meetings. The building was valued as a center of education in its early years of service, and today is valued for its architectural style. For one family it is home.

Top: School clerk certificate, September 10, 1868, from Adnah McMurtry testifying that the contents of the school register report are accurate and truthful. (Nancy Childs Knobloch)

Bottom: A portion of a report from the clerk of School District 1, Franklin Corner School, shows: amount of tuition collected during the school year, amount paid for teachers' salaries, present value of school property, number of schoolchildren ages five to 18 residing in the district, number of months the school has been kept open, number of children enrolled in the school register, the number who have attended ten months, between eight and ten months, between six and eight months, and between six and four months. This information was followed by the names of parents or guardians, the children's names, and their ages. (Nancy Childs Knobloch)

—*Rory Hand, Divya Krishnan, Jake Massa, and Emily McCormick*

A view of the Bernardsville Mountain, ca. 1900. (Special Collections and University Archives, Rutgers University Library)

Mine Mount and Mine Brook Schoolhouses

Dear Sir,

The "Mystery Photograph" in the January 12th issue of the Bernardsville News is described as: A rural school during late 1800 and located on a road to Mine Brook Railroad Station at Mine Brook, N.J.

(The building still stands on an adjacent property used for farm purposes). A few of our present local residents of this territory traveled to this school where in winter they sat around a potbelly stove to keep warm.

I attended this school in early 1900 being taught by a Miss Kuntz and our present Mrs. Homer Brookins (whose grandfather was President of the Board of Education for Bernards Township).

Pupils whom I can remember are George I. Frost, Irving Frost, Mrs. Lena Nuse, Mrs. Harry Higgins, Mrs. James Foster, Mrs. Fred Gutleber and our present Chief of Police, Clarence Pope.

I have a photograph of the pupils that was taken in 1903. Many of the faces shown have passed on.

Yours very truly,
A reader of the News since 1898

The land for the Mine Mount School, School District 13, was purchased in 1839. The school was situated on half an acre on what today is Mountain Top Road. Known as the Mountain School, it was located in the vicinity of the northern part of Bernardsville near Mine Mountain. At various times, there were two different schools in the Mine Mountain area.

Religious organizations that lacked church facilities met in the schoolhouses. Many rural church groups regularly met there. Presbyterian, Baptist, Lutheran, Methodist, Adventist, and Catholic ministers and priests all used the schools as places of worship. According to Gulliford, country schools served many purposes. "Circuit-riding ministers, in addition to conducting services, would hold baptisms, confirmations, weddings and even funerals at the schools."

The schoolhouses were important multi-purpose sites. Unfortunately, many also burned, as was the case with the original schoolhouse in Mine Mount. It went up in flames in 1872, and a second schoolhouse replaced it. That schoolhouse later was abandoned and its students transported to improved school facilities in the village. In February 1917 the second schoolhouse also burned.

Most one-room schoolhouses were made of wood—material that is flammable. Numerous fires were started by the kerosene used for lighting the classroom. Sometimes, old chimneys caught fire. A spark that landed on the roof or the wooden floorboards could ignite the structure.

When the schoolhouses were standing, a traveler could find one nearly every mile or at every other crossroad.

Both male and female teachers taught in the one-room schoolhouses. Many male teachers were retired soldiers who knew how to read and write. If, however, they were left-handed, chances were they were not hired. Writing with one's left hand was considered to be "unacceptable."

An 1875 map of schoolhouses, school districts, and boundaries. (The Historical Society of the Somerset Hills)

The Mine Brook School, named for a nearby brook, was located in the western section of the Township. It was one of three early schools located in the general vicinity of what was at one time known as District 14. The names of the other two schools have slipped from public records. One of the two schools whose names are unknown was located south of the Mine Brook. The second of the nameless schoolhouses was located on the left side of the road leading to Far Hills.

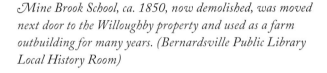

Mine Brook School, ca. 1850, now demolished, was moved next door to the Willoughby property and used as a farm outbuilding for many years. (Bernardsville Public Library Local History Room)

Side view of Mine Brook School, ca. 1850s. It was located at the intersection of Whitenack Road and Mine Brook Road. (Bernardsville Public Library Local History Room)

Mine Brook School at Mine Brook, October 29, 1896. Left to right: teacher unknown, small boy in center front row with large bowtie, Irving Frost; other students include Grace Barker, Bertha Frost, (first name unknown) Dobbs. (Bernardsville Public Library Local History Room)

Mine Brook School students sit outside their school, ca. 1887. Pictured are: Roderick Garrity, John Simpson, Louise Whitenack, Lizzie Dobbs, Laura Frost, Linne Barker, Sam Haines, and George Dobbs; Julia Hines, Harry Douglas, Ada Martin, Jessie Card, Joe Dobbs, Luella Riker, George Henry, Charles Vestlecraft, Miss Voorhees, teacher, center right, Frank Whitenack, James Woods, Ed Carry, Charlie Dobbs, Emma Woods, Molly Garrity, Vince Whitenack, Cora Ludlow, Lizzie Frost, Anna Woods, Ruth Voorhees, Will Douglas, Irving Ludlow, Robert Dunster, Charlie Henry, Matie Frost, and Pearl Allen. (The Historical Society of the Somerset Hills)

An account of money transactions due to teacher Josiah B. Wilkison, 1821. Elias Frost owed $9.625 for six-week tuition at one of the Mine schools. (Bernardsville Public Library Local History Room)

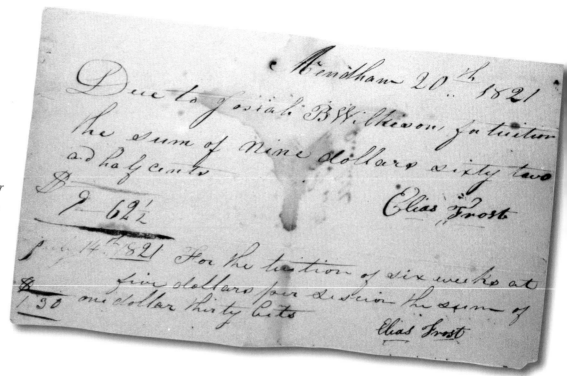

Opposite where the Liberty Corner Road began, the third school was located on the north side of the road. This school, known as Mine Brook, did not have a bell tower; instead, the teacher rang a hand-held bell. James Freeman and John Voorhees donated the land. They owned the

A receipt written by teacher, 1821. (Bernardsville Public Library Local History Room)

two adjoining fields, which they set aside for school use. Prior to its final location, the school was "moved across the fields: first to the right of one field, then to the left of two fields," recounts Anna W. Lines in "Early Schools in Bernards Township."

During 1871 there were 67 students enrolled in Mine Brook School. Unlike most other schools, this one had a janitor, and the teacher did not have to assume those duties. Erastus Ballentine, a trustee for the school, paid a local boy living near the school $4 a year to tend the fire in the school's stove and prepare the building for Sunday School. Later, a new stove was purchased, and the janitor's salary rose to $5 a year. Families in various communities took turns sending their children to school with armfuls of wood. This practice ensured that the school had enough wood and was kept warm.

The Mine Brook Schoolhouse served as a place for Sunday School and prayer meetings. Like the schools of today, the school also provided space for debates, musical productions, magic lantern shows [an early form of the slide projector], and other forms of entertainment.

Almost a century later, local residents enthusiastically responded to a "Mystery Photograph" inquiry featured in the January 12, 1956, edition of the *Bernardsville News*. In the Letters to the Editor published on February 2, 1956, folks unanimously identified the structure as the Mine Brook School:

> *In this rural school all grades were taught by one instructor. . . . I believe it is presently being used to store hay and grains.* —Theresa Eiltzer

> *Just to the right of the building can be seen the chain and bucket pump from which the "teacher's pet" drew many a pail of refreshing drink.* —George Frost

> *Your mystery picture is that of the Old Mine Brook School house which my mother attended 50 years ago.* —Charles Higgins

> *It was used as a schoolhouse and Sunday school; also a prayer meeting room.* —Lloyd Conrad

> *This school was situated on what was originally a part of my father's farm.* —Emma Allen

> *The picture on page 11 looks like the old schoolhouse on the Mine Brook road that my father said he went to when he was a lad. It's located on a knoll on the right hand side of the road near a farm, past a pond by Westlecraft's property, at the foot of the steep Mine Hill. I'd better draw a map.* —Vera Dobbs Lighthipe

—Allison Casar, Roman Hatala, Charlie Kritzmacher, and Lisa Wooldridge

Mount Prospect School, built during the mid-1860s. (The Historical Society of the Somerset Hills)

Mount Prospect Schoolhouses

————◆————

Teachers' desks varied from standard four-legged oak tables to elaborate desks with a top that lifted up to disclose secret drawers or slots for books.

—*America's Country Schools* by Andrew Gulliford

Around the 1850s, the Union School District, known to most as Mount Prospect, built the one-room Mount Prospect School on a 0.74-acre woodlot. It was located in a corner of the William Ludlow Allen property near the north side of a public road leading from Liberty Corner to Far Hills. This land was set aside for school purposes only. The school was dedicated in 1862, according to W. V. D. Layton's diary.

The schoolhouse had standard desks for the students and a large wooden desk for the teacher. Most teachers' desks had a shelf running across the top that acted as a storage compartment for class registers, a hand bell, primers, a wooden ruler, and a dictionary. The teacher's desk sat in the front of the room on a six- to eight-inch raised platform. The platform was used for recitations, plays, and spelling bees.

The Mount Prospect Schoolhouse had a bell tower located above the double doorway entry. Such a tower was a status symbol.

Anna D. Merrell, 1900, taught at the one-room Mount Prospect School. (Mary Guest Kenney)

In most early schools, the teacher used a hand-held bell. When communities became more prosperous, a collection was taken up for a bell tower that would serve both decorative and practical purposes. The tower was an ornament, and the bell called the children to school. It also was rung to indicate when someone was lost or hurt, to warn the community of danger, or to telegraph joy at Christmas. Communities with bell towers had a great sense of pride.

By the 19th century, bell towers had become more common. Placed above the entrance to the schoolhouse, some had simple roofs, but others had ornate gingerbread woodwork and copper roofs with hand-hammered or etched designs. Some schools flew flags above the bell towers.

Mount Prospect School's bell was loaned to a local fire company until 1947, when it was sent to the Oldwick Fire Company. Later, it was returned and placed in the bell tower of the new Liberty Corner Fire House on Church Street.

Over time, a long roster of teachers rang that bell. They included W. V. D. Layton, who was a teacher at the Mount Prospect School from 1885 to 1890, and earlier had been a student there. Layton attended Sunday worship at the school.

Other Mount Prospect teachers were G. Lizzie Wyckoff, George Whitten, Robert S. Boyle, Sara Adeline Layton McLaughlin, Sarah Redford English, Emma Schumaker, and Anna Merrill, who became Mrs. Amos Guest. Her daughter, Mary Guest Kenney, led the Liberty Corner School as principal from 1953 to 1969.

Mount Prospect School served the community until Liberty Corner School was built in 1905. In 1910 Mount Prospect School was bought by William Conkling for $300. The schoolhouse was converted into a four-room dwelling and moved to Liberty Corner-Far Hills Road, where it became a private residence of the Yates family in 1947.

Almost a century later, a new Mount Prospect School opened. Robin Swider, a fourth-grade student from Old Coach Road in Basking Ridge, suggested the name for the new school; it was the same as the school that stood on Mount Prospect Road in 1862.

In 1997, construction costs were at an all-time high, and the price tag for the new school was $37.7 million. The bond referendum presented to voters included expansions to Ridge High School and William Annin Middle School. Despite the costs, the bond was approved in June of that year.

The new Mount Prospect School was erected on a twelve-acre tract at Allen and Hansom Roads in a residential area of Bernards Township known as The Hills. The school originally had 25 classrooms and a seating capacity of 550. However, the cafeteria, gymnasium, and media center were added to accommodate 800 students. Mount Prospect School opened in September 1999 with Judith Slutzky as principal, former principal at Oak Street School.

In 2001, Mount Prospect School was identified in *New Jersey Monthly* magazine as one of thirty-one top elementary schools in the State.

Today Mount Prospect School is home to seven hundred children in kindergarten through grade five. One of many character education programs the school has is the Doer of Unusual Deeds of Excellence Award, which is given to recognize students, teachers, parents, or community members who have demonstrated exemplary actions.

In addition, students participate in community service projects that benefit a wide range of organizations, such as:

- A clothing drive that benefits Native American Indians
- A bird feed drive for endangered animals and raptor birds
- Participation in the annual holiday giving tree, which sponsors five charities in the local area

The schoolyard has grown from less than an acre to a twelve-acre tract. Even more significant is the difference in student populations of yesterday and today. There are at least thirty-two languages spoken by this student body! This school clearly celebrates its diversity and, as a result, enriches the educational experiences of all its students.

—*Rachel Conklin, Alexander Liao, Laurence Liao, Jack Kimzey, and Kate Kostecky*

Valley Road leading to Liberty Corner is a pastoral scene with cows in the outlying fields and grazing horses set against white picket fences, ca. 1900s. (Betty King Sisto)

Liberty Corner Schoolhouses

A school "should overlook a delightful country, present a choice of sunshine and shade, or trees and flowers, and be sheltered from the prevailing winds of winter by a hill-top," advised Henry Barnard in his plan book, School Architecture: Or, Contributions to the Improvement of School-Houses in the United States *(1838). Rolling meadows and wildflowers, however, were not the typical view from most rural schoolrooms.*

—*America's Country Schools* by Andrew Gulliford

Children living during the American Revolution in the area of Annan's Corner, later renamed Liberty Corner, were most likely educated in the basement of the old Stone House.

In "About Liberty Corner" (1952) Anna W. Lines writes:

> The Annan family were large landowners living in the village of Liberty Corner. In 1766 William Annan at the age of 51 built the famous old Stone House whose walls were made of massive blocks from a neighboring quarry. Here school was kept and here was fostered the religious life of the community by visits of Pastors Kennedy, Finley and Brownlee of the Basking Ridge Presbyterian Church.

In the early 1800s a traditional one-room schoolhouse, known as "the old red schoolhouse" or "the Academy," was built on the Annan property. Details of this schoolhouse's history are sparse, making it easy to confuse it with the Brick Academy on West Oak Street.

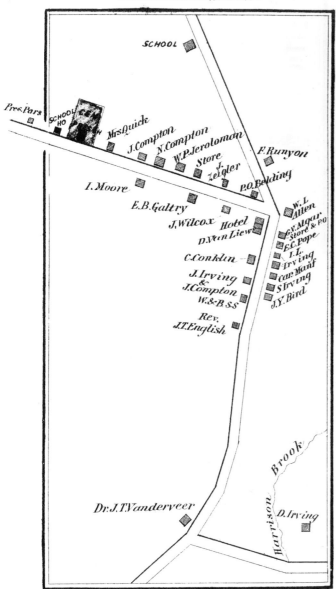

LIBERTY CORNER

BERNARD TSP.

Scale 30 Rods to the inch

Map of Liberty Corner, ca. 1873. (Somerset County Historical Society)

We do know the building's demise, however. Lines recounts how the old red schoolhouse was destroyed by fire: The story goes that a slave of the Annan family saw the fire first and called to his master to hurry as the schoolhouse was burning, and added that he would fight the fire as soon as he could get his pipe.

A second wooden schoolhouse, referred to as the Jefferson School, was built in 1856 on land owned by Francis Runyon near the road that led from Liberty Corner to Lyons. Construction was begun with fewer than $10. In the 1975 article "Liberty Corner School is gone, but its long history remains," Donna Hagemann explains the circumstances surrounding the purchase of the land:

> Evidently the growing school population had expanded beyond the original schoolhouse, so a new tract of land was partitioned off—for $6.36—and a new building constructed at the same time. The deed notes the Jefferson School trustees were granted the land and the inordinately low price, so they "shall have and hold for the use of the school and no other purpose."

Land was cheap in those days, as Andrew Gulliford makes clear in *America's Country Schools* (1984), but selecting an appropriate site "often caused serious squabbles among rural neighbors, according to John R. Stilgoe in *Common Landscapes of America, 1580–1845* (1982)."

Gulliford notes that a farmer or rancher who owned land near families with schoolchildren would often deed an acre of land to the school district. However, in certain instances, the schoolhouse would be moved closer to other residents in the district when the families moved away from the first site. In those cases, "the land reverted to the original donor." Gulliford points out:

> Many farmers did not want the school near their land because the schoolchildren would trample the crops and their dogs would harass livestock while the children were at school. So farmers often put schools in swamps, mudholes, floodplains, or even sites adjacent to pigsties. Any sliver of land unfit for agricultural use was likely to be chosen as the site of the district school. Rural schools had to be located within walking distance or at least pony-riding distance of the homes of the pupils.

Old Stone House in decline, pictured in the 20th century. It was built in 1766 by William Annin of massive blocks of quarried stone, brownish in color, from a local quarry. Located in Liberty Corner, it originally stood 36 feet wide by 48 feet long but was later enlarged to 40 feet by 50 feet. There were projecting eaves and a small porch. The remains are gone except for a stonewall foundation that is still visible on the Annin site in the southern corner of Liberty Corner. (The Historical Society of the Somerset Hills)

Liberty Corner School, 1906. Students include: Ed Froehling, Pearl Stantial, Ora Haines, Art King, Charlette Frost, Ella Lare, Belle Acken, Alma Haines, Marion Allen, Addie Woods, Minnie Allen, Olga Gutleber, Tom Allen, George Green, Andrew Martin, Elmer David, Henry Wright, Laura Martin, Hattie Thompson, Elsie Wright, Sybilla Wright, Fred Fee, Gladys Burnett. Teachers pictured in back row include Miss Elliott and Miss Harmon. (The Historical Society of the Somerset Hills)

The old schoolhouse at Liberty Corner was originally called the Jefferson School, ca. 1856. The small one-and-a-half-story, one-room wooden structure served as one of eleven structures where children in Bernards Township were educated. Students entered through a door in the middle of the short north wall. In 1905 the structure was purchased and converted for living purposes with a small addition made to the building. (The Historical Society of the Somerset Hills)

Liberty Corner School [Jefferson School], ca. 1900, as a residence. Note the gabled front wall and the open-shuttered windows in front and side of the structure. The 119-year-old schoolhouse was demolished in 1975 because it was considered a fire and safety hazard. (The Historical Society of the Somerset Hills)

As the population of Liberty Corner grew, so did the number of students at the Jefferson School. There were 126 students in attendance in 1871.

Liberty Corner schoolhouse was maintained by landowners until 1893, when it was turned over to "School District 17 of Somerset County" for $50. By the early 1900s, however, the Board of Education determined there no longer was a need for the old wooden Jefferson Schoolhouse.

Shortly thereafter, Liberty Corner residents voted to build a more spacious structure. In 1904 an article, "New Schoolhouse for Liberty Corner," appeared in the *Bernardsville News*:

> Vote at Special School Meeting Unanimous-Building to be Two-Room Stone Structure
>
> The building will be 32 x 68 feet in size, two stories high and constructed of quarry stone. There will be two rooms on the ground floor, each 24 x 28 feet, with 12-foot ceilings. Each room will have ample light and ventilation. The second floor will not be finished at present beyond the laying of the floor. The cost of the building and furnishings will be about $7,600.

Until this time, the schoolhouses of Liberty Corner were one-room structures built mostly of wood. However, the new Liberty Corner School was a big improvement, a two-story building constructed of quarry stone.

It was common in New Jersey to have schools built by skilled craftsmen who used masonry materials native to the area. These stone schoolhouses typically had a stone foundation and eighteen-inch-thick stone walls. They also had "deep-set windows and sills, stone lintels above

William J. Howes, principal, and his wife, Grace, a teacher at Liberty Corner, in the eighth-grade classroom. (Liberty Corner School)

No. 3.—New School House, Liberty Corner, N. Y.   J. KOEHLER, N.   *New Jersey.*   H. B. ROM

Liberty Corner School, built in 1905, originally consisted of two large rooms housing grades one through eight. Note: during publication, the incorrect state was stamped on the postcard. Because it was too expensive to reprint, "New Jersey" was stamped over the error. (The Historical Society of the Somerset Hills)

Liberty Corner School with addition in rear of building pre–World War II. More students arrived in 1915 from the defunct Pleasant Valley School, which prompted the addition of a classroom on the second floor and the hiring of another teacher. Enrollment continued to increase, with two more classrooms constructed in 1921, followed by another two and a nurse's office in 1950. By 1960, Liberty Corner School served 206 students in kindergarten and grades one, two, and three. The staff consisted of eight teachers, a principal, Mary Guest Kenney, and teachers of special subjects such as art and music. (The Historical Society of the Somerset Hills)

The Johnston family changed its name to Annan, after Annandale, their Scotland home, which they left in the pursuit of religious freedom. The family of Annandale, Scotland, settled in Bernards Township in 1722. John Johnston's father, Marquis James, and his mother, the Countess Sophie of Annandale, purchased one thousand acres of land from William Penn for their son, John, and his young family, which included two sons and a daughter. The area was called Annan's Corner until the Revolutionary War when a patriot planted a liberty pole on the village green; hence, the village was renamed Liberty Corner. The main supply route from Bound Brook to Morristown was through this area.

The Annans's two sons, John and William, fought in the French and Indian Wars, with John a fatality at Mackinac Island. William returned from the French and Indian Wars in 1760, married, and in 1766 built a splendid stone house, one of only three stone homes built before the American Revolution. Three generations of the Annan family would live in the quaint building with projecting eaves. The initials W. A. and H. S. M. and the year 1766 were cut in the stone; the letters identify the builder, William Annan, and the mason, Hugh Sunderland. The spelling of the family name soon after was changed to Annin.

During the American Revolution, the old Stone House served as a military hospital, church, school, and recreational area for Colonial troops. Mrs. Annin nursed General Lafayette's troops who had smallpox; she later died of the disease. William Annin served as a captain in the Somerset County militia from 1776 to 1780. He and several of his sons were members of the New Jersey Legislature.

During the 1800s, "the little red schoolhouse" served as both school and church. Close ties continued, and in 1831 people gathered there to discuss building a church in the village. The Annin family donated land for the Liberty Corner Presbyterian Church.

In 1829, descendants of William Annin became ship chandler and flag suppliers for the nautical trade. Today,

the Annin Flag Company supplies all United Nations flags and is the largest flag supplier in the world.

The Annin family of Liberty Corner continued their involvement with education when, in 1844, a descendant of the Annan family, also named William Annin, became a trustee of this district and was paid $36.48 to operate the school.

William Annin's homestead, ca. 1766. (The Historical Society of the Somerset Hills)

❖

Mary Guest Kenney, who was born in Liberty Corner in 1907, attended Liberty Corner School as a student and later became a teacher and a principal. In 1926, her first year at Liberty Corner, she taught a class of 44 students. It included 20 Bonnie Brae School boys who resided in a supervised correctional facility. After 43 years of service, of which she was principal for 15, she retired in 1969. Liberty Corner Media Center was renamed Mary Kenney Media Center.

However, when she began attending as a student at Liberty Corner School, it had only two classrooms—one housing grades one through four and the other, grades five through eight. Many boys dropped out after eighth grade and never attended high school, choosing instead to work for local builders.

As a student, Kenney missed much of the eighth grade because of a bout with scarlet fever, which kept her quarantined for six weeks. Prior to her own illness, her teacher had caught scarlet fever in November, and the school was closed through Christmas.

Liberty Corner School, left, and teacherage, white building, ca. 1925. The teacherage, built in 1923, was a small-framed house used only as housing for teachers. Tenants included William J. Howes, the school principal, and his wife, Grace, also a teacher and later a principal. In the mid-1950s, the structure was torn down to make way for a school playground. (The Historical Society of the Somerset Hills)

the windows and door, and stone entrance steps. As the walls rose higher, the mason often chose smaller, lighter stones because the top of the walls could be thinner."

When the new building was completed, the old Mount Prospect School closed, and its students transferred to the new Liberty Corner School. The student population still continued to grow, and in 1915 a new room and a new teacher were added. In the same year, students from the West Millington School, known then as Pleasant Valley School, were transferred to Liberty Corner School.

The Liberty Corner School was unique as the first stone school in the village and also as the last known school in the area to have a teacherage. Mary Louise Shaw describes the teacherage in the 1974 article "Annin Held Classes in His Home before 1800," which appeared in the *Bernardsville News*:

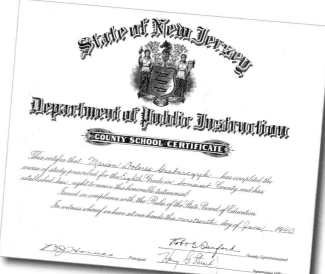

A copy of a teaching certificate received by Dolores Grabarczyk in June 1940 certifying her qualifications to teach grade eight. (Liberty Corner School)

> Liberty Corner had the distinction of having one of the last surviving "teacherages" in the State before the small frame house was torn down to make room for a playground. A teacherage was a home for teachers only, and it was badly needed in the small village where "spare rooms" were few and far between. Teachers had to live near the school, as starting teachers in 1923, when the residence was built, were paid only $1,200 a year—far too little to own a car or even a horse and cart. And the roads were mostly dirt-topped, morasses of mud in rainy months and impassable in snow. Teacherage tenants paid $30 per month, and were required to house any teacher who wanted quarters there.

May Day 1919. Local students from Basking Ridge, Liberty Corner, Bernardsville, and Far Hills participate in this annual celebration at the Far Hills Fairgrounds. Every school's colored streamers were wound around a maypole (Basking Ridge's colors were blue and gold, Liberty Corner's yellow and white). Activities included Indian clubs, track and field events, group calisthenics, baton drills, and other acrobatic feats. (The Historical Society of the Somerset Hills)

Through time, Liberty Corner School housed countless students and teachers and became a center of community activity. At 102 years old, it is the oldest schoolhouse in use in Bernards Township. It has undergone a total of four additions and other renovations. It has hosted many community celebrations, including a centennial celebration on June 1, 2005.

In *America's Country Schools* (1984), Gulliford spotlights school programs of the day:

> People from miles around came to country schools to attend school programs throughout the school year—at Halloween, Thanksgiving, Christmas, Easter, and eighth grade graduation in early June. Spring and fall programs usually included a basket social. The Young Citizens League, a youth group, also held programs twice a year in many schools. National holidays frequently were occasions for programs and community get-togethers. Small schools were the center of rural social life, so teachers would organize special programs for Valentine's Day, Washington's and Lincoln's Birthdays, Arbor Day, Memorial Day, Parent's Day, and May Day, with its maypole dance and recessional.
>
> A typical program featured community singing, two or three readings of humorous or inspirational pieces and then musical solos on accordions, violins, pianos, or whatever instruments

LIBERTY CORNER SCHOOL
Bernards Township Public Schools

A Century of Excellence ✏ *1905-2005*

61 Church Street
Liberty Corner, New Jersey 07938

Liberty Corner School

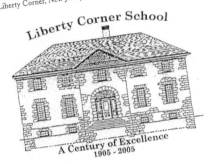

A Century of Excellence
1905 - 2005

Centennial Station
JUNE 1, 2005
Liberty Corner, NJ 07938

Celebrating
A Century
Of Excellence
1905-2005

No. 86 from a limited edition of 800

Thank you!

*Your Official Commemorative Souvenir Envelope from
The United States Postal Service
celebrates an important moment in history.*

May you enjoy this gift from the Liberty Corner School for years to come.

*If you wish to purchase additional Antique Old Glory Stamps
or receive the Centennial cancellation,
please visit the Liberty Corner Post Office
before July 1st, 2005.*

Top: A commemorative souvenir envelope of Liberty Corner School's 100th anniversary. (Liberty Corner School)

Bottom: Enclosed in the souvenir envelope is a note of appreciation. (Liberty Corner School)

Second-grader Elizabeth "Betty" Dent King poses for her school photo in 1936 at Liberty Corner School, where second- and third-graders shared a classroom. Mary Guest Kenney, the teacher, had Betty hold a writing slate to identify the grade of the photographed students. (Betty King Sisto)

were handy. Programs concluded with an address by a local resident who reported community news. A teacher who did not have a successful program might not be rehired for the coming term. Teachers' contracts often stipulated that they present at least two programs a year.

Old school bus in the background owned by Art Burnett, whose route included the Martinsville Road to Sunset Lane, Old Somerville Road, and Pigtail Mountain. L. V. Acken stands in front of his new 1939 bus. Children pictured walking home are (far left) Harry Allen and John Burnett. (Liberty Corner School)

In 1974, Liberty Corner School housed students in kindergarten through grade four, plus one special-education class; 518 children attended the school. Today, under the direction of Principal Dr. Kathleen Pecoraro, the school serves 616 children in kindergarten through grade five. An array of student service projects, including the following activities, represent the school's efforts to involve its students in character education:

- Costume collection for Morristown Neighborhood House and Goryeb Children's Hospital in Morristown

- Stuffed animal collection for Buddies & Books program to benefit the former Paige Whitney Babies Center in Basking Ridge (shelter for women and children)

- Sale of a school-authored cookbook to benefit the Seeing Eye of Morristown

- Foster care of a black Labrador retriever named Jethro for the Seeing Eye

Liberty Corner has evolved into a modern multi-room building. Yet, a visitor to the Liberty Corner School is reminded of its historical past by the wainscoting on classroom walls, the sunlight that streams through its tall basement windows, and the original quarry stone exterior.

Liberty Corner School has lost neither its historical charm nor its educational commitment—it embodies both.

—*Stephanie Campo, Tommy Carpenter, Marisa Dour, Alyssa Drews, and Howard Wei*

[Note: *The early schooling of Liberty Corner children began in 1766, but two centuries later a new school was built, named after William Annin, the patriot and ancestor of the original Annan family. The school called William Annin Junior High School is discussed in Chapter 13.*]

Eighth-grade boys in June 1941 include, left to right: (front row) Archie Burnett, Fred Suhr, and Warren Clark; (back row) Roger Kline, George England, Harry Allen, and Victor Burton. (Liberty Corner School)

Eighth-grade girls in June 1941 include, left to right: (front row) Madelyn Boxwell, Barbara Simonet, Doris Ruggerio, Ann Mellick, and Phyllis Merdinger; (second row) Nancy Lester, Doris Hilmer, Mildred Bird, and Doris Beatty peeking through. (Liberty Corner School)

Liberty Corner School students and teacher display Bicentennial flag, a school project, 1976. (Ray Jones)

Students at the Maple Avenue School, 1911. School desks were anchored to the floor and the teacher's desk placed in front of the room. On the left, blackboards, chalk tray, erasers, and chalk line the side of the classroom. Fourth row, third student down, is holding a book titled The Bible Story. *(The Historical Society of the Somerset Hills)*

Maple Avenue School

This is a spirit of concern, cooperation, and community interest. The mechanical aspects of moving to Oak Street are completed. However, there is an emotional factor, which is quite different to resolve.

—Andrew Long, principal

By the 1900s, one-room schoolhouses were no longer the trend. Gradually, they gave way to larger elementary school structures, with high ceilings and tall windows, furnace heat, large schoolyards, and separate classrooms for each grade.

The Maple Avenue School, also known as the Basking Ridge School, characterized this movement of constructing larger schoolhouses. It was built in 1903 on South Maple Avenue at a cost of $7,000. The building of the school made possible the consolidation of smaller nearby schools. Its student body came from Franklin Corners School and the Brick Academy, both of which closed.

The Maple Avenue School began as a one-story building with a small attic, four recitation rooms, a principal's office on the ground floor, and a playroom in the basement. It was built of gray quarry stone taken from the Millstone Quarry. It seated more than 30 students in its classrooms; the desks were furnished by the Favorite Seating Company of Cleveland, Ohio.

The Maple Avenue School. The flagpole was donated by New Jersey State Senator Samuel S. Childs, and later transferred from the Franklin Corner School to the new Maple Avenue School. (The Historical Society of the Somerset Hills)

The typical turn-of-the-century desks had a fixed seat, a wooden desk top, and a seat that folded. Desks were arranged in rows. In *America's Country Schools* (1984), Andrew Gulliford explains how in this formation, the back of one desk became the writing space for the student in the next desk.

Several furniture companies from New York, Chicago, Cleveland, Minneapolis, and Richmond, Indiana, offered at least six different desk sizes to accommodate students ages five to 20. The desks were often made of oak and featured ornate ironwork as part of the frame. On this grillwork, manufacturers stamped their name, location, and, sometimes, a motto.

The desks came in an assortment of colors and wood types. Gulliford notes, "However, no desk could maintain its surface for long against the penknives of children eager to leave their initials."

The local historical society acquired a few old student desks, the wooden open-box top flanked with intricate iron supports, ca. 1900s. The seat folds up; behind it is an attached desk equipped with a pencil holder and inkwell. The desktop provided a surface to write on and was easily raised for storage. Desks such as these were lined up in rows of six and secured to the classroom floor. (Josephine M. Waltz)

It is likely that at Maple Avenue School, the desks were bolted to the hardwood floors at first. In many schools, bolting desks down was accepted practice. However, in buildings where dances and box socials were often held, it was preferable to keep moveable furniture there.

Most classrooms of the time, such as those at Maple Avenue School, were sparsely decorated. But in 1908, the

Third- and fourth-grade students at the Maple Avenue School, 1914. Sarah Bockoven, teacher, is standing in rear of classroom. (The Historical Society of the Somerset Hills)

Painting of General George Washington hung at Maple Avenue School and now is located in the Brick Academy. (Josephine M. Waltz)

The Maple Avenue School's assembly hall benches were placed on the second floor of the building. They later were used as public seating when the Brick Academy became the municipal building. Today many of the benches have been donated by The Historical Society of the Somerset Hills to the existing Township schools, local library, and Board of Health, and can be seen in the main entrance of these buildings. (Josephine M. Waltz)

Maple Avenue School play, ca. 1935. Fourth-graders perform Tom Thumb's Wedding. *Left to right: (front row) Paul Bettler, Lucy Jane Vaughn, Virginia Moore, unknown, Nancy Childs, unknown, Jean Gutleber, Holman Head, and Irene Bettler. Back row: Truman Spencer, Gerard Bancker, Samuel Carswell, Muriel Lowe, unknown, Ken Turner, Reginald Lowe. (Nancy Childs Knobloch)*

Students outside Maple Avenue School. Principal Jack Twichell is seated in front row center, ca. 1930. (The Historical Society of the Somerset Hills)

Eighth-grade students from the Basking Ridge Grammar School, 1909. This class was the first to enter the Maple Avenue School and graduate in 1910. Left to right: (front row) Dorothy Connolly, Marion Roberts, Mary Walron, Myra Howlett, Marion Dayton, Frances Wilcox, Mildred Bennett, Lillian Bornmann, and Viola Sanders; (back row) Britton Everett, Charles Karston, Russell Pope, Carroll Allen, Willett Neer, principal, Garret Rutman, Charles Ehrler, and Leonard Bender. May Petty and Jessie Hendershot were not present when this photograph was taken. (The Historical Society of the Somerset Hills)

Maple Avenue teachers conducted a bread and cake sale. The profits were used to purchase four pictures for the school and one for the principal's office.

The small attic space of the Maple Avenue School was unfinished initially, but in 1905 it was equipped as an assembly room with two and three folding wooden oak seats. Unfortunately, the new space was used only briefly, for on April 30, 1906, at about 2 p.m. a fire broke out.

All students and staff were evacuated safely. The damage totaled $10,000, however. The school was closed for two weeks following the fire; during the summer months, the building was completely repaired.

As if in celebration, a new piano was purchased when the school reopened. Music then became an important part of the curriculum under William Childs and Samuel Edgar, who had been appointed to explore the introduction of music in the local schools.

Andrew Gulliford confirms in *America's Country Schools* (1984) just how important music programs were in early communities as a way of bringing people together from the community. "Music served as the great socializer," he said. He further explains that many non-English-speaking immigrants such as Italians, Swedes, Norwegians, and German-Russians benefited from attending these functions because "they learned to sing patriotic songs in English."

Many winter musical concerts featured fiddles, guitars, zithers, and accordions. When communities became prosperous, the school board saw to it that a piano or organ was purchased. Playing the piano was an impor-

Maple Avenue School, 1909. Standing left to right: Willett Neer, principal, Eleanor Schoenover, and others unknown. Seated: Jane Cheney and Louise Rich. (The Historical Society of the Somerset Hills)

Maple Avenue School, middle grades, 1910, teacher Miss Laura Frost pictured in the center. (The Historical Society of the Somerset Hills)

tant skill for teachers seeking employment then. In letters to the Board of Education, teachers provided not only their educational background, but also included their musical talents.

The school's early teaching staff consisted mostly of women who probably had some musical background. They included: Rebecca Smith, Lizzie Henry, Mary Lum, and Ms. Bingham. In 1904 Laura Frost joined the faculty. In 1910 the Maple Avenue School teachers were involved in cooperative housekeeping in the Methodist Church parsonage, which they rented. Teachers who came from out of state included Eleanor Schoonover of New York State, Louise Rich of Pennsylvania, and Martha Fleming of Nova Scotia.

By this time, teachers were, overwhelmingly, women. Part of the reason was economics. In 1906 a female faculty member at Maple Avenue School might earn $50 a month, and the men, more. Donna Hagemann notes the traditional salary disparity between men and women in the article "Liberty Corner School is Gone . . . and things have changed since 1905 opening" (1975):

> Equal rights advocates would cringe at budget figures for Bernards Township in 1905. The maximum male salary was $700 annually, while women reached their peak at $500. On the average a male teacher earned $650 with a women teacher earning $450.

Another part of the male/female equation had to do with social dynamics. In *Going to School in 1876* (1984), John J. Loeper discusses the commonly held attitude toward women teachers.

"*Godey's Lady's Book* is a respected magazine published in Philadelphia. Most American women of this period respect its views":

> Young women must become the teachers. . . . They are the best teachers . . . because of the superior tact and moral power natural to the female character. Women can afford to teach for one half, or even less, the salary which men would ask, because the female teacher has only to care for herself. She does not look forward to the duty of supporting a family, should she marry. Where female teachers have been hired, they are found faithful and useful.

"Eventually, teaching became a woman's profession by default," said Loeper. "She would work for half the salary a man expected, and her 'gentle nature' helped children to learn." Not all officials were in agreement on the subject, however. The following was written by a Michigan school official:

> Tho' the cheapest guardian and teacher of childhood, can she prepare children for the intellectual demands of the superior male teacher?

As the times changed and the community grew, it became clear that the Maple Avenue School needed more space, for students and for community events. A second story was added in 1911 at a cost of $6,000. The roof was literally raised, and two additional rooms and a very large auditorium were added.

The teachers at Maple Avenue School in 1915. From left to right: (front row) Sue Tuttle, Irma Siebert; (rear row) Agatha Greulock, Elizabeth Steele, Willett Neer, principal, Minnie S. Tewes, Sarah Bockoven. (The Historical Society of the Somerset Hills)

Maple Avenue School, 1911, raising the roof. It consisted of two additional classrooms and an auditorium. (The Historical Society of the Somerset Hills)

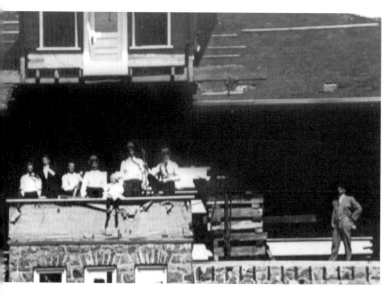

A close-up of Maple Avenue School undergoing construction, 1911. Man on the right side of ledge is holding a four-foot open-ended sized wrench, used to turn massive jacks. The man on the far right is the contractor for the project. (The Historical Society of the Somerset Hills)

Three local unidentified boys pose for the photographer in the entrance of Maple Avenue School while it was undergoing renovations. (The Historical Society of the Somerset Hills)

A side view of the Maple Avenue School, complete with fire escape. The adjacent lot holds a display of vehicles from the pre-WWII era. (The Historical Society of Somerset Hills)

In 1912 the student body and the staff enjoyed the new auditorium for a special presentation made by Civil War veteran George Terry, who had served with a regiment from New York. The benefits of the auditorium were short-lived, however. As a result of increasing enrollment, the Board of Education decided to convert the auditorium into two classrooms to accommodate eight grades.

In the following account, Katherine Kearns Connolly describes her school days at the Maple Avenue School:

> In the autumn of 1935, my brother Kevin and I were enrolled at the Maple Avenue School, a large, square stone building—an unforgettable structure that, to our dismay, was razed years ago. During our lightly-populated time in rural Somerset County, when kindergarten was not an option, Kevin and I were admitted to first grade, (up a wide wooden staircase, first door to the left), as taught by Eleanor Dobbs, a perceptive, intelligent young woman and the most delightful teacher I ever had. No teacher in my academic experience ever measured up to her level of gentle, courteous instruction. Right off the bat, on the first welcoming day, she endeared herself to us by allowing each child to select his/her own seating location. Kevin and I chose neighboring desks.
>
> A blackboard ran across the front wall behind Miss Dobbs' adult-size desk, and a long cloakroom was accessed by doors at either end of the same wall. (This basic layout was, I believe, repeated in all eight classrooms.) To Kevin's and my delight, an upright piano sat in a corner near the north-facing windows, with several boxes of rhythm instruments close by.

A large center hall complete with drinking fountain, two lavatories and four generous corner classrooms (grades 1 to 4) made up the first floor. Grades 5 to 8 were on the second floor, where the older students, not the teachers, moved from classroom to classroom—an emancipating privilege longed for by the students in the lower grades. A short flight of wooden steps near the door of the sixth-grade classroom led to the office of the principal, Jack B. Twichell, exemplary leader of the school as well as teacher of arithmetic and health.

On two sides of each classroom, just above the wainscoting, were tall windows that were designed to accommodate each classroom's needs for fresh air. The windows rattled audibly on windy days. They were opened and closed by the use of long wooden poles with hooked metal ends that slid into window slots. In the higher grades the biggest and strongest boys were often given the job of opening and closing the windows. Oh yes, and near the door of each classroom hung a large wall clock that seemed to take forever to work its slow, poky way around the dial to the most popular hour of the day, 3:00 p.m.

The playground provided a site for the much anticipated summer carnival run by the men who tended the fire station just across the street. Every summer we were astonished at the transformation wrought by lively music and brightly-lighted booths stocked with refreshments and stuffed toys and prizes guaranteed to tempt anyone with pitching or shooting skills. We were always delighted to see our friends running around freely, whereas during the rest of the year, we usually had to line up quietly.

As for the attic, although Kevin and I used to imagine ourselves climbing the last flight of reputedly "dangerous" steps leading to its mysterious, out-of-bounds rooms, we never did succeed in getting a look at that forbidden area. We used to entertain ourselves by imagining its contents: stage props and costumes stored in trunks and barrels, stacks of ancient books and maps, boxes of students' property confiscated by overwrought teachers on rainy days, countless enormous cobwebs, ghosts.

Every school day began with "The Lord's Prayer." When our turn came to read, we were allowed to choose a favorite passage that provided us with a bit of wisdom from the Bible. It was followed by the Pledge of Allegiance to the Flag. . . .

First-graders of Maple Avenue School, 1924. From left to right are: (bottom row) Lorraine Wolfe, Shirley Berman, Janet Carswell, June Merritt, Nellie Fennimore, unknown, Helen Riker, unknown, and Edson Riker; (top row) Ransford Crane, Alexander Truppi, Thomas Fargey, unknown, William Scheuerman, Frank Graback, Austin Spencer, Eddie Jones, Fenn Crafferty, and Sidney Brown. The teachers are Sarah Bockoven and Miss Light. (The Historical Society of the Somerset Hills)

Maple Avenue School, lower grade, 1913. (The Historical Society of the Somerset Hills)

Seventh- and eighth-grade students, with girls in nautical attire, ca. 1921, at Maple Avenue School. The male instructor is standing on left. (The Historical Society of the Somerset Hills)

First-grade students at Maple Avenue School, 1921. Teacher on right is Sarah Bockoven. (The Historical Society of the Somerset Hills)

Maple Avenue School, middle grade, 1913. Teacher Miss Dupay, in center, wears a traditional lapel watch on the left side of her dress; students are unknown. (The Historical Society of the Somerset Hills)

Maple Avenue School baseball team with Jack Twichell, principal, standing in center back row, ca. 1930. (The Historical Society of the Somerset Hills)

Boys in their starched white knickers pose for eighth-grade graduation picture, 1934. (The Historical Society of the Somerset Hills)

Eighth-grade students at Maple Avenue School, 1939. (Nancy Childs Knobloch)

Students at Maple Avenue School, ca. 1930. (The Historical Society of the Somerset Hills)

In the fourth grade we studied Stone-Age people, whom we referred to as "cave men." Under the tutelage of Miss Arena, we tacked our painted depictions of these plucky prehistoric beings to the classroom walls. On one special day, just before lunch hour, we took turns, girls first, going into the cloakroom to remove our school clothes and wrap ourselves in the cotton sheets we'd painted to resemble animal skins. Mrs. Kurgier handed out large meaty bones and arranged us on the dark wooden floor while a professional photographer took pictures of us as our best Stone-Aged selves.

Certain smells associated with that old school live on in memory: the smell of wet galoshes in the cloakroom and wet mittens drying on radiators; the smell of Miss Mussen's rubber-soled saddle oxfords as she walked quietly around the fifth grade classroom while we were taking written tests; the smell of the new pad of lined paper each student was given every month; the smell of pencil shavings packed inside the sharpener attached to the window sill.

There was always a kind of mystery attached to the worn lift-top desks that often bore unfamiliar inky initials worked into their wooden surfaces. And what about the scribbles, notes and declarations of love scattered throughout used textbooks? Somehow everything about that Maple Avenue School resonated with intimations of the generations of students and teachers who had over the years climbed its aged-warped stairs and trod its dark floor boards.

By the time Kevin and I learned that the public library was no longer located at the corner of Finley Avenue and Oak Street, but had taken over the very space where our stalwart old stone school had stood, we were long gone from Basking Ridge and our "country life" was over.

The teachers were the last to leave the Maple Avenue School, 1939. Left to right: Jack Twichell, principal; Louise Flint, front far right; Agatha Greulock, far right, rear; and other staff members. (The Historical Society of the Somerset Hills)

As in many other places, the community eventually outgrew its school building. In 1937 the Board of Education declared Maple Avenue School inadequate. The school, situated on an acre and a half, provided little play space. It also lacked an auditorium, gymnasium, library, and a home economics room. Because the building was located thirty feet from what had become a busy street, the Maple Avenue School also was deemed unsafe.

The community, along with the country, was outgrowing the regular school curriculum. As industry flourished, there was a greater demand to teach skilled trades, manual arts, and other subjects, such as bookkeeping, shorthand, and typing. Many communities had already started junior high schools equipped for their classes. Maple Avenue School need updating to provide education in these disciplines.

Thus, plans were prepared for Oak Street School, to be built on West Oak Street. Maple Avenue School was closed in 1939, and the Board of Education sold the building to the Township Committee. The Township anticipated locating its offices there, but plans changed, and the building remained unused for ten years.

The municipal offices were never relocated there, but as it turned out, activity at Maple Avenue School was not over. To relieve overcrowding conditions at the Oak Street School, the

Maple Avenue School was reopened in 1948 with a one dollar-a-year lease. Agatha Greulock became its principal.

Initially, the reopened Maple Avenue School housed grades one through eight, but by 1968 all eight rooms were used exclusively for grades K through three. Eleven classroom teachers and three substitutes taught 305 students.

During Maple Avenue School's 57-year history, principals included Mary G. Kenney, Agatha Greulock, William O. Losey, Willett Neer, Jack Twichell, and Andrew Long.

Five thousand kindergarten and primary-grade students passed through the school's doors during those years. Those who taught at Maple Avenue School say they witnessed a spirit of camaraderie that lasted to the end. Mr. Long was one of the last principals of Maple Avenue. He wrote the farewell for the final issue of the school paper, *Maple Leaves*, which opens this chapter.

On June 19, 1969, about 250 young students raised their voices in song to mark the end of local education, when Maple Avenue School closed. These words were written for the farewell assembly:

Maple Avenue School, ca. 1960. (Bernards Township Library Local History Room)

> *Maple Avenue's served us well*
> *For many, many years*
> *So now before we say goodbye*
> *Let's give her three big cheers.*
> *Fare you well dear old school*
> *Fare you well dear old school*
> *Fare you well we say*
> *We'd better be on our way.*

Several years after the school closed, it was judged to be a "firetrap" because raw linseed oil had been applied to the classroom floors as a way to manage dust and maintain the wood. Over the objection of many townspeople, the historic building was demolished in early 1973.

The Bernards Township Public Library now occupies the location of the school. On April 20, 1991, the former grammar school was memorialized with a plaque marking the site.

The building is gone, but its nostalgic spirit remains in the hearts of many students who attended Maple Avenue School.

—Samantha DiMaggio, Brian Patchett, Sam Schraer, and Ria Talsania

Second-grade students at Maple Avenue School, ca. 1968, wave a last farewell to teacher Mrs. Alma Corcoran and Principal Andrew Long as they walk to Oak Street School. The school served Bernards Township well for years and closed permanently because of outdated conditions. (Bernards Township Public Library Local History Room)

At the closing of the Maple Avenue School, Basking Ridge, New Jersey, June 19, 1969, three graduates examine class pictures with Superintendent Myron D. Headington. From left are: Miss Myra Howlett and Mrs. Kenneth Turner, both of the eighth-grade graduating Class of 1910, and Mrs. Fred Kampmier, from Class of 1909. (The Historical Society of the Somerset Hills)

Demolition of the Maple Avenue School, 1973. (Bernardsville Public Library Local History Room)

Demolition of the Maple Avenue School in 1973 made way for the new Township library. Left to right: Helen R. Mallon, Building Committee chairperson, Anne C. Ryan, library director, Jane D. Steinkopf, Board of Trustees president. (Bernards Township Public Library Local History Room)

115

Mr. Jack Twichell, principal of Oak Street School, back row at far left, William Keeler, teacher, back row, far right. Louise Flint, social studies teacher, second row from the front, far left, and Earl Houtz, manual training and mathematics teacher, second row, far right. Photograph taken in 1949. (The Historical Society of the Somerset Hills)

Oak Street School

To Our Graduates:

Congratulations to you, the first graduating class from our new junior high school. In years ahead you may look back with considerable pride as being the "pioneers" in establishing the first junior high school in Somerset County. Many thanks for the fine spirit of cooperation you have extended in helping us to work out the problems in a new school organization. I hope each of you has enjoyed this year as much as I have. With best wishes for continued success.

—Myron D. Headington, Superintendent, 1957

In January 1937 the Board of Education purchased a tract from the daughter of Dr. Horatio Gates Whitnall. The twelve and one-half acres varied in elevation from a low-lying field along the northern boundary to a level plateau on the southern boundary.

The school, initially built for children grades one through eight, housed nine classrooms, an auditorium, a gymnasium, a manual arts shop, a home economics room, and an office. Although the school was scheduled to open in September 1939, it was not ready, and students returned to the Maple Avenue School until November 23, 1939. On the day before Thanksgiving, more than 200 students from the old school gathered their belongings and marched by twos to the new Oak Street School.

Dr. Horatio Gates Whitnall, ca. 1900, owned land that housed the Whitnall farm, where Oak Street School would eventually be built. His property extended from the west line on Brownlee Place and South Finley Avenue across the railway line and down to Harrison's Brook. (The Historical Society of the Somerset Hills)

Dr. Horatio Whitnall's home was on the site that today houses the Bank of America. He was a Civil War surgeon in the Union Army and one of the richest men in town in the late 1800s. He donated his car to the Basking Ridge Fire Company. When he died in the early 1900s, his daughter inherited his estate, then sold the extensive property to the Board of Education in the 1930s.

The construction of Oak Street School marked a significant change in school facilities, costing the district $200,000. It was the third school built in the community in 139 years. On the day of the school's dedication, an article in the *Bernardsville News* reported, "Residents of Basking Ridge, particularly the parents of children, may well look with pride on this beautiful building, one of the most modern structures of its kind, which will stand for many years to come as a monument to the courage and forethought of those responsible for its building."

The building was distinctive inside and out; designers borrowed historic elements to create a classic structure. The school's exterior was Colonial-style brick architecture. The interior held a grand chandeliered auditorium and a distinctive ticket window booth, both visible today.

Approximately 500 parents and interested taxpayers attended the dedication on November 21, 1939. During that ceremony, the Neill Card American Legion Post 114 presented the platform flag for the auditorium.

Oak Street School began with a relatively small staff of five teachers and a few special-areas teachers. Jack B. Twichell was the school's principal until 1948, when he became the supervising principal of the Bernards Township schools. He held this position until he was appointed the County Superintendent of Schools in Mercer County in 1953.

Katherine Kearns Connolly, a former student, writes about attending the new school:

> The idea of leaving the old Maple Avenue School and moving to a different location didn't really take hold of us until the day when, led by Jack B. Twichell, all eight grades, together with their respective teachers, set out on foot to make the switch from old to new. Until then, the reality of the transition had been a fantasy goal to be achieved at some hazy point in the distant future. But the great day came, and when it did, equipped with pencil boxes, lunch boxes and book bags, we lined up on the sidewalk and began our march westward. Turning left at the end of Maple Avenue, we passed the beautiful white-columned Presbyterian Church, crossed Finley Avenue, passed the public library and headed down Oak Street where we beheld the reality of our new school as it stood there dressed in splendid red brick, waiting for us.
>
> A major change in the curriculum for grades 6 through 8 was the introduction of shop classes for boys

and sewing for girls. Both of these subjects were presented on Tuesday mornings for several hours in spacious well-lighted rooms. A bank of storage boxes lining part of one wall gave each sewing student a safe place in which to keep her work-in-progress. Our country was at war at the time, but in the new Basking Ridge Grammar School (Oak Street School), we were treated to what was then state-of-the-art equipment.

World War II, of course, had a commanding influence on our lives. We became accustomed to air raid drills during which we practiced going down to the lower level to sit on the floor in the hallway outside the doors to the new cafeteria and new gymnasium. We also saved our pennies to buy war stamps, planted victory gardens, and kept our eyes and ears open for information about where to buy shoes that could be bought without using ration coupons. My father was the air raid warden for our district, but when he was away on business and the sirens sounded at night, my brother Kevin would put on the white helmet and identifying arm band and go out alone to check on the darkened houses of our few neighbors.

The graduating exercises of 1943 went off as Mr. Twichell had envisioned. Each of us took our turn at standing up, walking to the front of the stage and delivering our well-rehearsed three-minute talk on whatever topic we had chosen. It was a rattling experience, but when it was over we began to breathe normally again. We were given a copy of "Our Great State Papers," a small blue hard-covered book, as well as our diplomas with our full names written in perfect Palmer-method script by Louise M. Flint. Even now, the words to that first school song we ever learned slip back into my head and I seem to hear children's voices from the past singing:

> Here's to you, Basking Ridge
> Proud of you we are
> We will not shirk our work
> Success will be our guiding star,
> Although the day will come
> When we must part,
> We'll keep the grammar school
> Of Basking Ridge forever in our hearts!

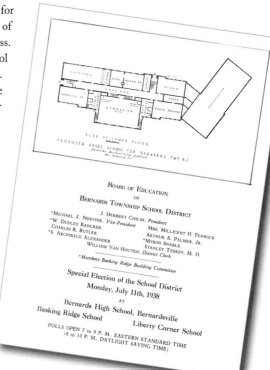

Building plans for the new, modern Oak Street School as it was presented to the voters of the Township on July 11, 1938. Note: Millicent Fenwick of Bernardsville was a school board member! (The Historical Society of the Somerset Hills)

Left: Brochures sent to local residents invited them to vote on the proposed building, Oak Street School. Elections were held at the three existing schoolhouses: Bernards High, Maple Avenue School, and Liberty Corner School. (The Historical Society of the Somerset Hills)

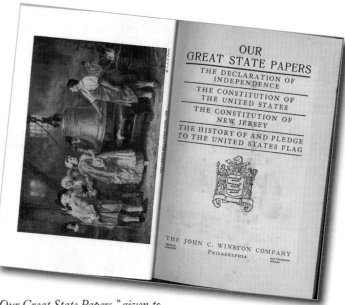

"Our Great State Papers," given to graduates from Oak Street School. (The Historical Society of the Somerset Hills)

In my nostalgic recollection of our last day in the "new" school on Oak Street, I like to think that we sang those words before we said our farewells, but in truth, I don't believe that we did either of those things. We didn't sing, and we didn't say goodbye. We simply climbed onto the waiting school bus outside, sat down on its worn brown leather seats, and rode away. The summer and the rest of our lives stretched out before us.

Bernards Township continued to grow; in 1952, eight additional rooms, along with administrative offices and a nurse's room, were added to Oak Street School. A year later, William Keeler succeeded Jack Twichell as principal. The school was used for grades five through eight, but in 1956 it became a junior high school for grades seven through nine. (See quote at beginning of chapter.)

Construction at the Oak Street School, latter part of 1938. Local students pose for photographer. (The Historical Society of the Somerset Hills)

Oak Street Junior High School offered many activities for its students. Among the most popular were the annual science fairs of the 1950s. More than 1,000 people attended the third annual science fair, which had 342 projects on exhibit. Students in grades seven through nine were awarded first, second, and third prizes. Exhibits included: "The World of Medicine," "Working Generator Model," "Geiger Counter," "The Eye," "Heart-Aches," "Wildlife Display," and an "Antibiotic Production and Fermentation Exhibit."

Students Nona Strauss and Jeff Stiles contributed editorials and news articles events to the Bernardsville newspaper in a column titled "Oak Street Junior High Jottings" (1958). These articles provide a glimpse into school life:

The eighth and ninth grade girls of the Junior High School heard on Wednesday, April 30, Mr. and Mrs. Robert Cole, admissions counselors of Katherine Gibbs School, speak at the seventh vocational talk in the school auditorium. Mrs. Cole spoke of manners and dress in business as well as the duties of a secretary.

Mr. Cole mentioned that since the school was founded in 1911, no employer has ever requested that his secretary be either beautiful or glamorous. The employers do expect their secretaries to be well groomed and well trained. The need for secretaries is great, as is shown by the fact that Katherine Gibbs had 60,000 calls for secretaries last year.

Mrs. Cole emphasized the importance of manners and dress. She stressed the necessity for girls to make introductions. Thoughtfulness, consideration for others, and the ability to be able to get along with others were also stressed.

In dress the girls were informed that sweaters and skirts, while being proper for school wear, are taboo in offices. Personal cleanliness is most important in order that other people will enjoy working with you.

Mr. Cole concluded with a short, but completely negative approach to the subject of chewing gum. "This," he said, "is a completely unnecessary American institution!"

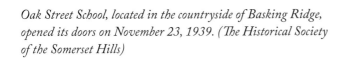

Oak Street School, located in the countryside of Basking Ridge, opened its doors on November 23, 1939. (The Historical Society of the Somerset Hills)

Foundation of Oak Street School, 1938. Erected arched white windows stand in the background. (The Historical Society of the Somerset Hills)

Construction crew works on the new Oak Street School, 1938, located on West Oak Street. The school was built in Colonial-style brick to complement buildings of similar style in the village, notably the Presbyterian Church, public library, and Brick Academy. Workers lay bricks around a few of the many planned arched windows. (The Historical Society of the Somerset Hills)

Oak Street School provided much-needed space for the 424 children who eventually attended Bernards Township schools. Left to right: Louise Flint, who taught history and geography in grades six through eight, Principal Jack B. Twichell, and staff member. (The Historical Society of the Somerset Hills)

Original ticket booth in foyer of Oak Street School, 1938. Photo taken in 2006. (Josephine M. Waltz)

Auditorium is lit with six chandeliers, 1938. Original seats have long since been replaced. Photo taken in 2006. (Josephine M. Waltz)

Eighth-grade girls from Oak Street School sitting on rear of car wearing bobby socks, penny loafers, and saddle oxfords, 1953. (Pauline Hilmer Merrill)

Oak Street School staff enjoy a softball game. Far right, Principal William Keeler, 1953. (Pauline Hilmer Merrill)

Basking Ridge teachers' barbecue, June 1941, at end of school year at Louise Flint's house on West Oak Street. Left to right (seated in front): Frances Kuriger, Jack B. Twichell, principal, Audrey Treacey, and Dorothy Cichon; (standing) Katharine Schmelzer, Bernice Frost, Mrs. J. B. Twichell, and Agatha Greulock. (The Historical Society of the Somerset Hills)

The following is another of the students' contributions to "Oak Street Junior High Jottings" (1958):

> Another big improvement was accomplished this past week when the installation of a school inner communication system was completed in the Junior High School. The two-way system, which operates between the office and all classrooms, auditorium, cafeteria, and gymnasium, makes it possible to eliminate the messenger system. It allows the administration to make announcements simultaneously to the entire school. It also is possible to have FM music played over the speakers during the noon hour.

The school population grew to 425 students and the staff to 25. The community saw to it that new programs and modern facilities were introduced to enrich the lives of its children. By the 1960s, the following programs existed:

- Progressive science instruction
- Industrial and fine arts instruction
- Home economics
- Real-life application of mathematical concepts
- Integrated language arts curriculum that included: speaking, listening, handwriting, creative writing, spelling, and literature

Literature about Oak Street School Bond Issue Referendum, June 10, 1952. (June O. Kennedy)

Robert Haycock, far left, Board of Education president, presents trophies to Carol McSkimin, Elizabeth Chapin, and Joan O'Gureck. To the far right are: Myron D. Headington, superintendent of schools, and William Keeler, Oak Street principal, ca. 1950. (Oak Street School Library)

Oak Street School when it was a junior high school, ca. 1960. Students enjoyed many social events with a live band. Lower left-hand corner shows line dancing. (William Annin Media Center)

Student demonstration during a science fair at Oak Street School, ca. 1940. (The Historical Society of the Somerset Hills)

Oak Street School band, 1955. Edward Dorman, standing at rear right, was the instrumental music supervisor. (The Historical Society of the Somerset Hills)

Oak Street Junior High School industrial arts classroom, 1966. From left to right are: Arthur Busch, Joe Brogan, teacher Mr. Hoffman, David Fleming, and Mitchell Friber. (William Annin Media Center)

Industrial arts class, 1966. The sign above the tools reads: "These tools aren't orphans, so please don't adopt them." Pictured are Arthur Busch (left) and Joe Brogan. (William Annin Media Center)

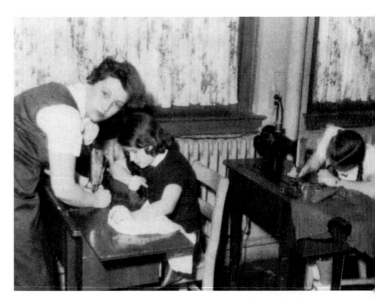

Home economics sewing classes, 1966. (William Annin Media Center)

Students, ca. 1940, give a presentation utilizing technology of the times, a 16mm Bell & Howell movie projector and hand-held microphone. (The Historical Society of the Somerset Hills)

Chartered buses line up outside Oak Street School, 1949, for seventh-grade class field trip to Philadelphia. (The Historical Society of the Somerset Hills)

Oak Street Junior High School left to right: Richard Hall, teacher Mr. Patela, Angie Post, Janice Dunken, 1966. (William Annin Middle School Media Center)

Oak Street students act as Township officials during Government Day, 1950. Left to right: (front row) Junior Committeemen Joseph Brush 2nd, Donald Vander Wyde, and Earl Polan; (second row) Junior Clerk Donald Davis, Assessor Chris Ward, Tax Collector Robert Beringer, Health Board Secretary Margaret Connolly, Engineer David Koppes, Road Superintendent John Deinert, attorney William Aitken, Police Chief Leonard Rembo, and Magistrate Carole Kennedy; (back row) Attorney Anthony P. Kearns, Engineer Kenneth A. Turner, Collector Scott F. Tarner, Assessor Robert Gutleber, Committeeman Herbert W. Graham, Mayor Harold B. Thomson, Warren M. Craft, Police Chief W. Robert Moore, Principal Jack B. Twichell, and Clerk Charles E. Anstedt. (The Historical Society of the Somerset Hills)

Brass arm badge worn by students who served on the School Safety Patrol at Oak Street School, ca. 1941. (Josephine M. Waltz)

Eighth-grade Oak Street student at assembly accepts storm coats for School Safety Patrol crossing guards, ca. 1950. (The Historical Society of the Somerset Hills)

The programs sought to develop in its students "sound habits" and "desirable attitudes," according to Louise Flint, a former social studies teacher at Oak Street Junior High School. She writes in *Education in Bernards Township* (1960):

> Because of improved transportation and communication, no part of the world is far from us, and it is desirable to know how people in other parts of the world live, work, and play. Social Studies include much more than the simple facts of geography and history taught years ago. Students are taught to realize and appreciate the advantages of democracy over other forms of government, to trace the development of those political ideas, which are fundamental in the American government of today, and to understand the future prospects of democracy as a way of life. Social Studies develop in the child an understanding of his responsibilities as a member of his social group and create understanding of and tolerance for all peoples of the world.

Oak Street Junior High School, 1959. (William Annin Media Center)

Today, almost 70 years later, Oak Street School's exterior consists of large, imposing white columns that stand proudly at its entrance. The original arched, white-framed cathedral windows still adorn the side. Once inside the school, visitors experience a sense of nostalgia. Twelve-inch wooden moldings surround the walls of the auditorium, doorways, and halls. There are many reminders of a bygone era; one needs but to stop and look.

Oak Street School, run by Principal Dr. Jane Costa, now is home to kindergarten through grade five and has an enrollment of approximately 600 students. The school activities foster literacy throughout the community. On Family Reading Night, children dress in pajamas and meet with their teachers to spend an evening reading in a café setting. The menus list books rather than food, and students serve as the café's waiters and waitresses.

Crown molding trim and simple pilaster on the right, still adorn the auditorium at Oak Street School, 2007. (Josephine M. Waltz)

Oak Street School has many child-centered community service projects, including:

- Annual Food Bank collection
- Valentine's Day cards for veterans
- Candy canisters made for the seniors at Ridge Oak Senior Citizen Housing
- Three-year project to collect one million soda tabs to benefit the Ronald McDonald House

At Oak Street School, students benefit from the seeds of high educational standards planted years before, when the community embraced a changing world. This school made a difference then, and it continues to do so today.

—*Adam Freides, Jameson Lochhead, Aditi Pai, and Daniel Piros*

Fruit trees and orchards on Cedar Hill Farm, originally owned by Samuel Owen, 1912, no longer exist, but their location is adjacent to where Cedar Hill School now is situated. In place of the orchards are Ridge High School's athletic fields. (The Historical Society of the Somerset Hills)

Cedar Hill
School

The school grounds were covered in salt hay to keep the newly planted seeds from blowing away. When the children played on the playground, balls rolled in the ground and they'd chase after them—both the children and the balls got covered in mud grass that entered the school for some time!

—Connie Malisky, former faculty member

Cedar Hill School was named after the Samuel Owen estate, Cedar Hill. Owen was a Newark pharmaceutical manufacturer. In 1912 he erected a 20-room brick English Tudor manor house on 100 acres that extended to the northern boundary of Homestead Village, just off South Finley Avenue on Collyer Lane. The manor was designed for his wife, Alice Burford, who was of British ancestry.

On 35 acres of his 100-acre estate, Owen planted 5,000 peach trees and 1,500 apple trees. The orchards produced large, plump peaches. Being a generous man, Owen invited the townspeople to enjoy the flowering fruit trees and picnic on his property. Visitors also collected the "drops" from the orchard, fruit that had fallen on the ground. "Drops" cost 50¢ per bushel.

Melvina M. Oehlers writes in "Look to your schools," about schoolchildren taking hikes to the orchards. "Old-timers like to recall that, when they were attending Maple Avenue School, field trips took them to Cedar Hill, and the highlight of the outing was always when the time came to gather the bunch of violets to be carried home to Mama."

In 1940 the Owen estate was sold to George Ludlow Lee, chairman of the Red Devil Tool Company (the inspiration for Ridge High's mascot, the Red Devil). The estate passed through several owners from 1940 until 1968, when the Township purchased it. Today the manor house serves as Bernards Township Municipal Building.

By the mid-1950s, Bernards Township had three schools: Maple Avenue, Liberty Corner, and Oak Street, and yet again the Township faced overcrowding. Fortunately, Lee and his wife donated sixty acres of land. Cedar Hill School was constructed on a portion of the land; Bernards Township's Ridge High School was built on another part of the former estate a few years later.

In a booklet titled "The Heritage of a School—Cedar Hill" (1982), Richie Cavallaro writes:

A Newark pharmaceutical manufacturer and builder, Samuel Owen, ca. 1930, stands outside his estate home, Cedar Hill, on Collyer Lane. (Township of Bernards)

The Board of Education had a special meeting Friday, August 19, 1955, at 8 p.m. at the Oak Street School. Mr. Sutherland introduced the resolution for the new [Cedar Hill] school, and Mr. Back seconded the motion:

"WHEREAS at a special election on the 30th of June 1955 all legal voters of the School District adopted the following proposal. . .

To construct a new schoolhouse on the tract of land owned by the Board of Education, approximately twelve acres in extent, situated in the school district between South Finley Avenue and South Maple Avenue northerly of Homestead Village, purchase the school furniture and other equipment necessary therefore, and improve the said tract of land:
. . . all necessary plans pursuant to this proposal shall be activated."

The motion was approved unanimously by roll call vote.

In September 1957 the new building was completed at a cost of $780,000. The school opened on August 1, 1957, with G. William Allabach as its first principal. His annual salary was $7,000. Allabach held the position for many years. William Losey succeeded him as Cedar Hill School's principal.

Cedar Hill School was considered a most modern structure in its time. The school originally had 18 classrooms equipped with skylights and a combination gymnasium, cafeteria, and auditorium. There also were administrative offices, a teachers' room, and a nurse's office.

A former schoolteacher recalls when Cedar Hill School was set to open but was not fully completed:

The cafeteria equipped for hot meals was unfinished, so students brought bagged lunches. There were cords and electrical wires scattered throughout the hallways, and a lament made by the Superintendent: "If you give the construction crew more time, they'll never finish, but when they have to work with the kids around. . .they hurry up!"

One problem that was not anticipated was the glare that entered from the skylights, though they were covered with shades. The lighting was such that it became necessary to remove the skylights from the classrooms altogether.

A distinguishing characteristic of Cedar Hill School was its courtyards. One very small inner courtyard was located in the front between the café/auditorium and the administrative offices; it still exists today. A much larger second courtyard was left as an open grassy area for many years, until another wing was added, closing the fourth side of the courtyard.

In the following excerpts from "The Heritage of a School—Cedar Hill" (1982), former students recall their experiences:

Samuel Owen built this house on 100 acres in 1912. From 1940 through 1968, the property was owned by three other families [Lee, Bissell, and Astor]. In 1975 it became the official Municipal Building of Bernards Township. (Township of Bernards)

Joan Wagner writes:

Everyone was excited about going to a brand new school. We were impressed with how modern it was. We were introduced to a new word: cafetorium.

Bombardment [similar to dodge ball] was the all-time favorite sport.

Girls wore skirts or dresses and penny loafers. No pants or jeans were allowed.

A sure sign of the times was noted in Bob Frieber's recollections of Cedar Hill School's dress code:

One thing that I remember which I'm sure you will get a kick out of, is the dress code of the early '60s. We were not permitted to wear blue jeans, and the girls had to wear dresses no matter how cold it got outside. Hair had to be kept cut above the ears if you were a guy. We always had to consult the dress code whenever there was a question about a new style. Finally, during one cold winter, the argument was raised to let girls wear pants to school for health reasons. The girls wore their pants, and thus began the slow decay of the dress code. Soon after, the rest of the educational system began to find its way into the 20th century.

Evelyn Hamann recalls sixth grade at Cedar Hill School in 1967–68:

When I was in sixth grade, we were the first group of students to change classes for math, English, social studies, and science, instead of having one teacher for all subjects. That was exciting for us, and the transition into junior high school was much easier.

Peter Miller, a longtime resident of Basking Ridge, details the lunchtime routine when he attended Cedar Hill School in 1957:

All our classes were conducted in the same room with the exception of art, music, gym and lunch. Mr. Styles, my first male teacher, was a good teacher as far as we knew in 4th grade.

When it was time for our class to go to lunch, we would get our lunch boxes, for those who brought their lunch, line up and in a single file line head for the cafetorium.

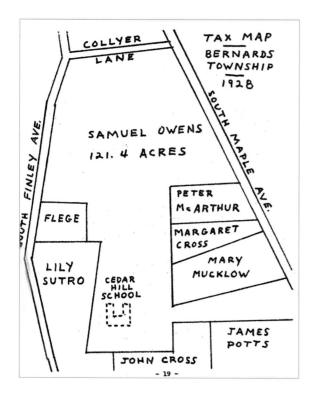

Map from 1928 of homestead property shows Owen's acreage and location of Cedar Hill School added in later years. (Cedar Hill School Media Center)

The area and the hand washing equipment was like none I had ever seen. Mr. Styles explained how this hand washing equipment worked. The two vessels were round, approximately 4 to 5 feet in diameter. There was a foot apparatus that you placed your foot on. This would activate a circular, single row shower of warm water in a continuous flow around the circumference of the large stainless steel sink. Picture a champagne fountain and that is what these units remind me of. Just up from the stream were liquid soap dispensers where you pushed a device to get soap and then wash your hands. There were also paper towel dispensers on the unit. The units accommodated approximately 10 to 12 students each and made the hand washing process quick. Like we really cared about how well we washed our hands—we wanted lunch!

During the mid-1970s, a few adventurous teachers and students established an herb and rock garden in the larger courtyard, where a few sapling shade trees grew. Today those gardens have been replaced with extensive annual and perennial flowerbeds. All classrooms adjacent to the interior of the school can easily view this courtyard.

Cedar Hill School's grade-level configuration changed over the years, as did those of Liberty Corner and Oak Street schools. In the 1970s, Cedar Hill School housed all the district's fifth and sixth grades and a portion of the fourth-graders. While the fifth and sixth grades were located at Cedar Hill School, students were organized in ability groups. There were 11 to 12 instructional levels in reading and math.

Following a drop in student enrollment in the early 1980s, Cedar Hill School was closed. Joseph Kaufman, its principal since 1976, was assigned to lead Liberty Corner School. Its students were transferred to Liberty Corner and Oak Street schools. Space at Cedar Hill was rented to outside child care providers.

When enrollment increased, the school reopened in 1982 with Kaufman as its principal. In 1994 Cedar Hill School was home to 575 students in grades three, four, and five, and during that same year, ten classrooms were added to the rear of the building, thus providing an additional wing.

Cedar Hill School, known for its exceptional music programs, produced wonderful

Entrance to Cedar Hill School at Christmas time. Photo taken in 2006. (Josephine M. Waltz)

Side view of Cedar Hill School shows one of its many additions jutting out beyond classrooms. In the far back right corner is Ridge High School. Photo taken in 2006. (Josephine M. Waltz)

musicals, such as *Alice in Wonderland*, *Robin Hood*, and *Cinderella*. Nancy Childs Knobloch, staff music teacher, directed the performances.

Today Cedar Hill School is home to 642 students in preschool through grade five. Joseph Mollica, principal since January 1994, is known as both a genuine educator with high standards and a warm, caring individual.

Students take an active role in Invention Day; student mock trials; Immigration Day, when they display exhibits about diversity and ethnic groups; Talent Showcase Day, and the school science fair. Each year, students design Valentine's Day cards for local veterans and contribute $1,000 worth of collected food items to needy families in nearby towns during Thanksgiving and the winter holidays. These are but a few of the many student-driven programs at Cedar Hill School.

Over the years, changing teacher requirements and rigorous curriculum standards have reshaped education, ensuring that the quality of instruction remains strong. And although the school building now is larger than the original structure, a small community still lies within this school that has celebrated learning for half a century.

Not coincidentally, its address is 100 Peachtree Road, Basking Ridge.

—Garrett McComb, Lauren Pizzi, and Liz Pires

Students arrive at Ridge High School via school buses, ca. 1960.
(Bernards Township Public Library Local History Room)

Ridge
High School

… Another sad note: This was the last school year that students from Basking Ridge and Liberty Corner attended Bernards High School. The 1961–62 school year opened with students from Basking Ridge and Liberty Corner attending their own new high school—Ridge High School. There was a pervading sense of loss, especially among the seniors. The 1962 Bernardian *described the situation, saying they were still one class, although in different schools. Because the winter vacation schedules were different, they were able to visit each other's schools.*

These two schools hold their reunions together to this day.

—Germaine McGrath, alumna, Class of 1966
—Mary Elizabeth Young, teacher 1957–66,
librarian 1966–98

In 1924, Bernardsville became a borough and separated from Bernards Township, yet the two school districts operated as one school system. It wasn't until 1947 that the two systems separated and Bernards High became the property of Bernardsville. However, the Township continued to pay tuition to send its students to Bernards High School.

George Ludlow Lee Sr., chairman of Red Devil Tool Company, donated sixty acres of land for the Cedar Hill and Ridge High Schools and sold twelve acres to the American Legion Post 114 for the War Memorial Field. Left to right are unknown; son, John Lee; George L. Lee Sr.; unknown; son, George Lee Jr.; and son, Todd Lee. (The Historical Society of the Somerset Hills)

Groundbreaking ceremony, 1960. Pictured are left to right, student, Jim Morris; Myron Jack D. Headington, superintendent; William Keeler, Oak Street School principal; Floyd Bragg, Board of Education, students Chip Sahler, Scott Bruenner, and Jack Welch (in dark suit), who is today a local restaurant entrepreneur. (Bernards Township Public Library Local History Room)

Steel beams are positioned, 1960, as Ridge High School begins to take shape. (Bernards Township Public Library Local History Room)

The area grew rapidly during the 1940s, more so in Bernards Township than in Bernardsville. At one point, Bernardsville, with fewer children attending school, was paying a larger share of the school district's operating costs.

Louise Flint writes in *Education of Bernards Township* (1960):

> In 1946 the school boards of nine or ten communities met to discuss the advisability of solving the secondary problem through a cooperative or consolidated plan. As the years passed, some of these districts included in the earlier study broke away to join with other neighbors in solving their high school problem. Mendham and Chester joined together with their western neighbors to form the West Morris Regional Districts.
>
> Eventually, six districts were included in Bernards High School . . . with Bernards Township, Far Hills, Peapack-Gladstone, Bedminster, and Passaic Township attending as sending tuition districts.

The idea of consolidating schools to manage shifting populations was not new. Andrew Gulliford includes a perspective in *America's Country Schools* (1984):

> The American Association of School Administrators, which had always favored consolidation, made this prophetic statement in 1939 in "*Schools in Small Communities*":
>
> > Keep the schools and the government of the schools close to the people, so that the citizens generally, including the parents and taxpayers, may know what their schools are doing, and may have an effective voice in the school programs. . . The relationship of the schools to the natural community and the closeness of the school to the people are of first rate educational significance and are not to be sacrificed in the interest of "efficiency." If such a sacrifice is made to establish economical districts, we will find in a generation that something of deep significance which money cannot buy has been destroyed.

Ridge High School was dedicated on November 5, 1961, two months after it welcomed students and faculty. (Bernards Township Public Library Local History Room)

The communities' values were tested repeatedly when space shortages and spending came into conflict. Serious overcrowding conditions in Bernards High continued despite actions intended to provide relief. In 1956 ninth-graders attended Oak Street School instead of Bernards High, and in 1957 Passaic Township withdrew its remaining students from the high school.

For a while, this solution alleviated the problem, but "The Columbia Report," prepared by the Columbia Teachers College in 1956, recommended a regional high school supported by the five neighboring districts: Bernards Township, Bernardsville, Bedminster, Peapack-Gladstone, and Far Hills.

In *Among the Blue Hills . . . Bernardsville . . . a History* (1974), the Bernardsville History Book Committee explains conflicts within the two school districts:

> The Bernards Township board refused to submit this plan to its voters, and instead proposed establishing its own high school. The New Jersey State authorities rejected this proposal on

Jim Schoenberg of Ridge clears hurdles in contest against Bernards High School, 1976. (Ray Jones)

the basis that it would create an imprudent debt ratio in the Township. More studies ensued by a committee of the combined boards under directive of the State Commissioner. Two different regional plans were offered for referendum, one in 1958 and the other in 1959, and both were turned down by some of the districts. Since now it was evident that a satisfactory regional plan was impossible, Bernardsville acted to stop accepting Bernards Township pupils after June 1961, and thus forced the State to authorize a separate Township high school.

Bernards Township Board of Education explored the idea of building a high school of its own. On October 6, 1959, the Bernards Township residents voted to build a high school, calling for a bond issue of $1,532,000. The voters enthusiastically approved the referendum by a four-to-one majority. By May 1960, construction of the new high school began on the property shared with Cedar Hill School—the northwestern section of the former Owen Estate. William J. Keeler, who had been principal at Oak Street Junior High School, became the new principal at Ridge High School, and Robert C. Stoll assumed Keeler's former position at Oak Street School. Ridge High School opened in September 1961 as planned with 492 pupils in grades nine through twelve.

The original building had 23 classrooms, a two-station gym, and administrative and guidance offices. The Township's juniors from Bernards High School became the first graduating class at Ridge. The ninth through tenth grades came from Oak Street School. The building was constructed with a 670-student capacity. Three years later, the second referendum was passed, and nine classrooms and special-area rooms were added. In 1969 Ridge became a senior high school for grades ten, eleven, and twelve, and for a few years William Annin Junior High School accepted the ninth-graders.

Ridge High School football team, 1962. (Bernards Township Public Library Local History Room)

Football coach Harry Bush with Ridge High School player, 1976. (Ray Jones)

Pom-pom girls during halftime football game at Ridge High School, 1976. (Ray Jones)

Students attend a Board of Education meeting at Cedar Hill School's auditorium to protest exams held during week of the Senior Prom at Ridge High School, 1978. (Ray Jones)

Band members entertain during halftime session at football game, 1976. (Ray Jones)

Rear of Ridge High School, where orchards once stood, shows additions made to support the increasing school population. Photo taken in 2006. (Josephine M. Waltz)

The trend of population growth continued in the decades that followed. In an effort to relieve the overcrowded conditions, more modifications and additions were made. Today, the school's four computer labs with wireless Internet connections help the district keep pace with changing technology. The school's principal, Francis Howlett, former principal of William Annin Middle School (2003–06), is overseeing major additions to the high school. Planned for September 2008 are: a 1,400-seat gymnasium and 1,000-seat auditorium; a conversion of the current auditorium space to guidance offices, along with refurbishing of science labs. An additional 18 classrooms will provide much-needed space. Howlett hopes to create "houses" for its incoming freshman, thus forming small communities within the larger school community.

Ridge High School is home to 1,600 students in grades nine through twelve. Because of its long tradition of comprehensive course offerings, it is not surprising that the May 8, 2006, issue of *Newsweek* ranked Ridge High School 118 on its list of the top 1,000 high schools in the United States, and the second-highest-ranked school in New Jersey. Ridge High School also was ranked 91 out of 1,000 high schools nationally in *Newsweek's* 2005 school survey. And most recently, RHS was ranked 98th nationally, making it the highest ranking of Central Jersey high schools in *Newsweek's* 2007 list of the top 1,200 high schools nationwide.

This highly regarded institution can trace its roots to 1764 and 1795 when Reverends Samuel Kennedy and Robert Finley set high educational standards for their classical school students, many of whom went on to attend Princeton University. With the school's tradition of excellence, it is not surprising that approximately 89 percent of today's 364 Ridge High School graduates continue their education at two- and four-year institutions.

Our forefathers would be proud!

—*Lisa Wooldridge*

William Annin Junior High School, 1974. (Ray Jones)

William Annin Junior High School

— · ◆ · —

In our study we discern six qualities of character. William Annin had superb self-reliance, a sense of family responsibility, a justifiable pride in accomplishment, an independence of judgment, strong religious faith, and sense of community responsibility.

—Archibald Carswell, president, Basking Ridge Historial Society dedication ceremony, September 28, 1969

Williaam Annin School was built on a site that likely lies within the bounds of where the Annin family homestead was built in 1766. Though the home of the Annin family is no longer in existence, the family name lives on through what some have called an "outwardly plain structure."

When the Board of Education proposed in 1966 to build a $2.7 million junior high school, the plan was rejected as "too fancy." Bernards Township Superintendent Myron D. Headington expressed the reality that "exterior beauty costs a lot, and today we have to concentrate on making the interior of our schools appealing." The board returned with a new school plan for nearly $2.5 million, which was approved in May 1967.

Laying of the cornerstone at William Annin Junior High School, September 28, 1969. Left to right: Assistant Principal James Dowden, Superintendent Myron D. Headington, and Principal Paul Wagner. (William Annin Media Center)

The planned site was a 45-acre tract off Quincy Road in the Heather Farms development. The tract originally consisted of 37 acres, but it was enlarged through two gifts of land totaling eight acres from Mr. and Mrs. Anthony Kearns of South Finley Avenue, Basking Ridge. (Mr. Kearns, a Bernards Township resident, was the municipal attorney.)

When selecting the name for the new school, the Board of Education considered honoring William Penn, John Harrison, or Samuel Kennedy. However, in late January 1969, Phyllis Johnson, the Board of Education's public relations chairman, explained that William Annin's name had been chosen:

> First, we pay a tribute to a man who was the father of his community and who embodied the finest ideals: love of his country, a belief in the need for education, and a desire to give public service. Second, in choosing the name of one of her sons, and the original settler, we honor the fastest-growing area of our Township. Third, and perhaps most important, we hope to instill in our schoolchildren some knowledge of and feeling for the long historical tradition of this pre-Revolutionary town of ours. We have much to be proud of in our past, and even more to be proud of in the future, which will be in the hands of many of the children educated in the school named William Annin. May they be inspired by his example.

In 1969 William Annin Junior High School became the sixth major school building constructed in Bernards Township. During the dedication ceremony on September 28, the Board of Education President Roger Conover remarked that many attendees had not seen the original

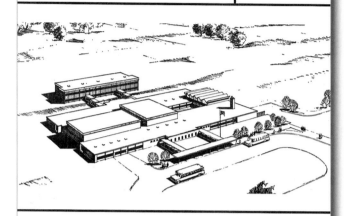

REVISED PROPOSAL

PUBLIC
HEARING
MAY 3, 1967

REFERENDUM
MAY 16, 1967

BERNARDS TOWNSHIP JUNIOR HIGH SCHOOL

A public hearing notice in 1966 for the revised proposal of a $2.7 junior high school. (The Historical Society of the Somerset Hills)

William Annin family, descendants of the original Annan settlers, 1969. From left to right are: William, eight, Sarah, four, Mr. William Annin, John, fourteen, Mrs. Nelle Annin, and Susan, fifteen. William Annin is the great-great-great-great-grandson of the local Colonial patriot for whom the school was named. (William Annin Media Center)

William Annin Junior High School, 1969, was called a "marvel of functional beauty." (William Annin Media enter)

Dedication ceremony program held on September 28, 1969. (The Historical Society of the Somerset Hills)

Sixth-graders busy with class work, 1969. (William Annin Middle School Media Center)

The hub of the school, a two-level spacious library, accommodated children throughout the day, 1969. In the late 1990s, new construction and remodeling saw the library converted to guidance offices and choral music rooms, while a much larger media center was added to the school. (William Annin Middle School Media enter)

148

Front entrance to William Annin Junior High School, located at 70 Quincy Road, Basking Ridge, 1974. (Ray Jones)

proposal for the structure. He explained what the school would have looked like had the first plan been accepted—and proceeded to hold up a picture of the Taj Mahal!

When William Annin Junior High School opened, it had 45 classrooms for students in grades six through eight. Although the building had a functional capacity of 960, the three grades consisted of 859 students. An octagonal two-level library held 6,000 volumes with room for 10,000. The cafeteria, with a cathedral ceiling, contained 300 seats and was equipped with a sliding room divider; it also served as a study hall. The auditorium held 632 seats. In addition, there were two science laboratories, a graphic arts room, a three-station gym, a home economics room, soundproof music rooms, art rooms, and a school store run by the student council. A two-story wing in the rear of the building contained 24 classrooms. Sixth-graders occupied 12 classrooms on the second floor; seventh- and eighth-graders were located in the remaining classrooms.

Today, William Annin is a middle school that houses 1,312 students in grades six through eight. This vibrant middle school is led by Principal Nick Markarian. There is a unique sense of commitment from the administration. Besides managing personnel and school facilities, school principals are known to roll up their sleeves and tutor students themselves. In addition, innovative learning opportunities for students abound:

- The school's industrial arts classes were featured in 2007 on New Jersey Network Public Television's "Classroom Close-up, NJ." The technical education program offers disciplines such as robotics and woodworking, with an emphasis on math and science.

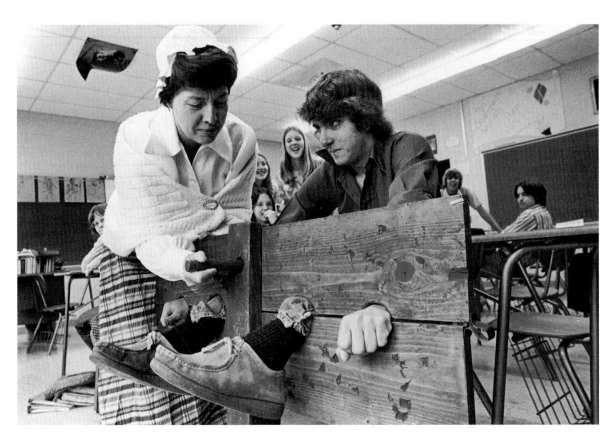

A lesson for the misbehaved is illustrated by a William Annin Junior High teacher to a student during Arts at Annin week, 1976. (Ray Jones)

Teachers don Revolutionary War uniforms for Arts at Annin week, much to their students' delight, 1976. (Ray Jones)

William Annin Middle School Cafeteria, with its original cathedral-style windows, shows the middle beam on the ceiling once used for a sliding room-divider. To the right is the annex built to accommodate the school lunch population, and to the left is the media center, 2007. (Josephine M. Waltz)

- Instruction in history is brought to a personal level when students learn about the Holocaust and World War II with an assembly program presented by Holocaust survivors.

- Students benefit from dynamic PTO-funded programs such as "Amazing Grace," an assembly about Martin Luther King Jr. and the issue of racial prejudice.

- Eighth-graders participate in an annual trip to Washington, D.C., where they get a first hand look at our nation's democratic process.

Character education is at the forefront of this school. At William Annin, students are encouraged to participate in schoolwide character education programs and charitable events, including:

- An annual can drive for the Somerset County Food Bank and coat drive for the Market Street Mission in Morristown

- WAMS Slams, a students vs. staff basketball game to benefit the American Cancer Society

- The Buy a Star program for diabetes research

- Fundraising activities in support of the Leukemia and Lymphoma Society

Within the last 37 years, William Annin Middle School has undergone many changes, but one thing has not changed—the rich legacy of the man for whom the school was named and the school's efforts to exemplify his character of unyielding service to community and country.

—*Patrick Burns, Julia Farley, and Stephen Santini*

Afterword

As new settlements sprang up, establishing a schoolhouse was a sign of settlers' optimism and commitment to the future. A schoolhouse represented their determination to build a home, a permanent community, and to prepare the next generation for whatever it might face.

—Elisabeth Deffner, author of "The One-Room Schoolhouse"

Bernards Township settlers built the area's first schoolhouses so that their children might benefit from having formal education and learning about the world beyond their farms and neighborhoods. The early efforts of community leaders to address the needs of the next generation spun threads of hope and enterprise, which bound the community together for good. The plans they made and the steps they took ensured that their children would receive the best education they could provide and that the area would grow and prosper.

We have come a long way from simple one-room schoolhouses to the contemporary multi-room structures in which our children are educated today. Buckets of drinking water have long been replaced by water fountains. Slates have given way to computers. And the basic instruction of reading and writing has extended to global problem solving.

Yet, the basic challenges remain the same. Significant construction projects in four schools and maintenance and remodeling in the others are ongoing.

These efforts are being made to meet the needs of the Township's growing school population; these expansive activities echo the settlers' early efforts to enlarge play areas and provide larger schoolhouses as more families put down roots in the community. Just as we once outgrew the traditional one-room schoolhouses, we are moving to create a better future for the next generation of students who must find their place in an ever-larger, yet ever-shrinking, world.

With education, they will be best prepared to meet those challenges. The threads spun by the early Township settlers continue to bind this hardworking, spirited community. This is the hallmark of our schools.

—J. M. W.

About the Author

Josephine Waltz has lived in New Jersey for most of her life. As a six-year-old she immigrated with her Sicilian-born parents to the United States from Buenos Aires, Argentina, where she was born.

A graduate of Fairleigh Dickinson University at Madison, New Jersey, she received her Master's in Education from Seton Hall University. She has been a mother, teacher, gardener, and photographer.

A public school teacher since graduating from college, Waltz has taught many subjects including reading, science, and social studies to students in grades five through eight. In addition, she has developed curricula for and taught gifted children and enrichment classes.

Beginning in 1998, her students have won writing awards for eight consecutive years in the New Jersey Council of Teachers of English Writing Contest.

In January 2005, her first book, *Write Out of the Oven! A Collection of Letters and Recipes from Children's Authors*, was published by Teacher Ideas Press, with proceeds going to the Children's Literacy Foundation (CLiF).

She was featured in the September/October 2006 issue of *New Jersey Countryside* magazine as "a New Jerseyan we are proud to know."

Her article "Recipes for Life" appeared in the March 2007 issue of *Teaching PreK-8*, a national magazine for educators. She has also appeared in *NEA Today*, November 2006, "Bulletin Board."

She resides in Belle Mead, New Jersey, with her family.

Author's Note

When I first began teaching, I knew that Bernards Township was a place of distinction, in which knowledge and education were highly regarded. I perceived this in the teaching staff, the parents, and my 11-year-old students. The children were eager to learn, and I was eager to teach.

I vividly recall teaching the unit "A Look at the Social Sciences." The culminating project was to explore the early settlement of Bernards Township by assuming the roles of anthropologists, historians, and geographers. I discovered an excellent resource, *Township of Bernards Bicentennial 1760–1960*, which had been prepared by local historians.

A bulletin board display, titled "Baskin on the Ridge," showcased my class's reports, illustrations, and maps. A vintage pair of white knickers, on loan from a student, added a touch of authenticity to the presentation.

Just over 30 years later, much has changed, and like many other small rural communities in central New Jersey, Bernards Township has experienced significant growth.

In response to those changes, I developed a unit in which students research the Township's early schoolhouses and compile their findings in a single lasting collection. I felt it was valuable for the students to experience, even on a small scale, a first-hand attempt to trace and record local history from a personal perspective.

This book is the result of our efforts.

I hope readers find our book discoveries interesting, informative, and nostalgic.

—Josephine M. Waltz

Bibliography

Allen, Mrs. Charles M. "Early Education in Basking Ridge." *Bernardsville News*. 31 Oct. 1929, Vol. 47, #37, page 13.

Allen, Samuel A. "Basking Ridge's New $200,000 School Which Will Open Monday, November 27." *Bernardsville News*. 16 Nov. 1939, Vol. XLVII, #40, page 7.

Becker, William B. *The American Photography Museum of Photography*. E-mail to images@photographymuseum.com from jowaltz@gmail.com, 9 Jan. 2007.

Bernardsville History Book Committee. *Among the Blue Hills . . . Bernardsville . . . a History*. Bernardsville, New Jersey: Bernardsville History Book Committee, 1974. Pages 5, 6, 36–38, 47–48, 121–134.

Barber, John Warner, Henry Howe & the WPA Writers. Somerset County, NJ. *Historical Observations of New Jersey*. New Haven, Connecticut: Benjamin Olds, 1861.

Basking Ridge Historical Society. *The Brick Academy*. Basking Ridge, NJ: Basking Ridge Historical Society, 1978. Pages 1–10, 12.

Bernards Crimson. Vol. X. No. 7, 13 March 1928.

Carter, Leslie. "Knott's Little Schoolhouse." *The History Magazine for Young People*. Cobblestone. Nov. 1981. Page 29.

Century Book Committee. *Bernards High School—100 Years of Excellence 1905–2005*. Berkley Heights, NJ: Twill Printing Services, 2005.

Deffner, Elisabeth. "The One-Room Schoolhouse." 2 Aug. 2006: 1–2. <http://www.americanprofile.com/issues/20031026/20031026-3434.asp>

Doyle, Marian I. "Going back to school was much tougher in the past." *Antique Week*, 14 Sept. 1992.

_____ "The Faithful Teacher Could Find her Reward in Heaven." *Antique Week* 13 Sept. 1992.

Dubroff, Henry. "The Story of America's Schools," *The History Magazine for Young People*, Cobblestone. Nov. 1981. Pages 14–15.

Evans, Timothy. "Cedar Hill Pupils Pen, Plan Farewell for Principal," *Star-Ledger*. 23 June 1994.

Flint, Louise, M. *Education in Bernards Township 1760–1960*. Basking Ridge, New Jersey. May 1960. Pages 1–24.

Franklin Academy. Archival records and documents at The Historical Society of the Somerset Hills, Basking Ridge, New Jersey.

Franklin Corners. Archived papers at The Historical Society of the Somerset Hills, Basking Ridge, New Jersey.

Gulliford, Andrew. *America's Country School*. Washington, D.C.: The Preservation Press, 1984. Pages 44, 45, 79, 81, 86, 131, 159, 161, 162, 174, 175, 178, 179, 183, 190, 191.

Hagemann, Donna. "Liberty Corner School is gone, but its history remains." *Courier News*. 5 Sept. 1975.

"Historic Institute of Basking Ridge." *Bernardsville News*. 24 Jan. 1902.

Hoops, Judy. "Academy, Sweet Academy." *Daily Record*. 5 April 1979.

Johnson, Clifton. *Old-Time Schools and School-books*. New York: Dover Publication Inc., 1963. Pages 101–102.

Judd, Rev. W. B. "School Question to Date." *Bernardsville News*, 8 June 1900. Vol. 4, #13.

Kalman, Bobbie. *A One-Room School*. New York: Crabtree Publishing Company, 1994. Pages 6, 8, 11, 12, 25.

Kampmier, Fred W., Norman J. Convery, Herbert F. Noll, Mrs. John Serafin, and Kenneth A. Turner Jr. "Historical booklet of Bernards Township, New Jersey, published to commemorate the bicentennial, 1760–1960." Basking Ridge, New Jersey: May 1960. Pages 6, 24.

Kennedy, June O. *A History of the Maple Avenue School, Basking Ridge, NJ.* April 20, 1991. Pages 1–5.

—————. *Around and About Basking Ridge, Liberty Corner, and Lyons.* Dover, New Hampshire: Arcadia Publishing, 1995.

—————. "Legendary Annin Homestead depicted in current display in Bernards Township." *Bernardsville News.* 19 Aug. 1999, Vol. 101, #38, Page 12.

—————. "Liberty Corner's Outstanding Annin Family." "Bernards Township Focus." August 24, 2000.

————— "A Brief History of the Maple Avenue School, Basking Ridge, NJ." 1991.

—————. "Mount Prospect School." 23 May 2002.

—————. "Some Random Notes about the Pleasant Valley School, Basking Ridge, NJ." August 7, 2004.

Kooser, Ted. "Country School." Official entry blank. Lincoln, Nebraska: University of Nebraska Press, 1969.

League of Women Voters of Bernards Area. "Inside Bernards Township," a "Know Your Town" publication. Bernards Township, NJ: League of Women Voters. 1977.

Lines, Anna W. "About Liberty Corner." March 31, 1952.

—————. "Early Schools in Bernards Township." *Bernardsville News.* 1948.

Loeper, John J. *Going to School in 1876.* Atheneum, New York: Macmillan Publishing Company, 1984. Pages 45–46.

"Longtime residents take a look back, simpler times of 1900s recalled." *Bernardsville News.* 30 Dec. 99.

Matson, Velma Fowler. "A Rural School as I Remember It." Newaygo County Historical Archive. 1999. 7 Jan. 2007. <http://ncha.ncats.net/data/Old_Rural_School/>

McCarron, Beverly. "Historian Elated as Bernards School Bell Turns Up." *Sunday Star-Ledger.* 30 Sept. 1990.

McFadden, Dorothy Loa. *A History of the Presbyterian Church in Basking Ridge, Part I, 1717–1961.* Basking Ridge, New Jersey: Johnston Letter Company Inc. 1961. Pages 18–19.

"New Schoolhouse for Liberty Corner." *Bernardsville News.* 20 May 1904.

New York Mercury, No. 807, April 20, 1767, as quoted in New Jersey Archives, 1st Series, XXV, newspaper extracts, I, VI, 1902, page 350.

Oehlers, Melvina M. Regent, Basking Ridge Chapter, Daughters of the American Revolution. *Look to Your Schools.* 1974. Pages 14, 16, 38, 45, 46, 52, 56, 57.

Perry, W. Jacob. "Former Maple Avenue School to be Memorialized April 20." *Bernardsville News.* 4 April 1991, Vol. 93, #17, Page 12.

—————. "Cedar Hill Principal Hailed after 25 Years." *Bernardsville News.* 19 June 2003.

—————. "When America Was on Alert 60 Years Ago." *Bernardsville News.* 28 Dec. 2001.

Reilly, Matthew. "Readington Students Toe the Line Back to Days of Quill Pens and Ink Wells." *Sunday Star-Ledger.* 28 April 1999.

Robinson, P. C. "He Still Loves a Parade." *Bernardsville News.* 7 Dec. 2006. Page 18.

Sanford, Betsy. *The Franklin Institute 1800–1906.*

Shaw, Mary Louise. "Annin Held Classes in His Home before 1800." *Bernardsville News.* 14 Feb. 1974, Vol. 76 #8, Page 7, Section 2.

Spinning, Edwin S. "One Room Schoolhouse was Standard in the Old Days." *Bernardsville News.* 9 July 1964, Vol. LXVI #22, Page 5, Section 2.

—————. "Schools Have Been a Sometime Thing." *Bernardsville News.* 22 August 1974, Page 16.

Stitcher, Felicia. "Bernards Township Shows Off Its New Annin Junior High." *Bernardsville News.* 2 Oct. 1969.

—————. "Annin School Dedication Evokes Sense of History." *Bernardsville News.* 2 Oct. 1969.

The Franklin Academy Built in 1851 in Basking Ridge, New Jersey. The Historical Society of the Somerset Hills, Basking Ridge, New Jersey.

The Heritage of a School—Cedar Hill 1957–1982. Pages 19–21, 27–28.

Van Horn, J. H. *Historic Somerset.* Printed by Uniman Printers. New Brunswick, New Jersey: Published by the compiler of the "Historical Societies of Somerset County, NJ," 1965. Pages 79, 80.

Voss, Hilda. Personal interview. 10 Feb. 2007.

Young, Kate. "The Kennedy Chronicle." *The Samuel Kennedy Family.* 2007. <http://freepages.genealogy.rootsweb.com/~kennedychronicle> (Accessed 5 July 2007).

Index

The Life of Lazarillo of Tormes
HIS FORTUNES AND
MISFORTUNES

THE LIFE OF

Lazarillo of Tormes

HIS FORTUNES AND MISFORTUNES
❁ As told by himself

Translated, and with an introduction,
by Robert S. Rudder

With a Sequel by Juan de Luna
Translated by Robert S. Rudder
with Carmen Criado de Rodríguez Puértolas

FREDERICK UNGAR PUBLISHING CO.
NEW YORK

Copyright © 1973 by Frederick Ungar Publishing Co., Inc.
Printed in the United States of America
Library of Congress Catalog Card Number: 70-125966
Designed by Irving Perkins
ISBN: 0-8044-2746-1 Cloth
0-8044-6772-2 Paper

This translation is for
LISA, PAULA,
and
CHRISTOPHER MICHAEL,
three small pícaros.

Contents

THE SECOND PART OF
THE LIFE OF
LAZARILLO OF TORMES

Introduction

Lazarillo of Tormes appeared in sixteenth-century Spain like a breath of fresh air among hundreds of insipidly sentimental novels of chivalry. With so many works full of knights who were manly and brave enough to fight any adversary, but prone to become weak in the knees when they saw their fair lady nearby, was it any wonder that Lazarillo, whose only goal was to fill a realistically hungry stomach, should go straight to the hearts of all Spain? The little novel sold enough copies for three different editions to be issued in 1554, and then was quickly translated into several languages. It initiated a new genre of writing called the "picaresque."

It seems certain that other editions, or at least other manuscripts, of *Lazarillo* were circulating previously, but the earliest we know of were the three published in 1554. One of these was printed at Burgos, another at Antwerp, and the third at Alcalá de Henares. They all differ somewhat in language, but it is the one from Alcalá de Henares that departs most radically from the other two. It adds some episodes not in the other editions, which were probably written by a second author.

Because *Lazarillo* was so critical of the clergy, it was put on the Index Purgatorius in 1559 and further editions were prohibited inside Spain. Then, in 1573, an abridged version was printed that omitted Chapters four and five, along with other items displeasing to a watchful

Inquisition; later additional episodes were suppressed. This mutilated version was reprinted until the nineteenth century, when Spain finally allowed its people to read the complete work once again.

The identity of the author of this novel has always been a mystery. A few names have been suggested over the years: Juan de Ortega, a Jeronymite monk; Sebastián de Horozco, a dramatist and collector of proverbs. But probably the most widely accepted theory was the attribution to Diego Hurtado de Mendoza, a famous humanist. Many early editions of *Lazarillo* carried his name as author, even though there has never been any real proof of his authorship. Some critics, following Américo Castro's lead, think the author was a Jewish convert to Christianity because of certain phrases which point in that direction. And some think he was a follower of Erasmus, despite the French critic Marcel Bataillon's emphatic statements to the contrary.

One of the first relationships we become aware of as we read this novel is the link of the name Lazaro (Lazarillo: little Lazaro) with the biblical Lazarus: either the figure who died and was brought back to life (John 16) or the beggar (Luke 16:20–31). This "historical" relationship is further compounded by the fact that many episodes of the novel are versions of material traditional in European folklore. There is, for instance, a thirteenth-century French theatrical farce, *Le garçon et l'aveugle,* in which a servant plays tricks on a blind man. And the British Museum manuscript of the *Decretals* of Gregory IX contains an illustration of a boy drinking through a straw from a blind man's bowl. The episode in which Lazarillo thinks a corpse is being brought to his house appears in the *Liber facetiarum et similitudinum Ludovici de Pinedo, et amicorum*, and may be a folktale. And the story of the constable and the pardoner is to be found in the fourth novel of *Il novellino* by Masuccio Salernitano, and may also be a folktale.

It has long been said that this novel is an accurate reflection of society in sixteenth-century Spain. And to some extent, this does seem to be true. The king of Spain, Charles I, became involved in several foreign wars, and had gone deeply into debt to German and Italian bankers in order to finance those wars. Soon the quantities of gold and silver coming from Spain's mines in the New World were being sent directly to the foreign bankers. The effects of inflation were to be seen everywhere, as were other social ills. Beggars and beggars' guilds were numerous. Men of all classes were affixing titles to their names, and refusing any work—especially any sort of manual labor—unless it suited their new "rank." The clergy was sadly in need of reform. And pardoners were—often unscrupulously—selling indulgences that granted the forgiveness of sins in return for money to fight the infidel in North Africa and the Mediterranean. All these things are to be found in *Lazarillo of Tormes*.

But is the book really an accurate reflection of all of Spanish society? If there were avaricious priests, and priests who had mistresses, were there none with strong moral principles? If poverty was felt so keenly by Lazarillo and others, was there no one who enjoyed a good meal? As another writer has suggested, the Spanish conquerors did not come to the New World on empty stomachs, nor was the Spanish Armada ill supplied. It is obvious, then, that while *Lazarillo* reflects Spanish society, it mirrors only one segment of that society. Its writer ignored uncorrupted men of generosity and high moral principles who surely existed alongside the others.

So just as the chivalresque novels distorted reality upward, this novel distorts reality downward and almost invariably gives us only the negative traits of society.

An important point is the unity, or nonunity, of the book. Earliest critics of *Lazarillo of Tormes* saw it as a loosely formed novel of unconnected episodes whose only point of unity happened to be the little rogue who told his life story, in which he is seen as serving one master after another. Later criticism has changed that point of view, however, by pointing to such unifying factors as wine, which is used as a recurring theme throughout (Lazarillo steals it; it is used for washing his wounds; he sells it). Then there is the "initiation" in which Lazarillo's head is slammed against a stone statue of a bull. Later the blind man smashes his own head against a stone post as poetic justice is meted out. Finally, Lazarillo's mother will "lie at the side—or stay on the side of good people," and as the novel ends Lazaro decides to do the same.

Claudio Guillén, a modern critic, has noted that time is also a unifying factor in this novel. Early incidents are told in detail, and at moments of pain specific amounts of time are measured ("I felt the pain from its horns for three days"). When Lazarillo is taken in by the squire, his hunger pangs become so great that he begins to count the hours. But as conditions improve for Lazarillo's stomach, he gradually forgets about the slow passage of time. In fact, time now begins to race past: four months with the pardoner, four years with the chaplain. This slow, then swift, passage of time is used by Guillén to explain the extreme brevity of some later chapters of the novel. It is a mature Lazaro, he says, who is telling the story and reflecting on his childhood. And we are really seeing the memory process of this older Lazaro who glosses over less important parts of his life and dwells on the moments that matter.

Other critics have responded to the question of "finality" in the work; that is, is *Lazarillo* an incomplete novel or not? Francisco Rico believes the novel is complete, and that there is a "circular" structure to it all. He notes that the novel is addressed to a certain fictional character ("You": *Vuestra merced*), and that Lazarillo intends to tell this character "all the details of the matter," the "matter" apparently being the questionable relations between the archpriest and Lazarillo's wife. So there is a continuity from the beginning of the work through the details of Lazarillo's life, until the last chapter ("right up to now") where the "matter" itself, alluded to previously in the Prologue, is finally given in some detail.

Another critic, Américo Castro, points out that *Lazarillo of Tormes* is different from other types of sixteenth-century prose fiction in at least one extremely important way that points toward the modern novel. The knights of chivalresque novels and the shepherds who sighed and lamented their way through pastoral novels were flat characters with no room to grow. Not so Lazarillo. Every action, every twist of fortune make an impression on him, form his way of looking at the world and shape his nature. From an innocent little boy he becomes a mischievous, then vengeful, blind man's boy. He observes the hypocrisy, avarice, false pride, materialism of his masters, and when he marries the archpriest's mistress for what he can gain, he applies all the lessons he has learned on the ladder to success—to the "height of all good fortune." Américo Castro also notes that *Lazarillo of Tormes* is a step toward the masterpiece of Cervantes, *Don Quixote of La Mancha*. As this critic said: "In addition to its intrinsic merits, the *Lazarillo de*

Tormes is supremely important viewed in its historic perspective. In many ways it made possible the *Quijote*. Among other things, it offered in the *intimate opposition* of the squire and his servant the first outline of the duality-unity of Don Quijote and Sancho."

Style is another point of great importance to this novel, particularly in the use of conceits. Lazarillo's father, for example, "suffered persecution for righteousness' sake," a clear reference to the beatitudes. But in this case "righteousness" is the law who is punishing him for being the thief that he is. Throughout the novel we see similar plays on words: the master, who "although he was *blind, enlightened* me;" or the squire who tried to coax certain young ladies one morning, and whose stomach was *warm*, but when he discovered that his pocketbook was *cold*, he suffered *hot-chills*.

It is not surprising that sequels promptly appeared, but the writers of these unfortunately lacked the genius of the author of the original *Lazarillo*. An anonymous sequel appeared in 1555 with the title, *The Second Part of Lazarillo of Tormes, His Fortunes and Misfortunes*. Its beginning words are the same as the final ones of the first *Lazarillo*, but there any similarity ends. In this novel Lazaro makes friends with some Germans, and his wife gives birth to a daughter. Lazaro then enlists to go on an expedition to fight the Turks, his ship sinks, and he is miraculously changed into a fish. He has many adventures in the sea, and is finally caught up in the nets of some fishermen and changes back into a man. The novel is a fantasy, and may be allegorical. The beginning is its most realistic point, and the first chapter of this novel became tacked onto the end of the first *Lazarillo*.

No further sequels were printed until 1620 when Juan Cortés de Tolosa's book, *Lazarillo de Manzanares*, was published. This novel imitates the first *Lazarillo* in its initial episodes, but is again far less successful than the original.

In the same year, 1620, Juan de Luna's *Second Part of the Life of Lazarillo of Tormes* was published in Paris. (Another edition was published simultaneously in Paris, but was marked as though printed in Zaragoza to facilitate the book's sale in Spain.) Little is definitely known about Luna. We do know that he was born in Spain—perhaps in Aragón. He apparently fled to France in 1612 as a political and religious refugee: in one of his books he refers to himself as "a foreigner who has left behind his homeland, his relatives, and his estate for a just and legitimate cause." It has been speculated that Luna may have been educated for the priesthood but then grown dissatisfied and even vehemently bitter toward the clergy. The reason for his flight to France has been interpreted as a flight from the Spanish Inquisition. In France, in Montauban, he began to study theology to prepare himself for the Protestant ministry. But soon afterward he became a Spanish teacher in Paris, and in 1619 published a book of proverbs and phrases for Spanish students. The following year his continuation of *Lazarillo* was published, along with a revised version of the original *Lazarillo* (revised because its style did not suit his tastes). Next he appeared in London, in 1622, attempting to have his sequel translated into English. His Spanish grammar was published there the following year. The last information we have of him is that he became a Protestant minister in England, and for three years delivered sermons to his fellow Spaniards each Sunday, in Mercer's Chapel, Cheapside, London.

Although the details of Juan de Luna's life are rather sketchy, a great deal more can be said about his novel.

His continuation of *Lazarillo* was the only sequel to meet with any success. The same characters—Lazarillo, the archpriest, the squire, etc.—are here, but their personalities are changed drastically. The squire is the one who is most noticeably different. He is no longer the sympathetic, poor, generous (when he has money) figure of the first part. Now he is a thief, a cowardly braggart, a dandy, and Lazaro has nothing but scorn for him. Lazaro himself is now fully grown, and there is no room for his personality to change as before. Perhaps the only character who is still the same is Lazaro's wife.

Other differences between the two novels are also evident. In the first *Lazarillo* we see a central protagonist who serves a different master or performs a different type of work in each chapter. But in Luna's sequel we do not have this same structure. In the first five chapters of Luna's book, for example, Lazarillo's adventures flow as they do in traditional novels: he goes to sea, the ship sinks, he is captured by fishermen and put on exhibition as a fish, and finally he is rescued. The following chapters, however, often divide his life into segments as he goes from one position to another.

Another difference to be noted is that while the first Lazarillo addresses a certain person ("You": *Vuestra merced*) who is not the reader but an acquaintance of the archpriest, in the *Second Part* something quite different occurs. Luna's Lazaro addresses the "dear reader," but hardly with flattering terms: he humorously suggests that we may all be cuckolds. Then he ironically refuses to tell us about—or even let us think about—certain promiscuous details because they may offend our pure and pious ears. The framework of the first novel is apparently a device whose purpose, like the "Arabic historian" and the "translators" of *Don Quixote*, is to create an atmosphere of realism, while Luna's "dear reader" is simply a device for humor.

Another important distinction to be made between the two books is the extent of word-play used. Almost one hundred years elapsed between the times the two books were published, and literary styles changed a great deal. While the first *Lazarillo* used some conceits, as we have previously noted, Luna's book abounds with them to the point where it becomes baroque. About people who are being flooded with water or are drowning, it is usually said that they are overcome by trifling, but watery, circumstances: "a drop in the ocean" (*ahogar en tan poca agua*). Lazarillo's child is "born with the odor of saintliness about her" (*una hija ingerta a cañutillo*); unfortunately this refers less to her as holy than it does to the fact that her father is really the archpriest. The use of antithesis is also evident throughout Luna's novel. From the beginning in which he dedicated his *small* work to a *great* princess, throughout the length of the book, we find Lazaro esteemed by his *friends* and feared by his *enemies*, begging from people who give money with *open* hands while he does not take it with *closed* ones, and so on. Another trick in language is Luna's plays on sounds: such combinations as *salí—salté* (left—leaped), *comedia—comida* (rituals—victuals) are abundant. Luna also uses obscene conceits for a humorous purpose, mixing them with religious allusions both for humor and to vent his own feelings of hostility against the church.

Yet another important difference between the two novels lies in Luna's emphasis on tying up loose ends. We know that in the first *Lazarillo* the protagonist leaves the blind man for dead, not knowing what happened to him, and we never do find out whether he survived the blow or not. Later the squire runs away from Lazaro, and we never see him again either. The author of the first *Lazarillo* gives us a series of vignettes in which the psychological interplay of the characters is stressed. The characters fade out of Lazaro's life just as people fade in and out of our own lives. Luna, however, was much more interested in telling a good story—and one that has an ending. So the squire appears, and tells what happened to him after leaving Lazaro: a complete story in itself. He steals Lazaro's clothes and runs off, and later we see him again—having got his just retribution almost by pure chance. The innkeeper's daughter runs off with her priest, and both turn up several chapters later; their account amounts to another short story. The "innocent" girl and the bawd disappear, then return to play a scene with Lazaro once more, and finally they fade out, presumably to live by their wits ever after. Related to this stress on external action is the importance Luna gives to descriptive rather than psychological detail. His minutely detailed descriptions of clothing are especially noteworthy: the squire's "suit"; the gallant's clothing as he emerges from the trunk; the costume worn by the girl who became a gypsy. These are descriptions we do not find in the original *Lazarillo* because the author of that work is much more interested in internal motivations than external description and action.

Let us move on to another point: the social satire in the two novels. We have seen the satire against the various classes, and particularly against the church, in the first *Lazarillo*. And Luna's satire has the same targets. The essential difference is in the way the two authors handle their darts. The first *Lazarillo* is fairly subtle in its attacks: men are avaricious, materialistic, unscrupulous, infamous—and these vices are sometimes only very loosely connected with the church. But Luna wants us to know definitely that the church is like this, so his satire of the church is blunt and devastating. The Inquisition, he tells us plainly, is corrupt, brutal, and feared throughout all of Spain. Priests and friars are always anxious to accept a free meal, they have mistresses, and they are less principled than thieves. Lawyers and the entire judicial system are corrupt. The Spaniards, Luna tells us from his position of exile in Paris, are too proud to work, and they will become beggars rather than perform any sort of manual labor. Lazaro himself is held up to us as a "mirror of Spanish sobriety." Apparently Luna's anger about having to leave Spain had no opportunity to mellow before he finished his novel.

Luna's *Second Part of Lazarillo of Tormes* is not the "First Part." But even so, it has its merit. Luna liked to tell stories, and he was good at it. Some scenes are witty and highly entertaining. When Lazaro meets his old friends, the bawd and the "maiden," at an inn, the action is hardly dull. The "quarter of kid" becomes the center of attraction from the time it appears on Lazaro's plate until he falls and ejects it from his throat, and it is used skillfully and humorously to tell us a great deal about each of the characters present.

Another scene worth calling to the reader's special attention is the chapter in which a feast is held that erupts into a brawl, after which the local constabulary arrives. Luna's account is a very close predecessor of the modern farce. Many of the elements seem to be present: a lack of reverence, a situation used for comic effects, the chase through many rooms to find the guests, the beatings that the constable's men are given by the pursued, being "breaded" in flour, "fried" in oil, and left out on the street where they run away, ashamed to be seen. It is as though we are catching a glimpse of the Keystone

Cops, seventeenth-century style. And the variations from seventeenth to twentieth century do not appear to amount to a great deal.

—ROBERT S. RUDDER

University of California at Los Angeles
December 1972

Translator's Note

My translation of the first *Lazarillo* follows Foulché-Delbosc's edition, which attempts to restore the *editio princeps* but does not include the interpolations of the Alcalá de Henares edition. The translation of the first chapter of the anonymous sequel of 1555 follows at the end of the first part because it serves as a bridge between the first novel and Luna's sequel. For Juan de Luna's sequel, the modern edition by Elmer Richard Sims, more faithful to the manuscript than any other edition, has been utilized.

A word of thanks is due to Professor Julio Rodríguez Puértolas, whose own work was so often interrupted by questions from the outer sanctum, and who nevertheless bore through it all with good humor, and was very helpful in clearing up certain mysteries in the text.

The seventy-three drawings were prepared by Leonard Bramer, a Dutch painter who was born in 1596 and died in 1674. Living most of his life in Delft, he is best known for his drawings and for his illustrations of Ovid's writings and of other works of literature. The original drawings are in the keeping of the Graphische Sammlung in Munich.

R.S.R.

The Life of
Lazarillo of Tormes,
His Fortunes
and Misfortunes

As told by himself

Prologue

I think it is good that such remarkable things as these, which may never have been heard of or seen before, should come to the attention of many people instead of being buried away in the tomb of oblivion. Because it might turn out that someone who reads about them will like what he reads, and even people who only glance lightly through this book may be entertained.

Pliny says along these lines that there is no book—no matter how bad it is—that doesn't have something good in it. And this is all the more true since all tastes are not the same: what one man won't even touch, another will be dying to get. And so there are things that some people don't care for, while others do. The point is that nothing should be destroyed or thrown away unless it is really detestable; instead, it should be shown to everybody, especially if it won't do any harm and they might get some good out of it.

If this weren't so, there would be very few people who would write for only one reader, because writing is hardly a simple thing to do. But since writers go ahead with it, they want to be rewarded, not with money but with people seeing and reading their works, and if there is something worthwhile in them, they would like some praise. Along these lines too, Cicero says: "Honor promotes the arts."

Does anyone think that the first soldier to stand up

and charge the enemy hates life? Of course not; a craving for glory is what makes him expose himself to danger. And the same is true in arts and letters. The young preacher gives a very good sermon and is really interested in the improvement of people's souls, but ask his grace if he minds when they tell him, "Oh, what an excellent sermon you gave today, Reverend!" And So-and-so was terrible in jousting today, but when some rascal praised him for the way he had handled his weapons, he gave him his armor. What would he have done if it had really been true?

And so everything goes: I confess that I'm no more saintly than my neighbors, but I would not mind it at all if those people who find some pleasure in this little trifle of mine (written in my crude style) would get wrapped up in it and be entertained by it, and if they could see that a man who has had so much bad luck and so many misfortunes and troubles does exist.

Please take this poor effort from a person who would have liked to make it richer if only his ability had been as great as his desire. And since you told me that you wanted me to write down all the details of the matter, I have decided not to start out in the middle but at the beginning. That way you will have a complete picture of me, and at the same time those people who received a large inheritance will see how little they had to do with it, since fortune favored them, and they will also see how much more those people accomplished whose luck was going against them, since they rowed hard and well and brought their ship safely into port.

I. Lazaro Tells about His Life and His Parents

You should know first of all that I'm called Lazaro of Tormes, and that I'm the son of Tome Gonzales and Antona Perez, who were born in Tejares, a village near Salamanca. I was actually born in the Tormes River, and that's how I got my name. It happened this way: My father (God rest his soul) was in charge of a mill on the bank of that river, and he was the miller there for more than fifteen years. Well, one night while my mother was in the mill, carrying me around in her belly, she went into labor and gave birth to me right there. So I can really say I was born in the river.

Then when I was eight years old, they accused my father of gutting the sacks that people were bringing to the mill. They took him to jail, and without a word of protest he went ahead and confessed everything, and he suffered persecution for righteousness' sake. But I trust God that he's in heaven because the Bible calls that kind of man blessed. At that time they were getting together an expedition to go fight the Moors, and my father went with them. They had exiled him because of the bad luck that I've already told about, so he went along as a muleteer for one of the men, and like a loyal servant, he ended his life with his master.

My widowed mother, finding herself without a husband or anyone to take care of her, decided to lie at the side—I mean, stay on the side—of good men and be like them. So she came to the city to live. She rented a little house and began to cook for some students. She washed clothes for some stableboys who served the Commander of La Magdalena, too, so a lot of the time she was around the stables. She and a dark man—one of those men who took care of the animals—got to know each other. Sometimes he would come to our house and wouldn't leave till the next morning; and other times he would come to our door in the daytime pretending that he wanted to buy eggs, and then he would come inside.

When he first began to come I didn't like him; he scared me because of the color of his skin and the way he looked. But when I saw that with him around there the food got better, I began to like him quite a lot. He always brought bread and pieces of meat, and in the winter he brought in firewood so we could keep warm.

So with his visits and the relationship going right along, it happened that my mother gave me a pretty little black baby, and I used to bounce it on my knee and help keep it warm.

I remember one time when my black stepfather was playing with the little fellow, the child noticed that my mother and I were white but that my stepfather wasn't, and he got scared. He ran to my mother and pointed his finger at him and said, "Mama, it's the bogeyman!" And my stepfather laughed: "You little son-of-a-bitch!"

Even though I was still a young boy, I thought about the word my little brother had used, and I said to myself: How many people there must be in the world who run away from others when they don't see themselves.

As luck would have it, talk about Zaide (that was my stepfather's name) reached the ears of the foreman, and when a search was made they found out that he'd been stealing about half of the barley that was supposed to be given to the animals. He'd pretended that the bran, wool, currycombs, aprons, and the horse covers and blankets had been lost; and when there was nothing else left to steal, he took the shoes right off the horses' hooves. And he was using all this to buy things for my mother so that she could bring up my little brother.

Why should we be surprised at priests when they steal from the poor or at friars when they take things from their monasteries to give to their lady followers, or for other things, when we see how love can make a poor slave do what he did?

And they found him guilty of everything I've said and more because they asked me questions and threatened me too, and I answered them like a child. I was so frightened that I told them everything I knew—even about some horseshoes my mother had made me sell to a blacksmith.

They beat and tarred my poor stepfather, and they gave my mother a stiff sentence besides the usual hundred lashes: they said that she couldn't go into the house of the Commander (the one I mentioned) and that she couldn't take poor Zaide into her own house.

So that matters wouldn't get any worse, the poor woman went ahead and carried out the sentence. And to avoid any danger and get away from wagging tongues, she went to work as a servant for the people who were living at the Solano Inn then. And there, while putting up with all kinds of indignities, she managed to raise my little brother until he knew how to walk. And she even raised me to be a good little boy who would take wine and candles to the guests and do whatever else they told me.

About this time a blind man came by and stayed at the

inn. He thought I would be a good guide for him, so he asked my mother if I could serve him, and she said I could. She told him what a good man my father had been and how he'd died in the battle of Gelves for the holy faith. She said she trusted God that I wouldn't turn out any worse a man than my father, and she begged him to be good to me and look after me, since I would be an orphan now. He told her he would and said that I wouldn't be a servant to him, but a son. And so I began to serve and guide my new old master.

After he had been in Salamanca a few days, my master wasn't happy with the amount of money he was taking in, and he decided to go somewhere else. So when we were ready to leave, I went to see my mother. And with both of us crying she gave me her blessing and said, "Son, I know that I'll never see you again. Try to be good, and may God be your guide. I've raised you and given you to a good master; take good care of yourself."

And then I went back out to my master who was waiting for me.

We left Salamanca and we came to a bridge; and at the edge of this bridge there's a stone statue of an animal that looks something like a bull. The blind man told me to go up next to the animal, and when I was there he said, "Lazaro, put your ear up next to this bull and you'll hear a great sound inside of it."

I put my ear next to it very simply, thinking he was telling the truth. And when he felt my head near the statue, he doubled up his fist and knocked my head into that devil of a bull so hard that I felt the pain from its horns for three days. And he said to me, "You fool, now learn that a blind man's servant has to be one step ahead of the devil." And he laughed out loud at his joke.

It seemed to me that at that very instant I woke up

8

from my childlike simplicity and I said to myself, "He's right. I've got to open my eyes and be on my guard. I'm alone now, and I've got to think about taking care of myself."

We started on our way again, and in just a few days he taught me the slang thieves use. When he saw what a quick mind I had he was really happy, and he said, "I can't give you any gold or silver, but I can give you plenty of hints on how to stay alive." And that's exactly what he did; after God, it was this fellow who gave me life and who, although he was blind, enlightened me and showed me how to live.

I like to tell you these silly things to show what virtue there is in men being able to raise themselves up from the depths, and what a vice it is for them to let themselves slip down from high stations.

Well, getting back to my dear blind man and telling about his ways, you should know that from the time God created the world there's no one He made smarter or sharper than that man. At his job he was sly as a fox. He knew over a hundred prayers by heart. He would use a low tone, calm and very sonorous, that would make the church where he was praying echo. And whenever he prayed, he would put on a humble and pious expression —something he did very well. And he wouldn't make faces or grimaces with his mouth or eyes the way others do.

Besides this he had thousands of other ways of getting money. He told everyone that he knew prayers for lots of different things: for women who couldn't have children or who were in labor; for those women who weren't happy in their marriage—so that their husbands would love them more. He would give predictions to expectant mothers about whether they would have a boy or a girl.

And as far as medicine was concerned, he said that Galen never knew the half of what he did about tooth-aches, fainting spells, and female illnesses. In fact, there was no one who would tell him they were sick that he wouldn't immediately say to them: "Do this, and then this; take this herb, or take that root."

And so everyone came to him—especially women—and they believed everything he told them. He got a lot out of them with these ways I've been telling about; in fact, he earned more in a month than a hundred ordinary blind men earn in a year.

But I want you to know, too, that even with all he got and all that he had, I've never seen a more greedy, miserly man. He was starving me to death. He didn't even give me enough to keep me alive! I'm telling the truth: If I hadn't known how to help myself with my wily ways and some pretty clever tricks, I would have died of hunger lots of times. But with all his know-how and carefulness I outwitted him, so that I always—or usu-ally—really got the better of him. The way I did this was I played some devilish tricks on him, and I'll tell about some of them, even though I didn't come out on top every time.

He carried the bread and all the other things in a cloth bag, and he kept the neck of it closed with an iron ring that had a padlock and key. And when he put things in or took them out, he did it so carefully and counted everything so well that no one in the world could have gotten a crumb from him. So I'd take what little he gave me, and in less than two mouthfuls it would be gone.

After he had closed the lock and forgotten about it, thinking that I was busy with other things, I would begin to bleed the miserly bag dry. There was a little seam on the side of the bag that I'd rip open and sew up again.

And I would take out bread—not little crumbs, either, but big hunks—and I'd get bacon and sausage too. And so I was always looking for the right time to score, not on a ball field, but on the food in that blasted bag that the tyrant of a blind man kept away from me.

And then, every time I had a chance I'd steal half-copper coins. And when someone gave him a copper to say a prayer for them—and since he couldn't see—they'd no sooner have offered it than I would pop it into my mouth and have a half-copper ready. And as soon as he stuck out his hand, there was my coin reduced to half-price. Then the old blind man would start growling at me. As soon as he felt it and realized that it wasn't a whole copper he'd say, "How the devil is it that now that you're with me they never give me anything but half-coppers, when they almost always used to give me a copper or a two-copper piece? I'd swear that this is all your fault."

He used to cut his prayers short, too; he wouldn't even get halfway through them. He told me to pull on the end of his cloak whenever the person who asked for the prayer had gone. So that's what I did. Then he'd begin to call out again with his cry, "Who would like to have me say a prayer for him?" in his usual way.

And he always put a little jug of wine next to him when we ate. I would grab it quickly and give it a couple of quiet kisses before I put it back in its place. But that didn't go on for very long: he could tell by the number of nips he took that some was missing. So to keep his wine safe he never let the jug out of reach; he'd always hold on to the handle. But not even a magnet could attract the way I could with a long rye straw that I had made for that very purpose. And I'd stick it in the mouth of the jug and suck until—good-bye, wine! But the old traitor was so wary that I think he must have sensed me, because from then on he stopped that and put the jug between his legs. And even then he kept his hand over the top to make sure.

But I got so used to drinking wine that I was dying for it. And when I saw that my straw trick wouldn't work, I decided to make a spout by carving a little hole in the bottom of the jug and then sealing it off neatly with a little thin strip of wax. When it was mealtime, I'd pretend I was cold and get in between the legs of the miserable blind man to warm up by the little fire we had. And the heat of it would melt the wax, since it was such a tiny piece. Then the wine would begin to trickle from the spout into my mouth, and I got into a position so that I wouldn't miss a blasted drop. When the poor fellow went to drink he wouldn't find a thing. He'd draw back, astonished, then he'd curse and damn the jar and the wine, not knowing what could have happened.

"You can't say that I drank it, Sir," I said, "since you never let it out of your hand."

But he kept turning the jug around and feeling it, until he finally discovered the hole and saw through my trick. But he pretended that he hadn't found out.

Then one day I was tippling on my jug as usual, without realizing what was in store for me or even that the blind man had found me out. I was sitting the same as always, taking in those sweet sips, my face turned toward the sky and my eyes slightly closed so I could really savor the delicious liquor. The dirty blind man saw that now was the time to take out his revenge on me, and he raised that sweet and bitter jug with both his hands and smashed it down on my mouth with all his might. As I say, he used all his strength, and poor Lazaro hadn't been expecting anything like this; in fact, I was drowsy and happy as always. So it seemed like the sky and everything in it had really fallen down on top of me. The little tap sent me reeling and knocked me unconscious, and that enormous jug was so huge that pieces of it stuck in my face, cutting me in several places and knocking out my teeth, so that I don't have them to this very day.

From that minute I began to hate that old blind man. Because, even though he took care of me and treated me all right and fixed me up, I saw that he had really enjoyed his dirty trick. He used wine to wash the places where the pieces of the jug had cut me, and he smiled and said, "How about that, Lazaro? The very thing that hurt you is helping to cure you." And he made other witty remarks that I didn't particularly care for.

When I had about recovered from the beating and the black and blue marks were nearly gone, I realized that with a few more blows like that the blind man would have gotten rid of me. So I decided to be rid of him. But I didn't run away right then; I waited until I could do it in a safer and better way. And although I wanted to be kind and forgive the blind man for hitting me with the jug, I couldn't because of the harsh treatment he gave me from then on. Without any reason he would hit me on the head and yank on my hair. And if anyone asked him why he beat me so much, he would tell them about the incident with the jug: "Do you think this boy of mine is just some innocent little fellow? Well, listen and see if you think the devil himself would try anything like this."

After they'd heard about it, they would cross themselves and say, "Well—who would ever think that such a little boy would do anything like that!"

Then they'd laugh at the prank and tell him, "Go on, beat him. God will give you your reward."

And this advice he followed to the letter.

So, for revenge, I'd lead him down all the worst roads on purpose to see if he wouldn't get hurt somehow. If there were rocks, I'd take him right over them; if there was mud, I'd lead him through the deepest part. Because even though I didn't keep dry myself, I would have given an eye if I could have hurt two eyes of that man who didn't even have one. Because of this, he was always beating me with the end of his cane so that my head was full of bumps, and with him always pulling on my hair a lot of it was gone. I told him I wasn't doing it on purpose and that I just couldn't find any better roads, but that didn't do any good. The old traitor saw through everything and was so wary that he wouldn't believe me any more.

So that you can see how smart this shrewd blind man was, I'll tell you about one of the many times when I was with him that he really seemed to show a lot of perception. When we left Salamanca, his plan was to go to Toledo because the people were supposed to be richer there, although not very free with their money. But he pinned his hopes on this saying: "You'll get more water from a narrow flowing stream than you will from a deep dry well." And we'd pass through the best places as we went along. Where we were welcomed and were able to get something, we stayed; where this didn't happen, we'd move on after a few days.

And it happened that as we were coming to a place called Almorox when they were gathering the grapes, a grape picker gave him a bunch as alms. And since the baskets are usually handled pretty roughly and the grapes were very ripe at the time, the bunch started to fall apart in his hand. If we had thrown it in the sack, it and everything it touched would have spoiled. He decided that we'd have a picnic so that it wouldn't go to

waste—and he did it to please me, too, since he'd kicked and beat me quite a bit that day. So we sat down on a low wall, and he said: "Now I want to be generous with you: we'll share this bunch of grapes, and you can eat as many as I do. We'll divide it like this: you take one, then I'll take one. But you have to promise me that you won't take more than one at a time. I'll do the same until we finish, and that way there won't be any cheating."

The agreement was made, and we began. But on his second turn, the traitor changed his mind and began to take two at a time, evidently thinking that I was doing the same. But when I saw that he had broken our agreement, I wasn't satisfied with going at his rate of speed. Instead, I went even further: I took two at a time, or three at a time—in fact, I ate them as fast as I could. And when there weren't any grapes left, he just sat there for a while with the stem in his hand, and then he shook his head and said, "Lazaro, you tricked me. I'll swear to God that you ate these grapes three at a time."

"No, I didn't," I said. "But why do you think so?"

That wise old blind man answered, "Do you know how I see that you ate them three at a time? Because I was eating them two at a time, and you didn't say a word."

I laughed to myself, and even though I was only a boy, I was very much aware of the sharpness of that blind man.

But, so that I won't talk too much, I won't tell about a lot of humorous and interesting things that happened to me with my first master. I just want to tell about how we separated, and be done with him.

We were in Escalona, a town owned by the duke of that name, at an inn, and the blind man gave me a piece of sausage to roast for him. When the sausage had been basted and he had sopped up and eaten the drippings with a piece of bread, he took a coin out of his purse and told me to go get him some wine from the tavern. Then the devil put an idea in my head, just like they say he does to thieves. It so happened that near the fire there was a little turnip, kind of long and beat up; it had probably been thrown there because it wasn't good enough for stew.

At that moment he and I were there all alone, and when I whiffed the delicious odor of the sausage, I suddenly got a huge appetite—and I knew that all I would get of it would be the smell. But the thought of eating that sausage made me lose all my fear: I didn't think for a minute what would happen to me. So while the blind man was getting the money out of his purse, I took the sausage off the spit and quickly put the turnip on. Then the blind man gave me the money for the wine and took hold of the spit, turning it over the fire, trying to cook the very thing that hadn't been cooked before because it was so bad.

I went for the wine, and on the way I downed the sausage. When I came back I found that sinner of a blind man holding the turnip between two slices of bread. He didn't know what it was yet, because he hadn't felt of it. But when he took the bread and bit into it, thinking he would get part of the sausage too, he was suddenly stopped cold by the taste of the cold turnip. He got mad then, and said, "What is this, Lazarillo?"

"You mean, 'Lacerated,'" I said. "Are you trying to pin something on me? Didn't I just come back from getting the wine? Someone must have been here and played a joke on you."

"Oh, no," he said. "I haven't let the spit out of my hand. No one could have done that."

I kept swearing that I hadn't done any switching around. But it didn't do me any good—I couldn't hide anything from the sharpness of that miserable blind man. He got up and grabbed me by the head and got close so he could smell me. And he must have smelled my breath like a good hound. Really being anxious to find out if he was right, he held on tight and opened my mouth wider than he should have. Then, not very wisely, he stuck in his nose. And it was long and sharp. And his anger had made it swell a bit, so that the point of it hit me in the throat. So with all this and my being really frightened, along with the fact that the black sausage hadn't had time to settle in my stomach, and especially with the sudden poking in of his very large nose, half choking me—all these things went together and made the crime and the snack show themselves, and the owner got back what belonged to him. What happened was that before the blind man could take his beak out of my mouth, my stomach got so upset that it hit his nose with what I had stolen. So his nose and the black, half-chewed sausage both left my mouth at the same time.

Oh, Almighty God! I was wishing I'd been buried at that very moment, because I was already dead. The perverse blind man was so mad that if people hadn't come at the noise, I think he would have killed me. They pulled me out of his hands, and he was left with what few hairs had still been in my head. My face was all scratched up, and my neck and throat were clawed. But my throat really deserved its rough treatment because it was only on account of what it had done that I'd been beaten. Then that rotten blind man told everyone there about the things I'd done, and he told them over and over about the jug and the grapes and this last incident.

They laughed so hard that all the people who were

going by in the street came in to see the fun. But the blind man told them about my tricks with such wit and cleverness that, even though I was hurt and crying, I felt that it would have been wrong for me not to laugh too.

And while this was going on I suddenly remembered that I'd been negligent and cowardly, and I began to swear at myself: I should have bitten off his nose. I'd had the opportunity to do it; in fact, half of the work had already been done for me. If only I'd clamped down with my teeth, I'd have had it trapped. Even though it belonged to that skunk, my stomach would probably have held it better than it held the sausage; and since there wouldn't have been any evidence, I could have denied the crime. I wish to God I'd have done it. It wouldn't have been a bad idea at all!

The lady running the inn and the others there made us stop our fighting, and they washed my face and throat with the wine I'd brought for him to drink. Then the dirty blind man made up jokes about it, saying things like: "The truth of the matter is I use more wine washing this boy in one year than I drink in two." And: "At least, Lazaro, you owe more to wine than you do to your father—he only gave you life once, but wine has brought you to life a thousand times."

Then he told about all the times he'd beaten me and scratched my face and then doctored me up with wine.

"I tell you," he said, "if there's one man in the world who will be blessed by wine, it's you."

And the people who were washing me laughed out loud, while I was swearing.

But the blind man's prophecy wasn't wrong, and since then I've often thought about that man who must have had a gift for telling the future. And I feel sorry about the bad things I did to him, although I really paid him

back, since what he told me that day happened just like he said it would, as you'll see later on.

Because of this and the dirty tricks the blind man played on me, I decided to leave him for good. And since I had thought about it and really had my mind set on it, this last trick of his only made me more determined. So the next day we went into town to beg. It had rained quite a bit the night before, and since it was still raining that day, he went around praying under the arcades in the town so we wouldn't get wet. But with night coming on and there still being no let up, the blind man said to me, "Lazaro, this rain isn't going to stop, and the later it gets the harder it's coming down. Let's go inside the inn before there's a real downpour."

To get there we had to cross over a ditch that was full of water from the rain. And I said to him; "Sir, the water's too wide to cross here, but if you'd like, I see an easier place to get across, and we won't get wet either. It's very narrow there, and if we jump we'll keep our feet dry."

That seemed like a good idea to him, and he said, "You're pretty clever. That's why I like you so much. Take me to the place where the ditch is narrow. It's winter now, and I don't care for water any time, and especially not when I get my feet wet."

Seeing that the time was ripe, I led him under the arcades, to a spot right in front of a sort of pillar or stone post that was in the plaza—one of those that hold up the overhanging arches of the houses. And I said to him, "Sir, this is the narrowest place along the whole ditch."

It was really raining hard and the poor man was getting wet. This, along with the fact that we were in a hurry to get out of the water that was pouring down on us—and especially because God clouded his mind so I

could get revenge—made him believe me, and he said, "Point me in the right direction, and you jump over the water."

I put him right in front of the pillar. Then I jumped and got behind the post like someone waiting for a bull to charge, and I said to him, "Come on, jump as far as you can so you'll miss the water."

As soon as I'd said that, the poor blind man charged like an old goat. First he took one step back to get a running start, and then he hurled himself forward with all his might. His head hit the post with a hollow sound like a pumpkin. Then he fell over backward, half dead, with his head split open.

"What? You mean to say you smelled the sausage but not the post? Smell it, smell it!" I said, and I left him in the hands of all the people who had run to help him.

I reached the village gate on the run, and before night fell I made it to Torrijos. I didn't know what God had done with him, and I never made any attempt to find out.

II. How Lazaro Took up with a Priest and the Things That Happened to Him with That Man

I didn't feel very safe in that town, so the next day I went to a place named Maqueda. There I met up with a priest (it must have been because of all my sins). I started to beg from him, and he asked me if I knew how to assist at mass. I told him I did, and it was the truth: even though that sinner of a blind man beat me, he'd taught me all kinds of good things, too, and this was one of them. So the priest took me in, and I was out of the frying pan and into the fire. Because even though the blind man was the very picture of greed, as I've said, he was an Alexander the Great compared to this fellow. I won't say any more, except that all the miserliness in the world was in this man. I don't know if he'd been born that way, or if it came along with his priest's frock.

He had an old chest that he kept locked, and he kept the key tied to his cassock with a leather cord. When the holy bread was brought from church, he'd throw it in the chest and lock it up again. And there wasn't a thing to eat in the whole place, the way there is in most houses: a bit of bacon hanging from the chimney, some cheese lying on the table or in the cupboard, a basket with some slices of bread left over from dinner. It seemed to me that even if I hadn't eaten any of it, I would have felt a lot better just being able to look at it.

The only thing around was a string of onions, and that was kept locked in a room upstairs. I was rationed out one onion every four days. And if anyone else was around when I asked him for the key to get it, he'd reach into his breast pocket and untie the key with great airs, and he'd hand it to me and say, "Here. Take it, but bring it back as soon as you're through, and don't stuff yourself." And this as if all the oranges in Valencia were up there, while there really wasn't a damned thing, as I said, besides the onions hanging from a nail. And he had those counted so well that if I (being the sinner that I am) had taken even one extra onion, I would really have been in for it.

So there I was, dying of hunger. But if he wasn't very charitable to me, he was to himself. A good five coppers' worth of meat was his usual fare for supper. I have to admit that he did give me some of the soup, but as for the meat—I didn't even get a whiff of it. All I got was a little bread: that blasted man wouldn't give me half of what I really needed! And on Saturdays everyone around here eats head of mutton, and he sent me for one that cost six coppers. He cooked it and ate the eyes, the tongue, the neck, the brains and the meat in the jaws. Then he gave me the chewed-over bones; he put them on a plate and said, "Here, eat this and be happy. It's a meal fit for a king. In fact, you're living better than the Pope."

"May God grant you this kind of life," I said under my breath.

After I had been with him for three weeks, I got so skinny that my legs wouldn't hold me up out of sheer hunger. I saw that I was heading right straight for the grave if God and my wits didn't come to my rescue. But there was no way I could trick him because there wasn't

a thing I could steal. And even if there had been something, I couldn't blind him the way I did the other one
(may he rest in peace if that blow on the head finished
him off). Because even though the other fellow was
smart, without that valuable fifth sense he couldn't tell
what I was doing. But this new guy—there isn't anyone
whose sight was as good as his was.

When we were passing around the offering plate, not a
penny fell into the basket that he didn't have it spotted.
He kept one eye on the people and the other on my
hands. His eyes danced in their sockets like quicksilver.
Every cent that was put in was ticked off in his mind.
And as soon as the offering was over, he would take the
plate away from me and put it on the altar.

I wasn't able to get a penny away from him all the
time I lived with him—or, to be more precise, all the
time I died with him. He never sent me to the tavern for
even a drop of wine: what little he brought back from
the offering and put in the chest he rationed out so that it
lasted him a whole week. And to cover up his terrible
stinginess, he would say to me, "Look, son, we priests
have to be very moderate in our eating and drinking, and
that's why I don't indulge the way other people do." But
that old miser was really lying, because when we prayed
at meetings or at funerals and other people were paying
for the food, he ate like a wolf and drank more than any
old, thirsty quack doctor.

Speaking of funerals, God forgive me but I was never
an enemy of mankind except during them. This was because we really ate well and I was able to gorge myself. I
used to hope and pray that God would kill off someone
every day. We'd give the sacraments to the sick people,
and the priest would ask everyone there to pray. And I
was certainly not the last to begin—especially at extreme

3 0

unction. With all my heart and soul I prayed to God—not that His will be done, as they say, but that He take the person from this world.

And when one of them escaped (God forgive me), I damned him to hell a thousand times. But when one died, I blessed him just as much. Because in all the time that I was there—which must have been nearly six months—only twenty people died. And I really think that I killed them; I mean, they died at my request. Because I think that the Lord must have seen my own endless and awful dying, and He was glad to kill them so that I could live. But at that time I couldn't find any relief for my misery. If I came to life on the days that we buried someone, I really felt the pangs of hunger when there wasn't any funeral. Because I would get used to filling myself up, and then I would have to go back to my usual hunger again. So I couldn't think of any way out except to die: I wanted death for myself sometimes just as much as for the others. But I never saw it, even though it was always inside of me.

Lots of times I thought about running away from that penny-pinching master, but I didn't for two reasons. First, I didn't trust my legs: lack of food had made them so skinny that I was afraid they wouldn't hold me up. Second, I thought a while, and I said: "I've had two masters: the first one nearly starved me to death, and when I left him I met up with this one; and he gives me so little to eat that I've already got one foot in the grave. Well, if I leave this one and find a master who is one step lower, how could it possibly end except with my death?" So I didn't dare to move an inch. I really thought that each step would just get worse. And if I were to go down one more step, Lazaro wouldn't make another peep and no one would ever hear of him again.

32

33

So there I was, in a terrible state (and God help any true Christian who finds himself in those circumstances), not knowing what to do and seeing that I was going from bad to worse. Then one day when that miserable, tight-fisted master of mine had gone out, a tinker came to my door. I think he must have been an angel in disguise, sent down by the hand of God. He asked me if there was anything I wanted fixed. "You could fix me up, and you wouldn't be doing half bad," I said softly but not so he could hear me. But there wasn't enough time so I could waste it on witty sayings and, inspired by the Holy Spirit, I said to him, "Sir, I've lost the key to this chest, and I'm afraid my master will beat me. Please look and see if one of those keys you have will fit. I'll pay you for it."

The angelic tinker began to try out the keys on his chain, one after the other, and I was helping him with my feeble prayers. Then, when I least expected it, I saw the face of God, as they say, formed by the loaves of bread inside that chest. When it was all the way open I said to him, "I don't have any money to give you for the key, but take your payment from what's in there."

He took the loaf of bread that looked best to him, and he gave me the key and went away happy, leaving me even happier. But I didn't touch a thing right then so that the loss wouldn't be noticeable. And, too, when I saw that I was the Lord of all that, I didn't think my hunger would dare come near me. Then my miserly old master came back, and—thank God—he didn't notice the missing loaf of bread that the angel had carried off.

The next day, when he left the house, I opened my breadly paradise and sank my hands and teeth into a loaf, and in a flash I made it invisible. And, of course, I didn't forget to lock up the chest again. Then I began to sweep the house very happily, thinking that from now on

36

my sad life would change. And so that day and the next I was happy. But it wasn't meant for that peace to last very long because on the third day real tertian fever struck.

It happened that I suddenly saw that man who was starving me to death standing over our chest, moving the loaves of bread from one side to the other, counting and recounting them. I pretended not to notice, and silently I was praying, hoping, and begging, "Saint John, blind him!" After he had stood there quite a while, counting the days and the loaves on his fingers, he said, "If I weren't so careful about keeping this chest closed, I'd swear that someone had taken some of the loaves of bread. But from now on, just to close the door on all suspicion, I'm going to keep close track of them. There are nine and a half in there now."

"May God send you nine pieces of bad news, too," I said under my breath. It seemed to me that what he said went into my heart like a hunter's arrow, and my stomach began to rumble when it saw that it would be going back to its old diet. Then he left the house. To console myself I opened the chest, and when I saw the bread I began to worship it—but I was afraid to "take any in remembrance of Him." Then I counted the loaves to see if the old miser had made a mistake, but he had counted them much better than I'd have liked. The best I could do was to kiss them over and over, and as delicately as I could, I peeled a little off the half-loaf on the side where it was already cut. And so I got through that day but not as happily as the one before.

But my hunger kept growing, mainly because my stomach had gotten used to more bread during those previous two or three days. I was dying a slow death, and finally I got to the point that when I was alone the only thing I did was open and close the chest and look at the face of God inside (or at least that's how children put it). But God Himself—who aids the afflicted—seeing me in such straits, put a little thought into my head that would help me. Thinking to myself, I said: This chest is big and old, and it's got some holes in it, although they're small. But he might be led to believe that mice are getting into it and are eating the bread. It wouldn't do to take out a whole loaf: he'd notice that it was missing right away, since he hardly gives me any food at all to live on. But he'll believe this all right.

And I began to break off crumbs over some cheap tablecloths he had there. I would pick up one loaf and put another one down, so that I broke a few little pieces off of three or four of them. Then I ate those up just as if they were bonbons, and I felt a little better. But when he came home to eat and opened the chest, he saw the mess. And he really thought that mice had done the damage because I'd done my job to perfection, and it looked just like the work of mice. He looked the chest over from top to bottom, and he saw the holes where he suspected they'd gotten in. Then he called me over and said, "Lazaro, look! Look at what a terrible thing happened to our bread this evening!"

And I put on a very astonished face and asked him what it could have been.

"What else," he said, "but mice? They get into everything."

We began to eat, and—thank God—I came out all right in this, too. I got more bread than the miserable little bit he usually gave me because he sliced off the parts he thought the mice had chewed on, and said, "Eat this. The mouse is a very clean animal."

So that day, with the extra that I got by the work of

my hands—or of my fingernails, to be exact—we finished our meal, although I never really got started.

And then I got another shock: I saw him walking around carefully, pulling nails out of the walls and looking for little pieces of wood. And he used these to board up all the holes in the old chest.

"Oh, Lord!" I said then. "What a life full of misery, trials, and bad luck we're born into! How short the pleasures of this hard life of ours are! Here I was, thinking that this pitiful little cure of mine would get me through this miserable situation, and I was happy, thinking I was doing pretty well. Then along came my bad luck and woke up this miser of a master of mine and made him even more careful than usual (and misers are hardly ever *not* careful). Now, by closing up the holes in the chest, he's closing the door to my happiness, too, and opening the one to my troubles."

That's what I kept sighing while my conscientious carpenter finished up his job with nails and little boards, and said, "Now, my dear treacherous mice, you'd better think about changing your ways. You won't get anywhere in this house."

As soon as he left, I went to see his work. And I found that he didn't leave a hole where even a mosquito could get into the sorry old chest. I opened it up with my useless key, without a hope of getting anything. And there I saw the two or three loaves that I'd started to eat and that my master thought the mice had chewed on, and I still got a little bit off of them by touching them very lightly like an expert swordsman.

Since necessity is the father of invention and I always had so much of it, day and night I kept thinking about how I was going to keep myself alive. And I think that hunger lit up my path to these black solutions: they say eat. He began to look around on the walls of the house again for nails and pieces of wood to keep them out. Then when night came and he was asleep, there I was on my feet with my knife in hand, and all the holes he plugged up during the day I unplugged at night.

That's how things went, me following him so quickly that this must be where the saying comes from: "Where one door is closed, another opens." Well, we seemed to be doing Penelope's work on the cloth because whatever he wove during the day I took apart at night. And after just a few days and nights we had the poor pantry box in such a shape that, if you really wanted to call it by its proper name, you'd have to call it an old piece of armor instead of a chest because of all the nails and tacks in it.

When he saw that his efforts weren't doing any good, he said, "This chest is so beat up and the wood in it is so old and thin that it wouldn't be able to stand up against any mouse. And it's getting in such bad shape that if we put up with it any longer it won't keep anything secure. The worst part of it is that even though it doesn't keep things very safe, if I got rid of it I really wouldn't be able to get along without it, and I'd just end up having to pay three or four pieces of silver to get another one. The best thing that I can think of, since what I've tried so far hasn't done any good, is to set a trap inside the chest for those blasted mice."

Then he asked someone to lend him a mousetrap, and with the cheese rinds that he begged from the neighbors, the trap was kept set and ready inside the chest. And that really turned out to be a help to me. Even though I didn't require any frills for eating, I was still glad to get the cheese rinds that I took out of the mousetrap, and even at that I didn't stop the mouse from raiding the bread.

When he found that mice had been into the bread and

eaten the cheese, but that not one of them had been caught, he swore a blue streak and asked his neighbors, "How could a mouse take cheese out of a trap, eat it, leave the trap sprung, and still not get caught?" The neighbors agreed that it couldn't be a mouse that was causing the trouble because it would have had to have gotten caught sooner or later. So one neighbor said to him, "I remember that there used to be a snake around your house—that must be who the culprit is. It only stands to reason: it's so long it can get the food, and even though the trap is sprung on it, it's not completely inside, so it can get out again."

Everyone agreed with what he'd said, and that really upset my master. From then on he didn't sleep so soundly. Whenever he heard even a worm moving around in the wood at night, he thought it was the snake gnawing on the chest. Then he would be up on his feet, and he'd grab a club that he kept by the head of the bed ever since they'd mentioned a snake to him, and he would really lay into that poor old chest, hoping to scare the snake away. He woke up the neighbors with all the noise he made, and he wouldn't let me sleep at all. He came up to my straw mat and turned it over and me with it, thinking that the snake had headed for me and gotten into the straw or inside my coat. Because they told him that at night these creatures look for some place that's warm and even get into babies' cribs and bite them. Most of the time I pretended to be asleep, and in the morning he would ask me, "Didn't you feel anything last night, son? I was right behind the snake, and I think it got into your bed: they're very cold-blooded creatures, and they try to find a place that's warm."

"I hope to God it doesn't bite me," I said. "I'm really scared of it."

45

He went around all excited and not able to sleep, so that—on my word of honor—the snake (a male one, of course) didn't dare go out chewing at night, or even go near the chest. But in the daytime, while he was at church or in town, I did my looting. And when he saw the damage and that he wasn't able to do anything about it, he wandered around at night—as I've said—like a spook.

I was afraid that in his wanderings he might stumble onto my key that I kept under the straw. So it seemed to me that the safest thing was to put it in my mouth at night. Because since I'd been with the blind man my mouth had gotten round like a purse, and I could hold twenty or thirty coppers in it—all in half-copper coins— and eat at the same time. If I hadn't been able to do that I couldn't have gotten hold of even a copper that the blasted blind man wouldn't have found: he was always searching every patch and seam on my clothes. Well, as I say, I put the key in my mouth every night, and I went to sleep without being afraid that the zombie master of mine would stumble onto it. But when trouble is going to strike, you can't do a thing to stop it.

The fates—or to be more exact, my sins—had it in store for me that one night while I was sleeping my mouth must have been open, and the key shifted so that the air I breathed out while I was asleep went through the hollow part of the key. It was tubular, and (unfortunately for me) it whistled so loud that my master heard it and got excited. He must have thought it was the snake hissing, and I guess it really sounded like one.

He got up very quietly with his club in hand, and by feeling his way toward the sound he came up to me very softly so the snake wouldn't hear him. And when he found himself so close, he thought that it had come over

4 6

to where I was lying, looking for a warm place, and had slipped into the straw. So, lifting the club up high, and thinking that he had the snake trapped down there and that he would hit it so hard that he'd kill it, he swung down on me with such a mighty blow that he knocked me unconscious and left my head bashed in.

Then he saw that he'd hit me (I must have really cried out when the blow leveled me), and—as he later told me—he reached over and shouted at me, calling my name and trying to revive me. But when his hands touched me and he felt all the blood, he realized what he'd done, and he went off to get a light right away. When he came back with it he found me moaning with the key still in my mouth: I had never let loose of it, and it was still sticking half out—just like it must have been when I was whistling through it.

The snake killer was terrified, wondering what it could be. He took it all the way out of my mouth and looked at it. Then he realized what it was because its ridges matched his key exactly. He went to try it out, and he solved the crime. Then that cruel hunter must have said: "I've found the mouse and the snake that were fighting me and eating me out of house and home."

I can't say for sure what happened during the next three days because I spent them inside the belly of the whale. But what I've just told I heard about from my master when I came to; he was telling what had happened in detail to everyone who came by. At the end of three days, when I was back in my senses, I found myself stretched out on my straw bed with my head all bandaged up and full of oils and salves. And I got scared and said, "What is this?"

The cruel priest answered, "It seems that I caught the mice and snakes that were ruining me."

47

I looked myself over, and when I saw how badly beaten up I was, I guessed what had happened.

Then an old lady who was a healer came in, along with the neighbors. And they began to take the wrappings off my head and treat the wound. When they saw that I was conscious again, they were very happy, and they said, "Well, he's got his senses back. God willing, it won't be too serious."

Then they began to talk again about what had happened to me and to laugh. While I—sinner that I am—I was crying. Anyway, they fed me, and I was famished, but they really didn't give me enough. Yet, little by little, I recovered, and two weeks later I was able to get up, out of any danger (but not out of my state of hunger) and nearly cured.

The next day when I'd gotten up, my master took me by the hand and led me out the door, and when I was in the street he said to me: "Lazaro, from now on you're on your own—I don't want you. Go get yourself another master, and God be with you. I don't want such a diligent servant here with me. You could only have become this way from being a blind man's guide."

Then he crossed himself as if I had the devil in me and went back into his house and closed the door.

III. How Lazaro Took up with a Squire and What Happened to Him Then

So I had to push on ahead, as weak as I was. And little by little, with the help of some good people, I ended up in this great city of Toledo. And here, by the grace of God, my wounds healed in about two weeks. People were always giving me things while I was hurt, but when I was well again, they told me, "You—you're nothing but a lazy, no-good sponger. Go on—go find yourself a good master you can work for."

"And where will I meet up with one of those," I said to myself, "unless God makes him from scratch, the way he created the world?"

While I was going along begging from door to door (without much success, since charity seemed to have gone up to heaven), God had me run into a squire who was walking down the street. He was well dressed, his hair was combed, and he walked and looked like a real gentleman. I looked at him, and he looked at me, and he said, "Boy, are you looking for a master?"

And I said, "Yes, sir."

"Well, come with me," he said. "God has been good to you, making you run into me. You must have been doing some good praying today."

So I went with him. And I thanked God that he asked me to go along because—with his nice-looking clothes and the way he looked—I thought he was just what I needed.

It was morning when I found my third master. And I followed him through most of the city. We went through squares where they were selling bread and different things. And I was hoping and praying that he would load me up with some of the food they were selling because it was just the right time for shopping. But very quickly, without stopping, we went right past those places. Maybe he doesn't like what he sees here, I thought, and he wants to buy his groceries somewhere else.

So we kept on walking until it was eleven o'clock. Then he went into the cathedral, and I was right behind him. I saw him listen to mass and go through the other holy ceremonies very devoutly, until it was over and the people had gone. Then we came out of the church.

We began to go down a street at a good clip. And I was the happiest fellow in the world, since we hadn't stopped to buy any food. I really thought my new master was one of those people who do all their shopping at once, and that our meal would be there, ready and waiting for us, just the way I wanted—and, in fact, the way I needed.

At that minute the clock struck one—an hour past noon—and we came to a house where my master stopped, and so did I. And pulling his cape to the left, he took a key out of his sleeve and opened the door, and we both went into the house. The entrance was dark and gloomy: it looked like it would make anyone who went in afraid. But inside there was a little patio and some fairly nice rooms.

Once we were in, he took off his cape: he asked me if my hands were clean, and then we shook it out and folded it. And blowing the dust very carefully off a stone bench that was there, he put the cape down on top of it. And when that was done, he sat down next to it and

asked me a lot of questions about where I was from and how I'd happened to come to that city.

I talked about myself longer than I wanted to because I thought it was more a time to have the table set and the stew dished up than to tell him about all that. Still, I satisfied him about myself, lying as well as I could. I told him all my good points but kept quiet about the rest, since I didn't think that was the time for them. When that was over, he just sat there for a while. I began to realize that that was a bad sign, since it was almost two o'clock and I hadn't seen him show any more desire to eat than a dead man.

Then I began to think about his keeping the door locked, and the fact that I hadn't heard any other sign of life in the whole house. The only thing I'd seen were walls: not a chair, not a meat-cutting board, a stool, a table, or even a chest like the one I'd had before. And I began to wonder if that house was under a spell. While I was thinking about this, he said to me, "Boy, have you eaten?"

"No, sir," I said. "It wasn't even eight o'clock when I met you."

"Well, even though it was still morning, I'd already had breakfast. And when I eat like that, I want you to know that I'm satisfied until nighttime. So you'll just have to get along as well as you can: we'll have supper later."

You can see how, when I heard this, I nearly dropped in my tracks—not so much from hunger but because fate seemed to be going completely against me. Then all my troubles passed before my eyes again, and I began to cry over my hardships once more. I remembered my reasoning when I was thinking about leaving the priest: I figured that even though he was mean and stingy, it

5 4

might turn out that I would meet up with someone worse. So there I was, moping over the hard life I'd had and over my death that was getting nearer and nearer.

And yet, keeping back my emotions as well as I could, I said to him, "Sir, I am only a boy, and thank God I'm not too concerned about eating. I can tell you that I was the lightest eater of all my friends, and all the masters I've ever had have praised that about me right up to now."

"That really is a virtue," he said, "and it makes me appreciate you even more. Because only pigs stuff themselves: gentlemen eat moderately."

I get the picture! I thought to myself. Well, damn all the health and virtue that these masters I run into find in staying hungry.

I went over next to the door and took out of my shirt some pieces of bread that I still had from begging. When he saw this, he said to me, "Come here, boy. What are you eating?"

I went over to him and showed him the bread. There were three pieces, and he took one—the biggest and best one. Then he said, "Well, well, this does look like good bread."

"It is!" I said. "But tell me, sir, do you really think so now?"

"Yes, I do," he said. "Where did you get it? I wonder if the baker had clean hands?"

"I can't tell you that," I said, "but it certainly doesn't taste bad."

"Let's see if you're right," said my poor master.

And he put it in his mouth and began to gobble it down as ferociously as I was doing with mine.

"Bless me, this bread is absolutely delicious," he said.

When I saw what tree he was barking up, I began to

5 6

eat faster. Because I realized that if he finished before I did, he would be nice enough to help me with what was left. So we finished almost at the same time. And he began to brush off a few crumbs—very tiny ones—that were left on his shirt. Then he went into a little room nearby and brought out a chipped-up jug—not a very new one—and after he had drunk, he offered it to me. But, so I would look like a teetotaler, I said, "Sir, I don't drink wine."

"It's water," he said. "You can drink that."

Then I took the jug, and I drank. But not much, because being thirsty wasn't exactly my trouble. So that's how we spent the day until nighttime: him asking me questions and me answering as best as I could. Then he took me to the room where the jug that we'd drunk from was, and he said to me, "Boy, get over there, and I'll show you how this bed is made up so that you'll be able to do it from now on."

I went down to one end, and he went over to the other, and we made up the blasted bed. There really wasn't much to do: it just had a bamboo frame sitting on some benches, and on top of that there was a filthy mattress with the bedclothes stretched over it. And since it hadn't been washed very often, it really didn't look much like a mattress. But that's what it was used for, though there was a lot less stuffing than it needed. We stretched it out and tried to soften it up. But that was impossible because you can't make a really hard object soft. And that blessed packsaddle had hardly a damned thing inside of it. When it was put on the frame, every strut showed through, and it looked just like the rib cage of a real skinny pig. And on top of that starving pad he put a cover of the same stamp: I never could decide what color it was. With the bed made and night on us, he said to me, "Lazaro, it's late now, and it's a long way from here to the square. And besides, there are a lot of thieves who go around stealing at night in this city. Let's get along as well as we can, and tomorrow, when it's daytime, God will be good to us. I've been living alone, and so I haven't stocked up any groceries: instead, I've been eating out. But from now on we'll do things differently."

"Sir," I said, "don't worry about me. I can spend one night—or more, if I have to—without eating."

"You'll live longer and you'll be healthier too," he answered. "Because as we were saying today, there's nothing in the world like eating moderately to live a long life."

If that's the way things are, I thought to myself, I never will die. Because I've always been forced to keep that rule, and with my luck I'll probably keep it all my life.

And he lay down on the bed, using his pants and jacket as a pillow. He told me to stretch out at his feet, so I did. But I didn't get a damned bit of sleep! The frame struts and my protruding bones didn't stop squabbling and fighting all night long. With all the pains, hunger, and trouble I'd been through, I don't think there was a pound of flesh left on my body. And since I'd hardly had a bite to eat that day, I was groveling in hunger—and hunger and sleep don't exactly make good bedfellows. So I cursed myself (God forgive me!) and my bad luck over and over, nearly all night long. And what was worse, I didn't dare to turn over because I might wake him up. So I just kept asking God for death.

When morning came we got up, and he began to shake out and clean his pants and jacket and his coat and cape (while I stood around like an idle servant!). And he took his own good time about getting dressed. I brought some

5 8

water for him to wash his hands, and then he combed his hair and put his sword in the belt, and while he was doing that, he said: "If you only knew what a prize this is, boy! I wouldn't sell it for any amount of money in the world. And I'll have you know that of all the swords the famous Toledan swordmaker Antonio made, there isn't one that he put as sharp an edge on as this one has."

And he pulled it out of the sheath and felt it with his fingers and said, "Look here. I'll bet I could slice a ball of wool with it." And I thought to myself: And with my teeth—even though they're not made of steel—I could slice a four-pound loaf of bread.

He put it back in the sheath and strapped it on, and then he hung a string of large beads from the sword belt. And he walked slowly, holding his body straight and swaying gracefully as he walked. And every so often he would put the tail of the cape over his shoulder or under his arm. And with his right hand on his side, he went out the door, saying, "Lazaro, while I go to mass, you watch the house. Make the bed and fill the pitcher up with water from the river just down below us. Be sure to lock the door so that nothing will get stolen, and put the key on the hinge here so that if I come back while you're gone I can get in."

Then he went up the street with such a stately expression and manner that anyone who didn't know him would think he was a close relative to the Count of Arcos, or at least his valet.

I stood there, thinking: "Bless You, Lord—You give us sickness and You cure us too! My master looks so content that anyone who saw him would think he'd eaten a huge supper last night and slept in a nice bed. And even though it's early in the morning, they'd think he'd had a good breakfast. Your ways are mighty mysterious,

Lord, and people don't understand them! With that refined way he acts and that nice-looking cape and coat
he'd fool anyone. And who would believe that that gracious man got by all day yesterday on a piece of bread
that his servant Lazaro had carried all day and night
inside his shirt for safekeeping—not really the most sani-
tary place in the world—and that today when he washed
his hands and face, he dried them on his shirttail because
we didn't have any towels? Nobody would suspect it, of
course. Oh Lord, how many of these people do You have
scattered around the world who suffer for the filth that
they call honor what they would never suffer for You!"

So I stood at the door, thinking about these things and
looking until my master had disappeared down the long,
narrow street. Then I went back into the house, and in a
second I walked through the whole place, both upstairs
and down, without stopping or finding anything to stop
for. I made up that blasted hard bed and took the jug
down to the river. And I saw my master in a garden,
trying hard to coax two veiled women—they looked like
the kind that are always hanging around that place. In
fact, a lot of them go there in the summer to take the
early morning air. And they go down to those cool river-
banks to eat breakfast—without even bringing any food
along; they're sure someone will give them some, since
the men around there have got them in the habit of doing
that.

As I say, there he was with them just like the trouba-
dor Macias, telling them more sweet words than Ovid
ever wrote. And when they saw that he was pretty well
softened up, they weren't ashamed to ask him for some
breakfast, promising the usual payment.

But his pocketbook was as cold as his stomach was
warm, and he began to have such hot chills that the color

drained from his face, and he started to trip over his tongue and make up some lame excuses.

They must have been pretty experienced women because they caught on to his illness right away and left him there for what he was.

I'd been eating some cabbage stalks, and that was my breakfast. And since I was a new servant, I went back home very diligently without my master seeing me. I decided I'd sweep out a little there, since that's what the place really needed, but I couldn't find anything to sweep with. Then I began to think about what I should do, and I decided to wait until noon for my master because if he came he might bring something to eat; but that turned out to be a waste of time.

When I saw that it was getting to be two o'clock and he still hadn't come, I began to be attacked by hunger. So I locked the door and put the key where he told me to, and then I went back to my old trade. With a low, sickly voice, my hands crossed over my chest, and with my eyes looking up to heaven and God's name on my tongue, I began to beg for bread at the doors of the biggest houses I saw. But I'd been doing this almost from the cradle—I mean I learned it from that great teacher, the blind man, and I turned out to be a pretty good student—so even though this town had never been very charitable, and it had been a pretty lean year besides, I handled myself so well that before the clock struck four I had that many pounds of bread stored away in my stomach and at least two more in my sleeves and inside my shirt.

I went back to the house, and on my way through the meat market I begged from one of the women there, and she gave me a piece of cow's hoof along with some cooked tripe.

When I got home my good master was there, his cape folded and lying on the stone bench, and he was walking around in the patio. I went inside, and he came over to me. I thought he was going to scold me for being late, but God had something better in store. He asked me where I'd been, and I told him, "Sir, I was here until two o'clock, and when I saw that you weren't coming, I went to the city and put myself in the hands of the good people there, and they gave me what you see here."

I showed him the bread and the tripe that I was carrying in my shirttail, and his face lit up, and he said: "Well, I held up dinner for you, but when I saw that you weren't going to come, I went ahead and ate. But what you've done there is all right because it's better to beg in God's name than it is to steal. That's my opinion, so help me. The only thing I ask is that you don't tell anyone that you're living with me because it will hurt my honor. But I think it would stay a secret anyway, since hardly anyone in this town knows me. I wish I'd never come here!"

"Don't worry about that, sir," I said. "No one would give a damn about asking me that, and I wouldn't tell them even if they did."

"Well then, eat, you poor sinner. If it's God's will, we'll soon see ourselves out of these straits. But I want you to know that ever since I came to this house nothing has gone right for me. There must be an evil spell on it. You know there are some unlucky houses that are cursed, and the bad luck rubs off on the people who live in them. I don't doubt for a minute that this is one of them, but I tell you that after this month is over, I wouldn't live here even if they gave the place to me."

I sat down at the end of the stone bench, and I kept quiet about my snack so that he wouldn't take me for a glutton. So, for supper I began to eat my tripe and bread, while I was watching my poor master out of the corner of my eye. And he kept staring at my shirttail that I was using for a plate. I hope God takes as much pity on me as I felt for him. I knew just what he was feeling, since the same thing had happened to me lots of times—and, in fact, it was still happening to me. I thought about asking him to join me, but since he told me that he'd already eaten I was afraid he wouldn't accept the invitation. The fact is, I was hoping that the sinner would help himself to the food I had gone to the trouble of getting and that he'd eat the way he did the day before so he could get out of his own troubles. This was really a better time for it, since there was more food and I wasn't as hungry.

God decided to grant my wish—and his, too, I guess. Because he was still walking around, but when I began to eat, he came over to me and said, "I tell you, Lazaro, I've never seen anyone eat with as much gusto as you put into it. Anyone watching you would get hungry on the spot, even if he hadn't been before."

The marvelous appetite you have, I thought to myself, makes you think mine is beautiful.

Still, I decided to help him, since he had opened up a way for me himself. So I said to him, "Sir, a man can do a good job if he has good tools. This bread is absolutely delicious, and the cow's hoof is so well cooked and seasoned that no one could possibly resist its taste."

"Is it cow's hoof?"

"Yes, sir."

"I tell you, there's no better dish in the world. I don't even like pheasant as much."

"Well, dig in, sir, and you'll see how good it really is."

6 4

I put the cow's hooves into his, along with three or four of the whiter pieces of bread. And he sat down beside me and began to eat like a man who was really hungry. He chewed the meat off of every little bone better than any hound of his would have done.

"With garlic sauce," he said, "this is an exceptional dish."

"You don't need any sauce with your appetite," I said under my breath.

"By God, that tasted so good you'd think I hadn't had a bite to eat all day."

That's true as sure as I was born, I said to myself.

He asked me for the water jug, and when I gave it to him it was as full as when I'd first brought it in. Since there was no water gone from it, there was a sure sign that my master hadn't been overeating that day. We drank and went to sleep, very content, like we'd done the night before.

Well, to make a long story short, that's the way we spent the next nine or ten days: that sinner would go out in the morning with his satisfied, leisurely pace, to dawdle around the streets while I was out hoofing it for him.

I used to think lots of times about my catastrophe: having escaped from those terrible masters I'd had and looking for someone better, I ran into a man who not only couldn't support me but who I had to support. Still, I really liked him because I saw that he didn't have anything and he couldn't do more than he was already doing. I felt more sorry for him than angry. And lots of times, just so I could bring back something for him to eat, I didn't eat anything myself.

I did this because one morning the pitiful fellow got up in his shirt and went to the top floor of the house to

66

take care of a certain necessity. And to satisfy my curiosity I unfolded the jacket and pants he'd left at the head
of the bed. And I found an old, crumpled-up little purse
of satiny velvet that didn't have a damned cent in it, and
there wasn't any sign that it had had one for a long
time.

"This man," I said, "is poor. And no one can give
what he doesn't have. But both the stingy blind man and
that blasted miser of a priest did all right in God's
name—one of them with a quick tongue and the other
one with his hand-kissing. And they were starving me to
death. So it's only right that I should hate them and feel
sorry for this man."

As God is my witness, even today when I run into
someone like him, with that pompous way of walking of
his, I feel sorry for them because I think that they may
be suffering what I saw this one go through. But even
with all his poverty, I'd still be glad to serve him more
than the others because of the things I've just mentioned.
There was only one little thing that I didn't like about
him: I wished that he wouldn't act so superior; if only
he'd let his vanity come down a little to be in line with
his growing necessity. But it seems to me that that's a
rule his kind always keeps: even if they don't have a red
cent to their name, they have to keep up the masquerade.
God help them or that's the way they'll go to their
graves.

Well, while I was there, getting along the way I said,
my bad luck (which never got tired of haunting me)
decided that that hard, foul way of life shouldn't last.
The way it happened was that, since there had been a
crop failure there that year, the town council decided to
make all the beggars who came from other towns get out
of the city. And they announced that from then on if they

found one of them there, he'd be whipped. So the law went into effect, and four days after the announcement was given I saw a procession of beggars being led through the streets and whipped. And I got so scared that I didn't dare go out begging any more.

It's not hard to imagine the dieting that went on in my house and the sadness and silence of the people living there. It was so bad that for two or three days at a time we wouldn't have a bite to eat or even say one word to each other. I knew some ladies who lived next door to us; they spun cotton and made hats, and they kept me alive. From what little they brought in they always gave me something, and I just about managed to get by.

But I didn't feel as sorry for myself as I did for my poor master: he didn't have a damned bite to eat in a week. At least, we didn't have anything to eat at the house. When he went out I don't know how he got along, where he went or what he ate. And if you could only have seen him coming down the street at noon, holding himself straight, and skinnier than a full-blooded grey-hound! And because of his damn what-do-you-call-it—honor—he would take a toothpick (and there weren't very many of those in the house either) and go out the door, picking at what didn't have anything between them and still grumbling about the cursed place. He'd say, "Look how bad things are. And it's this blasted house that's causing it all. Look how gloomy and dark and dismal it is. As long as we stay here, we're going to suffer. I wish the month were over so we could get out of here."

Well, while we were in this terrible, hungry state, one day—I don't know by what stroke of luck or good fortune—a silver piece found its way into the poor hands of my master. And he brought it home with him, looking

as proud as if he had all the money in Venice, and smiling very happily, he gave it to me and said: "Take this,
Lazaro. God is beginning to be good to us. Go down to
the square and buy bread and wine and meat. Let's shoot
the works! And also—this should make you happy—I
want you to know that I've rented another house, so
we'll only stay in this unlucky place until the end of the
month. Damn the place and damn the person who put
the first tile on its roof—I should never have rented it. I
swear to God that as long as I've lived here I haven't had
a drop of wine or a bite of meat, and I haven't gotten any
rest. And it's all because of the way this place looks—so
dark and gloomy! Go on now, and come back as quick
as you can: we'll eat like kings today."

I took my silver coin and my jug, and hurrying along,
I went up the street, heading for the square, very content
and happy. But what's the use if my bad luck has it
planned for me that I can't enjoy anything without trouble coming along with it? And that's the way this thing
went. I was going up the street, thinking about how I
would spend the money in the best way possible and get
the most out of it. And I was thanking God with all my
heart for letting my master have some money, when suddenly I came upon a corpse that a bunch of clergy and
other people were carrying down the street on a litter.

I squeezed up next to the wall to let them by, and after
the body had gone past there came right behind the litter
a woman who must have been the dead man's wife, all
dressed up in mourning (and a lot of other women with
her). And she came along, crying loudly and saying,
"My husband and lord, where are they taking you? It's to
that poor, unhappy house, that dark and gloomy house,
that house where they never eat or drink!"

And when I heard that, I felt like I had fallen through

the ground, and I said, "Oh—no! They're taking this dead man to my house."

I turned around and squeezed through the crowd and ran back down the street as fast as I could toward my house. And when I got inside I closed the door right behind me and called out for my master to come and help me. And I grabbed hold of him and begged him to help me block the door. He was a little stunned, thinking it might be something else, and he asked me, "What is it, boy? Why are you shouting? What's the matter? Why did you slam the door so hard?"

"Oh, sir," I said, "help me! They're bringing a dead man here."

"What do you mean?" he asked.

"I stumbled into him just up the way from here, and his wife was coming along saying, 'My husband and lord, where are they taking you? To the dark and gloomy house, the poor, unhappy house, the house where they never eat or drink!' Oh, sir, they're bringing him here."

And I tell you that when my master heard that, even though he didn't have any reason for being very cheerful, he laughed so hard that for a long time he couldn't even talk. In the meantime I had the bolt snapped shut on the door and my shoulder against it to hold them all back. The people passed by with their corpse, and I was still afraid that they were going to stick him in our house. And when he'd had his bellyful of laughter (more than of food) my good master said to me: "It's true, Lazaro, that taking the words of the widow at face value, you had every reason to think what you did. But since it was God's will to do something else and they've gone by, go on and open the door and go get us something to eat."

"Sir, wait until they've gone down the street," I said.

Finally my master came up to the door that led to the

street and opened it, reassuring me—and I really needed that because I was so upset and afraid. So I started up the street again.

But even though we ate well that day, I didn't enjoy it a damn bit. In fact, I didn't get my color back for three days. And my master would grin every time he thought about what I'd done.

So that's what happened to me during those days with my third poor master, this squire, and all the time I was wishing I knew how he'd come to this place and why he was staying here. Because from the very first day that I started serving him, I realized he was a stranger here: he hardly knew anyone, and he didn't associate with very many of the people around here.

Finally my wish came true, and I found out what I wanted to know. One day after we'd eaten fairly well and he was pretty content, he told me about himself. He said he was from Old Castile. And he said the only reason he'd left there was because he didn't want to take his hat off to a neighbor of his who was a high-class gentleman.

"Sir," I said, "if he was the kind of man you say he was and his status was higher than yours, it was only right for you to take your hat off first—after all, you say that he took off his hat, too."

"That is the kind of man he was: his status was higher and he did take his hat off to me. But considering all the time I took mine off first, it wouldn't have been asking too much for him to be civil and make the first move once in a while."

"It seems to me, sir," I told him, "that I wouldn't even think about that—especially with people who are my superiors and are better off than I am."

"You're just a boy," he answered, "and you don't understand honor. That is the most important thing to any self-respecting gentleman these days. Well, I want you to know that I'm a squire—as you can see. But I swear to God that if I meet a count on the street and he doesn't take his hat all the way off his head for me, the next time I see him coming, I'll duck right into a house and pretend that I have some business or other to do there. Or I'll go up another street, if there is one, before he gets up to me—just so I won't have to take off my hat to him. Because a gentleman doesn't owe anything to anyone except God or the King. And it isn't right, if he's a man of honor, for him to let his self-respect fall even for a minute.

"I remember one day when I put a craftsman from my town in his place, and I felt like strangling him, too, because every time I ran into him he would say, 'God keep you, friend.' 'You little peasant,' I said to him, 'How dare you address me with "God keep you" as if I were just anybody? Where were you brought up?' And from that day on, whenever he saw me, he took off his hat and spoke to me the way he was supposed to."

"But isn't that a good way for one man to greet another: to say 'God keep you'?"

"Damn it!" he said. "That's what they say to the lower classes. But to people who are higher up, like me, they're only supposed to say, 'I hope you are well today, sir.' Or, at least, 'I hope you feel well today' if the person talking to me is a gentleman. So I didn't want to put up with that man from my town who was filling me up to here with his 'God keep you.' And I wouldn't put up with him either. In fact, I won't stand for anyone—including the King himself—to say to me 'God keep you, friend.' "

"Well, I'll be. . . ," I said. "That's why God doesn't help you out. You won't let anyone ask Him to."

"Especially," he said, "because I'm not so poor. In

73

fact, where I'm from I have a huge estate (it's fifty miles from where I was born, right along Costanilla, the main street of Valladolid). And if the houses on it were still standing and kept up, it would be worth more than six thousand pieces of silver—just to give you an idea of how big and grand it would be. And I have a pigeon house that would produce more than two hundred pigeons a year if it hadn't fallen down. And there are some other things I won't mention, but I left them all because of my honor.

"And I came to this city, thinking I'd find a good position. But it hasn't turned out the way I thought it would. I meet lots of canons and other officials of the church, but those people are so tight with their money that no one could possibly get them to change their ways. Lesser men want me, too, but working for them is a lot of trouble. They want you to change from a man into a jack-of-all-trades, and if you won't, they give you the sack. And, generally, the paydays are few and far between; most of the time your only sure way of being paid is when they feed you. And when they want to have a clear conscience and really pay you for the sweat of your brow, your payoff comes from their clothes closet with a sweaty old jacket or a ragged cape or coat. And even when a man has a position with someone of the nobility, he still has his troubles.

"I ask you: aren't I clever enough to serve one of them and make him happy? Lord, if I ran into one, I really think I'd be his favorite—and I could do lots of things for him. Why, I could lie to him just as well as anyone else could. And I could flatter him like nothing he'd ever seen before. And I'd laugh at his stories and jokes even if they weren't exactly the funniest things in the world. I'd never tell him anything disturbing even if he

74

would be better off knowing it. I would be very conscientious in everything about him, both in word and in deed. And I wouldn't kill myself to do things he wouldn't see. Whenever he was around to hear me, I would always scold the servants so he'd think I was very concerned about him. And if he were scolding one of his servants, I'd step in with some pointed remarks about the culprit that would make the nobleman even madder, while I was appearing to take the servant's side. I would praise the things he liked, but I'd mock and slander the people of the house and even the ones who didn't live there. I would go prying and try to find out about other people's lives so I could tell him about them.

"And I'd do all sorts of other things like this that go on in palaces these days and that people in that sort of a position like. They don't want to see good men in their homes. In fact, they think they're useless, and actually, they hate them. They say they're stupid people you can't deal with and that a nobleman can't confide in them. And smart people these days act with the nobility, as I say, just the way I would. But with my bad luck, I haven't met one of them."

And so my master complained about his unhappy life, too, telling me how admirable he was.

Well, about this time, a man and an old woman came in the door. The man wanted the rent money for the house, and the old lady had rented him the bed and wanted the money for that. They figured up the amount, and for two months' rent they wanted what he couldn't have made in a year. I think it was about twelve or thirteen pieces of silver. And he answered them very courteously: he said that he would go out to the square to change a doubloon and that they should come back that afternoon. But when he left, he never came back.

So they returned in the afternoon, but it was too late. I told them that he still hadn't come back. And when night came and he didn't, I was afraid to stay in the house alone. So I went to the women next door and told them what had happened, and I slept at their place.

The next morning, the creditors returned. But no one was home, so they came to the door of the place I was staying at now and asked about their neighbor. And the women told them, "Here is his servant and the door key."

Then they asked me about him, and I told them I didn't know where he was and that he hadn't come back home after going to get the change. And I said that I thought he'd given both them and me the slip.

When they heard that, they went to get a constable and a notary. And then they came back with them and took the key and called me and some witnesses over. And they opened the door and went inside to take my master's property until he paid what he owed them. They walked through the entire house and found it empty, just as I've said. And they asked me, "What's become of your master's things—his chests and drapes and furniture?"

"I don't know anything about that," I answered.

"It's obvious," they said, "that last night they must have had it all taken out and carted somewhere else. Constable, arrest this boy. He knows where it is."

Then the constable came over and grabbed me by the collar of my jacket, and he said, "Boy, you're under arrest unless you tell us what's happened to your master's things."

I'd never seen myself in such a fix (I had, of course, been held by the collar lots of times before, but that was done gently so that I could guide that man who couldn't

see down the road), and so I was really scared. And while crying, I promised to answer their questions.

"All right," they said. "Then tell us what you know. Don't be afraid."

The notary sat down on a stone bench so he could write out the inventory, and he asked me what things my master had.

"Sir," I said, "according to what my master told me, he has a nice estate with houses on it and a pigeon house that isn't standing any more."

"All right," they said. "Even though it probably isn't worth much, it will be enough to pay off his bill. And what part of the city is it located in?" they asked me.

"In his town," I answered.

"For God's sake, we're really getting far," they said. "And just where is his town?"

"He told me that he came from Old Castile," I replied.

And the constable and notary laughed out loud, and said, "This sort of information would be good enough to pay off your debt even if it was bigger."

The neighbor ladies were there, and they said: "Gentlemen, this is just an innocent boy, and he's only been with that squire a few days. He doesn't know any more about him than you do. Besides, the poor little fellow has been coming to our house, and we've given him what we could to eat out of charity, and at night he's gone to his master's place to sleep."

When they saw that I was innocent, they let me loose and said I was free to go. And the constable and notary wanted the man and the woman to pay them for their services. And there was a lot of shouting and arguing about that. They said they weren't obligated to pay: there was no reason for them to, since nothing had been attached. But the men said that they had missed out on

7 8

some other more profitable business just so they could come here.

Finally, after a lot of shouting, they loaded the old lady's old mattress onto a deputy—even though it wasn't very much of a load. And all five of them went off, shouting at each other. I don't know how it all turned out. I think that sinner of a mattress must have paid everyone's expenses. And that was a good use for it because the time it should have spent relaxing and resting from its past strain, it had still been going around being rented out.

So, as I've said, my poor third master left me, and I saw the hand of my bad luck in this, too. It showed how much it was going against me, because it arranged my affairs so backward that instead of me leaving my master—which is what normally happens—my master left and ran away from me.

IV. *How Lazaro Went to Work for a Friar of the Order of Mercy and What Happened to Him*

I had to get a fourth master, and this one turned out to be a friar of the Order of Mercy. The women I've mentioned recommended me to him. They said he was a relative. He didn't think much of choir duties or eating in the monastery; he was always running around on the outside; and he was really devoted to secular business and visiting. In fact, he was so dedicated to this that I think he wore out more shoes than the whole monastery put together. He gave me the first pair of shoes I ever wore, but they didn't last me a week. And I wouldn't have lasted much longer myself trying to keep up with him. So because of this and some other little things that I don't want to mention, I left him.

V. How Lazaro Went to Work for a Pardoner and the Things That Happened to Him Then

As luck would have it, the fifth one I ran into was a seller of papal indulgences. He was arrogant, without principles, the biggest hawker of indulgences that I've ever seen in my life or ever hope to see—and probably the biggest one of all time. He had all sorts of ruses and underhanded tricks, and he was always thinking up new ones.

When he'd come to a place where he was going to sell these pardons, first he'd give the priests and the other clergy some presents—just little things that really weren't worth much: some lettuce from Murcia; a couple limes or oranges if they were in season; maybe a peach; some pears—the kind that stay green even after they're ripe. That way he tried to win them over so they'd look kindly on his business and call out their congregation to buy up the indulgences.

When they thanked him, he'd find out how well-educated they were. If they said they understood Latin, he wouldn't speak a word of it so they couldn't trip him up; instead he'd use some refined, polished-sounding words and flowery phrases. And if he saw that these clerics were "appointed reverends"—I mean that they bought their way into the priesthood instead of by going through school—he turned into a Saint Thomas, and for two hours he'd speak Latin. Or, at least, something that sounded like Latin even if it wasn't.

When they wouldn't take his pardons willingly, he'd try to find some underhanded way to get them to take them. To do that, he'd sometimes make a nuisance of himself, and other times he'd use his bag of tricks. It would take too long to talk about all the things I saw him do, so I'll just tell about one that was really sly and clever, and I think that will show how good he was at it.

In a place called Sagra, in the province of Toledo, he'd been preaching for two or three days, trying his usual gimmicks, and not one person had bought an indulgence, and I couldn't see that they had any intention of buying any. He swore up and down, and trying to think of what to do, he decided to call the town together the next morning so he could try to sell all the pardons.

And that night, after supper, he and the constable began to gamble to see who would pay for the meal. They got to quarreling over the game, and there were heated words. He called the constable a thief, and the constable called him a swindler. At that point my master, the pardoner, picked up a spear that was lying against the door of the room where they were playing. The constable reached for his sword, that he kept at his side.

The guests and neighbors came running at the noise and shouting we all began to make, and they got in between the two of them to break it up. Both men were really mad, and they tried to get away from the people who were holding them back so they could kill each other. But since those people had come swarming in at all the noise, the house was full of them, and when the two men saw that they couldn't use their weapons they began to call each other names. And at one point the constable said my master was a swindler and that all the pardons he was selling were counterfeit.

Finally, the townspeople saw that they couldn't make them stop, so they decided to get the constable out of the inn and take him somewhere else. And that made my master even madder. But after the guests and neighbors pleaded with him to forget about it and go home to bed, he left, and then so did everyone else.

The next morning my master went to the church and told them to ring for mass so he could preach and sell the indulgences. And the townspeople came, muttering about the pardons, saying that they were forgeries and that the constable himself had let it out while they were quarreling. So, if they hadn't wanted to take any pardons before, they were dead set against it now.

The pardoner went up to the pulpit and began his sermon, trying to stir up the people, telling them that they shouldn't be without the blessings and the forgiveness that would come to them by buying the indulgences.

When he was into the sermon in full swing, the constable came in the church door, and after praying he got up, and with a loud and steady voice he began to speak very solemnly: "My fellow men, let me say a word; afterward, you can listen to whoever you like. I came here with this swindler who's preaching. But he tricked me: he said that if I helped him in his business, we'd split the profits. And now, seeing how it would hurt my conscience and your pocketbooks, I've repented of what I've done. And I want to tell you openly that the indulgences he's selling are forgeries. Don't believe him and don't buy them. I'm not involved with them any longer—either in an open or a hidden way—and from now on I'm giving up my staff, the symbol of my office, and I

throw it on the ground so that you'll see I mean it. And if sometime in the future this man is punished for his cheating, I want you to be my witnesses that I'm not in with him and I'm not helping him, but that I told you the truth—that he's a double-dealing liar."

And he finished his speech.

When he'd started, some of the respectable men there wanted to get up and throw the constable out of church so there wouldn't be any scandal. But my master stopped them and told them all not to bother him under penalty of excommunication. He told them to let him say anything he wanted to. So while the constable was saying all that, my master kept quiet, too.

When he stopped speaking, my master told him if he wanted to say anything more he should go ahead. And the constable said, "I could say plenty more about you and your dirty tricks, but I've said enough for now."

Then the pardoner knelt down in the pulpit, and with his hands folded, and looking up toward heaven, he said: "Lord God, to Whom nothing is hidden and everything is manifest, for Whom nothing is impossible and everything is possible, Thou knowest the truth of how unjustly I have been accused. In so far as I am concerned, I forgive him so that Thou, Oh Lord, may forgive me. Pay no attention to this man who knows not what he says or does. But the harm that has been done to Thee, I beg and beseech Thee in the name of righteousness that Thou wilt not disregard it.

"Because someone here may have been thinking of taking this holy indulgence, and now, believing that the false words of that man are true, they will not take it. And since that would be so harmful to our fellow men, I beg Thee, Lord, do not disregard it; instead, grant us a miracle here. Let it happen in this way: if what that man

8 7

says is true—that I am full of malice and falseness—let this pulpit collapse with me in it and plunge one hundred feet into the ground, where neither it nor I shall ever be seen again. But if what I say is true—and he, won over by the devil to distrain and deprive those who are here present from such a great blessing—if he is saying false things, let him be punished and let his malice be known to all."

My reverent master had hardly finished his prayer when the crooked constable fell flat on his face, hitting the floor so hard that it made the whole church echo. Then he began to roar and froth at the mouth and to twist it and his whole face, too, kicking and hitting and rolling around all over the floor.

The people's shouts and cries were so loud that no one could hear anyone else. Some were really terrified. Other people were saying, "God help him." And others said, "He got what was coming to him. Anyone who lies like he did deserves it."

Finally, some of the people there (even though I think they were really afraid) went up to him and grabbed hold of his arms, while he was swinging wildly at everyone around him. Other people grabbed his legs, and they really had to hold him tight because he was kicking harder than a mule. They held him down for quite a while. There were more than fifteen men on top of him, and he was still trying to hit them; and if they weren't careful he would punch them in the nose.

All the time that master of mine was on his knees up in the pulpit with his hands and eyes fixed on heaven, caught up by the Holy Spirit. And all the noise in the church—the crying and shouting—couldn't bring him out of that mystical trance.

Those good men went up to him, and by shouting they

aroused him and begged him to help that poor man who was dying. They told him to forget about the things that had happened before and the other man's awful words because he had been paid back for them. But if he could somehow do something that would take that man out of his misery and suffering, to do it—for God's sake— because it was obvious that the other man was guilty and that the pardoner was innocent and had been telling the truth, since the Lord had shown His punishment right there when he'd asked for revenge.

The pardoner, as if waking from a sweet dream, looked at them and looked at the guilty man and all the people there, and very slowly he said to them: "Good men, you do not need to pray for a man in whom God has given such a clear sign of Himself. But since He commands us not to return evil for evil and to forgive those who harm us, we may confidently ask Him to do what He commands us to do. We may ask His Majesty to forgive this man who offended Him by putting such an obstacle in the way of the holy faith. Let us all pray to Him."

And so he got down from the pulpit and urged them to pray very devoutly to Our Lord, asking Him to forgive that sinner and bring back his health and sanity and to cast the devil out of him if, because of his great sins, His Majesty had permitted one to go in.

They all got down on their knees in front of the altar, and with the clergy there they began to softly chant a litany. My master brought the cross and the holy water, and after he had chanted over him, he held his hands up to heaven and tilted his eyes upward so that the only thing you could see was a little of their whites. Then he began a prayer that was as long as it was pious. And it made all the people cry (just like the sermons at Holy

8 9

Week, when the preacher and the audience are both fervent). And he prayed to God, saying that it was not the Lord's will to give that sinner death but to bring him back to life and make him repent. And since the man had been led astray by the devil but was now filled with the thought of death and his sins, he prayed to God to forgive him and give him back his life and his health so he could repent and confess his sins.

And when this was finished, he told them to bring over the indulgence, and he put it on the man's head. And right away that sinner of a constable got better, and little by little he began to come to. And when he was completely back in his senses, he threw himself down at the pardoner's feet and asked his forgiveness. He confessed that the devil had commanded him to say what he did and had put the very words in his mouth. First, to hurt him and get revenge. Secondly—and mainly—because the devil himself would really be hurt by all the good that could be done here if the pardons were bought up.

My master forgave him, and they shook hands. And there was such a rush to buy up the pardons that there was hardly a soul in the whole place that didn't get one: husbands and wives, sons and daughters, boys and girls.

The news of what had happened spread around to the neighboring towns, and when we got to them, he didn't have to give a sermon or even go to the church. People came right up to the inn to get them as if they were going out of style. So in the ten or twelve places we went to around there, my master sold a good thousand indulgences in each place without even preaching a sermon.

While the "miracle" was happening, I have to admit that I was astonished, too, and I got taken in just like the others. But when I saw the way my master and the constable laughed and joked about the business later, I real-

ized that it had all been cooked up by my sharp and clever master.

And even though I was only a boy, it really amused me, and I said to myself: I'll bet these shysters do this all the time to innocent people.

Well, to be brief, I stayed with my fifth master about four months, and I had some hard times with him, too.

VI. *How Lazaro Went to Work for a Chaplain and What Happened to Him Then*

After this I took up with a man who painted tambourines. He wanted me to grind the colors for him, and I had my trials with him, too.

By now I was pretty well grown up. And one day when I went into the cathedral, a chaplain there gave me a job. He put me in charge of a donkey, four jugs, and a whip, and I began to sell water around the city. This was the first step I took up the ladder to success: my dreams were finally coming true. On weekdays I gave my master sixty coppers out of what I earned, while I was able to keep everything I got above that. And on Saturdays I got to keep everything I made.

I did so well at the job that after four years of it, watching my earnings very carefully, I saved enough to buy myself a good secondhand suit of clothes. I bought a jacket made out of old cotton, a frayed coat with braid on the sleeves and an open collar, a cape that had once been velvety, and an old sword—one of the first ones ever made in Cuellar. When I saw how good I looked in my gentleman's clothes, I told my master to take back his donkey: I wasn't about to do that kind of work any more.

VII. How Lazaro Went to Work for a Constable and Then What Happened to Him

After I left the chaplain I was taken on as bailiff by a constable. But I didn't stay with him very long: the job was too dangerous for me. That's what I decided after some escaped criminals chased me and my master with clubs and rocks. My master stood there and faced them, and they beat him up, but they never did catch me. So I quit that job.

And while I was trying to think of what sort of a life I could lead so that I could have a little peace and quiet and save up something for my old age, God lit up my path and put me on the road to success. With the help of some friends and other people, all the trials and troubles I'd gone through up till then were finally compensated for, seeing as how I got what I wanted: a government job. And no one ever gets ahead without a job like that.

And that's what I've been doing right up to now: I work in God's service—and yours, too. What I do is announce the wines that are being sold around the city. Then, too, I call out at auctions and whenever anything is lost. And I go along with the people who are suffering for righteousness' sake and call out their crimes: I'm a town crier, to put it plainly.

It's been a good job, and I've done so well at it that almost all of this sort of work comes to me. In fact, it's

gotten to the point where if someone in the city has wine or anything else to put up for sale, they know it won't come to anything unless Lazarillo of Tormes is in on it.

About this time that gentleman, the Archpriest of San Salvador (your friend and servant), began to notice my abilities and how I was making a good living. He knew who I was because I'd been announcing his wines, and he said he wanted me to marry a maid of his. And I saw that only good, profitable things could come from a man like him, so I agreed to go along with it.

So I married her, and I've never regretted it. Because besides the fact that she's a good woman and she's hard-working and helpful, through my lord, the archpriest, I have all the help and favors I need. During the year he always gives her a few good-sized sacks of wheat, meat on the holidays, a couple loaves of bread sometimes, and his socks after he's through with them. He had us rent a little house right next to his, and on Sundays and almost every holiday we eat at his place.

But there have always been scandalmongers, and I guess there always will be, and they won't leave us in peace. They talk about I don't know what all—they say that they've seen my wife go and make up his bed and do his cooking for him. And God bless them, but they're a bunch of liars.

Because, besides the fact that she's the kind of woman who's hardly happy about these gibes, my master made me a promise, and I think he'll keep it. One day he talked to me for a long time in front of her, and he said to me: "Lazaro of Tormes, anyone who pays attention to what gossips say will never get ahead. I'm telling you this because I wouldn't be at all surprised if someone did see your wife going in and out of my house. In fact, the reason she goes in is very much to your honor and to hers: and that's the truth. So forget what people say. Just think of how it concerns you—I mean, how it benefits you."

"Sir," I said, "I've decided to be on the side of good men. It is true that some of my friends have told me something of that. The truth is, they've sworn for a fact that my wife had three children before she married me, speaking with reverence to your grace since she's here with us."

Then my wife began to scream and carry on so much that I thought the house with us in it was going to fall in. Then she took to crying, and she cursed the man who had married us. It got so bad that I'd rather I'd died than have let those words of mine slip out. But with me on one side and my master on the other, we talked to her and begged her so much that she finally quit her crying. And I swore to her that as long as I lived I'd never mention another word about the business. And I told her I thought it was perfectly all right—in fact, that it made me happy—for her to go in and out of his house both day and night because I was so sure of her virtue. And so we were all three in complete agreement.

So, right up to today we've never said another word about the affair. In fact, when I see that someone wants to even start talking about it, I cut him short, and I tell him: "Look, if you're my friend, don't tell me something that will make me mad because anyone who does that isn't my friend at all. Especially if they're trying to cause trouble between me and my wife. There's nothing and nobody in the world that I love more than her. And because of her, God gives me all sorts of favors—many more than I deserve. So I'll swear to God that she's as good a woman as any here in Toledo, and if anyone tells me otherwise, I'm his enemy until I die."

So no one ever says anything to me, and I keep peace in my house.

That was the same year that our victorious emperor came to this illustrious city of Toledo and held his court here, and there were all sorts of celebrations and festivities, as you must have heard.

Well, at this time I was prosperous and at the height of all good fortune.

VIII.   *In Which Lazaro Tells of the Friendship He Struck up in Toledo with Some Germans and What Happened to Them*

At this time I was prosperous and at the height of all good fortune. And because I always carried a good-sized pan full of some of the good fruit that is raised in this land as a sign of what I was announcing, I gathered so many friends and benefactors around me, both natives and foreigners, that wherever I went no door was closed to me. The people were so kind to me that I believe if I had killed a man then, or had found myself in difficult straits, everyone would have come to my side, and those benefactors would have given me every sort of aid and assistance. But I never left them with their mouths dry because I took them to the places where they could find the best of what I spread throughout the city. And there we lived the good life and had fine times together: we would often walk into a place on our own two feet and go out on the feet of other people. And the best part of it

This is the first chapter of an anonymous sequel to *Lazarillo of Tormes,* published in 1555. This chapter became attached to the original work in later editions, but is not to be considered part of the first *Lazarillo.* It is presented here because it serves as a bridge between the first *Lazarillo of Tormes* and the second part by Juan de Luna—TRANSLATOR.

was that all this time Lazaro of Tormes didn't spend a damned cent, and his friends wouldn't let him spend anything. If I ever started to open my purse, pretending that I wanted to pay, they were offended, and they would look at me angrily and say, *"Nite, nite, Asticot, lanz."* They were scolding me, saying that when they were there no one would have to pay a cent.

I was, frankly, in love with those people. And not only because of that, but because whenever we got together they were always filling my pockets and my shirt full of ham and legs of mutton—cooked in those good wines— along with many spices and huge amounts of beef and bread. So in my house my wife and I always had enough for an entire week. With all this, I remembered the past times when I was hungry, and I praised God and gave thanks that things and times like those pass away. But, as the saying goes, all good things must come to an end. And that's how this turned out. Because they moved the great court, as they do now and then, and when they were leaving, those good friends of mine urged me to go with them, and they said they would give me their help. But I remembered the proverb: Better certain evil than doubtful good.

So I thanked my friends for their good wishes, and with a great deal of clapping on the shoulders and sadness, I said goodbye to them. And I know that if I hadn't been married I would never have left their company because they were the salt of the earth and the kind of people that were really to my liking. The life they lead is a pleasant one. They aren't conceited or presumptuous; they have no hesitation or dislike for going into any wine cellar, with their hats off if the wine deserves it. They are simple, honest people, and they always have so much that I hope God gives me no less when I'm really thirsty.

But the love I had for my wife and my land ("The land you are born in, . . ." as they say) held me back. So I stayed in this city, and although I was well known by the people who lived here, I missed the pleasure of my friends and the court. Still, I was happy, and even happier when my family line was extended by the birth of a beautiful little girl that my wife had then. And although I was a little suspicious, she swore to me that the child was mine. But then fortune thought it had forgotten me long enough, and it decided to show me its cruel, angry, harsh face once more and disturb these few years of good, peaceful living by bringing others of affliction and bitterness. Oh, almighty God! Who could write about such a terrible misfortune and such a disastrous fall without letting the inkwell rest and wiping his eyes with the quill?

The Second Part of
The Life of
Lazarillo of Tormes

Juan de Luna

SECOND PART
OF THE LIFE OF
LAZARILLO
OF TORMES

·

Drawn Out Of The
Old Chronicles
Of Toledo

·

By J. De Luna, Castilian
and Interpreter of the
Spanish Language

·

Dedicated to the Most Illustrious
Princess
Henriette De Rohan

·

In Paris

·

In the House of Rolet Boutonne,
in the Palace, in the Gallery of the Prisoners;
Near the Chancery

·

M. DC. XX.
By Grant of the King

MOST ILLUSTRIOUS AND EXCELLENT PRINCESS.

It is common among all writers to dedicate their works to someone who may shelter those works with their authority and defend them with their power. Having decided to bring to light the Second Part of the life of the great Lazaro of Tormes, a mirror and standard of Spanish sobriety, I have dedicated and do dedicate it to Your Excellency, whose authority and power may shelter this poor work (poor, since it treats of Lazaro) and to prevent its being torn apart and abused by biting, gossiping tongues which with their infernal wrath attempt to wound and stain the most sincere and simple wills. I confess my boldness in dedicating such a small work to such a great princess; but its sparseness brings its own excuse—which is the necessity for greater and more effective shelter—and the kindness of Your Excellency, the pardon. So I humbly beseech Your Excellency to take this small service, putting your eyes on the desire of him who offers it, which is and will be to use my life and strength in your service.

Of whom I am a very humble servant,

J. DE LUNA

To The Reader

The reason, dear reader, that the Second Part of Lazarillo of Tormes is going into print is that a little book has come into my hands that touches on his life but has not one word of truth in it. Most of it tells how Lazaro fell into the sea, where he changed into a fish called a tuna. He lived in the sea for many years and married another tuna, and they had children who were fishes like their father and mother. It also tells about the wars of the tuna, in which Lazaro was the captain, and about other foolishness both ridiculous and erroneous, stupid and with no basis in truth. The person who wrote it undoubtedly wanted to relate a foolish dream or a dreamed-up foolishness.

This book, I repeat, was the prime motivation for my bringing to light this Second Part, exactly as I saw it written in some notebooks in the rogues' archives in Toledo, without adding or subtracting anything. And it is in conformity with what I heard my grandmother and my aunts tell, and on which I was weaned, by the fireside on cold winter nights. And as further evidence, they and the other neighbors would often argue over how Lazaro could have stayed under water so long (as my Second Part relates) without drowning. Some said he could have done it, others said he could not: those who said he could cited Lazaro himself, who says the water could not go into him because his stomach was full all the way up to his mouth. One good old man who knew how to swim, and who wanted to prove that it was feasible, interposed his authority and said he had seen a man who went swimming in the Tagus, and who dived and went into some caverns where he stayed from the time the sun went down until it came up again, and he found his way out by the sun's glow; and when all his friends and relatives had grown tired of weeping over him and looking for his body to give him a burial, he came out safe and sound.

The other difficulty they saw about his life was that nobody recognized that Lazaro was a man, and everyone who saw him took him for a fish. A good canon (who, since he was a very old man, spent all day in the sun with the weavers) answered that this was even more possible, basing his statement on the opinion of many ancient and modern writers, including Pliny, Phaedo, Aristotle, and Albertus Magnus, who testify that in the sea there are some fish of which the males are called Tritons, and the females Nereids, and they are all called mermen: from the waist up they look exactly like men, and from the waist down they are like fish. And I say that even if this opinion were not held by such well-qualified writers, the license that the fishermen had from the Inquisitors would be a sufficient excuse for the ignorance of the Spanish people, because it would be a matter for the Inquisition if they doubted something that their lordships had consented to be shown as such.

About this point (even though it lies outside of what I am dealing with now) I will tell of something that occurred to a farmer from my region. It happened that an Inquisitor sent for him, to ask for some of his pears, which he had been told were absolutely delicious. The poor country fellow didn't know what his lordship wanted of him, and it weighed so heavily on him that he fell ill until a friend of his told him what was wanted. He jumped out of bed, ran to his garden, pulled up the tree by the roots, and sent it along with the fruit, saying that he didn't want anything at his house that would make his lordship send for him again. People are so afraid of them—and not only laborers and the lower classes, but lords and grandees—that they all tremble more than leaves on trees when a soft, gentle breeze is blowing, when they hear these names: Inquisitor, Inquisition. This is what I have wanted to inform the reader about so that he can answer when such questions are aired in his presence, and also I beg him to think of me as the chronicler and not the author of this work, which he can spend an hour of his time with. If he enjoys it, let him wait for the Third Part about the death and testament of Lazarillo, which is the best of all. And if not, I have nevertheless done my best. *Vale.*

I. *Where Lazaro Tells about How He Left Toledo to Go to the War of Algiers*

"A prosperous man who acts unwisely should not be angry when misfortune comes." I'm writing this epigram for a reason: I never had the mentality or the ability to keep myself in a good position when fortune had put me there. Change was a fundamental part of my life that remained with me both in good, prosperous times and in bad, disastrous ones. As it was, I was living as good a life as any patriarch ever had, eating more than a friar who has been invited out to dinner, drinking more than a thirsty quack doctor, better dressed than a priest, and in my pocket were two dozen pieces of silver—more reliable than a beggar in Madrid. My house was as well stocked as a beehive filled with honey, my daughter was born with the odor of saintliness about her, and I had a job that even a pew opener in the church at Toledo would have envied.

Then I heard about the fleet making ready to sail for Algiers. The news intrigued me, and like a good son I decided to follow in the footsteps of my good father, Tome Gonzalez (may he rest in peace). I wanted to be an example—a model—for posterity. I didn't want to be remembered for leading that crafty blind man, or for nibbling on the bread of the stingy priest, or for serving that penniless squire, or even for calling out other people's crimes. The kind of example I wanted to be was one who would show those blind Moors the error of their ways, tear open and sink those arrogant pirate ships, serve under a valiant captain who belonged to the Order of Saint John (and I did enlist with a man like that as his valet, with the condition that everything I took from the Moors I would be able to keep, and it turned out that way). Finally, what I wanted to do was to be a model for shouting at and rousing the troops with our war cry: "Saint James be with us. . . . Attack, Spaniards!"

I said good-by to my adoring wife and my dear daughter. My daughter begged me not to forget to bring her back a nice Moorish boy, and my wife told me to be sure to send, by the first messenger, a slave girl to wait on her and some Barbary gold to console her while I was gone. I asked my lord the archpriest's permission, and I put my wife and daughter in his charge so he would take care of them and provide for them. He promised me he would treat them as his very own.

I left Toledo happy, proud, and content, full of high hopes—the way men are when they go to war. With me were a great number of friends and neighbors who were going on the same expedition, hoping to better their fortunes. We arrived at Murcia with the intention of going to Cartagena to embark. And there something happened to me that I had no desire for. I saw that fortune had put me at the top of its whimsical wheel and with its usual swiftness had pushed me to the heights of worldly prosperity, and now it was beginning to throw me down to the very bottom.

It happened that when I went to an inn, I saw a half-man who, with all the loose and knotted threads hanging from his clothes, had more the appearance of an old goat

than a man. His hat was pulled down so far you couldn't see his face, his cheek was resting on his hand, and one leg was lying on his sword, which was in a half scabbard made of strips of cloth. He had his hat cocked jauntily over one ear (there was no crown on it, so all the hot air coming out of his head could evaporate). His jacket was cut in the French style—so slashed there wasn't a piece big enough to wrap a mustard seed in. His shirt was skin: you could see it through the lattice work of his clothes. His pants were the same material. As for his stockings, one was green and the other red, and they barely covered his ankles. His shoes were in the barefoot style: worn both up and down. By a feather sewn in his hat, the way soldiers dressed, I suspected that he was, in fact, a soldier.

With this thought in mind, I asked him where he was from and where he was going. He raised his eyes to see who was asking, and we both recognized each other: it was the squire I had served under at Toledo. I was astonished to see him in that suit.

When the squire saw my look of amazement, he said: "I'm not surprised to see how startled you are to see me this way, but you won't be when I tell you what happened to me from that day I left you in Toledo until today. As I was going back to the house with the change from the doubloon to pay my creditors, I came across a veiled woman who pulled at my cloak and, sighing and sobbing, pleaded with me to help her out of the plight she was in. I begged her to tell me her troubles, saying that it would take her longer to tell them than for me to take care of them. Still crying, and with a maidenly blush, she told me that the favor I could do for her (and she prayed that I would do it) was to go with her to Madrid where, according to what people had told her,

the man was staying who had not only dishonored her but had taken all her jewelry without fulfilling his promise to marry her. She said that if I would do this for her, she would do for me what a grateful woman should. I consoled her as best I could, raising her hopes by telling her that if her enemy were to be found anywhere in this world, she would be avenged.

"Well, to make a long story short, we went straight to the capital, and I paid her expenses all the way. The lady knew exactly where she was going, and she led me to a regiment of soldiers who gave her an enthusiastic welcome and took her to the captain, and there she signed up as a 'nurse' for the men. Then she turned to me, and with a brazen look said, 'All right, fathead. Now push off!' When I saw that she had tricked me, I flew into a rage, and I told her that if she were a man instead of a woman I would tear her heart out by the roots. One of the soldiers standing there came up and thumbed his nose at me, but he didn't dare to strike me because if he had they would have had to bury him on the spot.

"When I saw how badly that business was turning out, I left without saying another word, but I walked out a little faster than usual to see if any brawny soldier was going to follow me so that I could kill him. Because if I had fought that first little soldier boy and killed him (which I would have done, without any doubt), what honor or glory would there have been in it for me? But if the captain or some bully had come out, I would have sliced more holes in them than there are grains of sand in the sea. When I saw that none of them dared to follow me, I left, very pleased with myself. I looked around for work, and since I couldn't find any good enough for a man of my station, here I am like this. It is true that I could have been a valet or an escort to five or six seamstresses, but I would starve to death before I'd take a job like that."

My good master finished by telling me that, since he hadn't been able to find any merchants from his home town to lend him money, he was penniless, and he didn't know where he was going to spend the night. I caught his hint and offered to let him share my bed and my supper. He called my hand. When we were ready to go to sleep, I told him to take his clothes off the bed because it was too small for so many varmints. The next morning, wanting to get up without making any noise, I reached for my clothes—in vain. The traitor had taken them and vanished. I lay in bed, thinking I was going to die from pure misery. And it might have been better if I had died because I could have avoided all those times I was in agony later.

I started shouting, "Thief! Thief!" The people in the house came up and found me naked as a jaybird, looking in every corner of the room for something to cover myself with. They all laughed like fools, while I was swearing like a mule driver. I damned to hell that thieving bragger who had kept me up half the night telling about all the splendor of himself and his ancestors. The remedy that I took (since no one was giving me any) was to see if I could use that hot-air merchant's clothes until God furnished me with some others. But they were a labyrinth, with no beginning or end to them. There was no difference between the pants and the jacket. I put my legs in the sleeves and used the pants as a coat, and I didn't forget the stockings: they looked more like a court clerk's sleeves—loose enough to put his bribes in. The shoes were like fetters around my ankles: they didn't have any soles. I pulled the hat down over my head, putting the bottom side up so it wouldn't be so grimy. I

won't say a word about the insects running all over me—either the crawling infantry or the galloping cavalry.

In this shape I went to see my master, since he had sent for me. He was astonished to see the scarecrow that walked in, and he laughed so hard his rear tether let loose, and—royal flush. Out of respect for him, I think we should pass over that in silence. After a thousand unsuccessful attempts to talk, he asked me why I was wearing a disguise. I told him, and the result was that instead of pitying me, he swore at me and threw me out of his house. He said that just as I had let that man come in and sleep in my bed, one day I would let someone else in, and they would rob him.

II. How Lazaro Embarked at Cartagena

By nature I didn't last very long with my masters. And it was that way with this one, too, although I wasn't to blame. So there I was, miserable, all alone, and in despair; and with the clothes I was wearing everyone scoffed and made fun of me. Some people said to me, "That's not a bad little hat you have, with its back door. It looks like an old Dutch lady's bonnet."

Others said, "Your rags are certainly stylish. They look like a pigsty: so many other fat little ones are in there with you that you could kill and salt them and send them home to your wife."

One of the soldiers—a packhandler—said to me, "Mr. Lazarillo, I'll swear to God your stockings really show off your legs. And your sandals look like the kind the barefoot friars wear."

A constable replied, 'That's because this gentleman is going to preach to the Moors."

They kept teasing and taunting me so much that I was nearly ready to go back home. But I didn't because I thought it would be a poor war if I couldn't get more than I would lose. What hurt me most was that everyone avoided me like the plague. We embarked at Cartagena: the ship was large and well stocked. They unfurled the sails, and a wind caught them and sent the ship skimming along at a good clip. The land disappeared from sight, and a cross wind lashed the sea and sent waves

6433.

123

hurling up to the clouds. As the storm increased, we began losing hope; the captain and crew gave us up for lost. Everyone was weeping and wailing so much I thought we were at a sermon during Holy Week. With all the clamor no one could hear any of the orders that were given. Some people were running to one place, others to another: it was as noisy and chaotic as a blacksmith's shop. Everyone was saying confession to whoever they could. There was even one man who confessed to a prostitute, and she absolved him so well you would have thought she had been doing it for a hundred years.

Churning water makes good fishing, they say. So when I saw how busy everyone was, I said to myself: If I die, let it be with my belly full. I wandered down to the bottom of the ship, and there I found huge quantities of bread, wine, meat pies, and preserves, with no one paying any attention to them. I began to eat everything and to fill my stomach so it would be stocked up to last me till judgment day. A soldier came up and asked me to give him confession. He was astonished to see how cheerful I was and what a good appetite I had, and he asked how I could eat when death was so near. I told him I was doing it so that all the sea water I would drink when I drowned wouldn't make me sick. My simplicity made him shake with laughter from head to foot. I confessed a number of people who didn't utter a word with the agony they were in, and I didn't listen to them because I was too busy eating.

The officers and people of high rank escaped safely in a skiff, along with two priests who were on board. But my clothes were so bad that I couldn't fit inside. When I had my fill of eating, I went over to a cask full of good wine and transferred as much as I could hold into my stomach. I forgot all about the storm, myself, and every-

6434.

125

thing. The ship started to sink and the water came pouring in as though it had found its home. A corporal grabbed my hands and as he was dying he asked me to listen to a sin he wanted to confess. He said he hadn't carried out a penance he had been given, which was to make a pilgrimage to Our Lady of Loreto, even though he had had many opportunities to do it. And now that he wanted to, he couldn't. I told him that with the authority vested in me, I would commute his penance, and that instead of going to Our Lady of Loreto, he could go to Santiago.

"Oh, sir," he said. "I would like to carry out that penance, but the water is starting to come into my mouth, and I can't."

"If that's the way it is," I said, "the penance I give you is to drink all the water in the sea."

But he didn't carry that out either because there were many men there who drank as much as he did. When it came up to my mouth I said to it: Try some other door, this one is not opening. And even if it had opened, the water couldn't have gotten in, because my body was so full of wine it looked like a stuffed pig. As the ship broke apart a huge swarm of fish came in. It was as though they were being given aid from the bodies on board. They ate the flesh of those miserable people who had been overcome by a drop in the ocean, as if they were grazing in the county pasture. They wanted to try me out, but I drew my trustworthy sword and without stopping to chat with such a low-class mob, I laid into them like a donkey in a new field of rye.

They hissed at me: "We're not trying to hurt you. We only want to see if you taste good."

I worked so hard that in less than half-a-quarter of an hour I killed more than five hundred tuna, and they were the ones that wanted to make a feast out of the flesh of this sinner. The live fish began to feed on the dead ones, and they left Lazaro's company when they saw it wasn't a very profitable place to be. I found myself lord of the sea, with no one to oppose me. I ran around from one place to another, and I saw things that were unbelievable: huge piles of skeletons and bodies. And I found a large number of trunks full of jewels and gold, great heaps of weapons, silks, linens, and spices. I was longing for it all and sighing because it wasn't back at home, safe, so that, as the buffoon says, I could eat my bread dipped in sardines.

I did what I could, but that was nothing. I opened a huge chest and filled it full of coins and precious jewels. I took some ropes from the piles of them there and tied up the chest, and then I knotted other ropes together until I had one I thought was long enough to reach to the surface of the water. If I can get all this treasure out of here, I thought to myself, there won't be a tavernkeeper in the world better off than I'll be. I'll build up my estate, live off my investments, and buy a summer house in Toledo. They'll call my wife "Madam," and me they'll call "Sir." I'll marry my daughter to the richest pastrycook in town. Everyone will come to congratulate me, and I'll tell them that I worked hard for it, and that I didn't take it out of the bowels of the earth but from the heart of the sea. That I didn't get damp with sweat but drenched as a dried herring. I have never been as happy in my life as I was then, and I wasn't even thinking about the fact that if I opened my mouth I would stay down there with my treasure, buried till hell froze over.

III. How Lazaro Escaped from the Sea

I saw how near I was to death, and I was horrified; how
near I was to being rich, and I was overjoyed. Death
frightened me, and the treasure delighted me. I wanted to
run away from the first and enjoy the second. I tore off
the rags that my master, the squire, had left me for the
services I had done him. Then I tied the rope to my foot
and began to swim (I didn't know how to do that very
well, but necessity put wings on my feet and oars on my
hands). The fish there gathered around to nip at me, and
their prodding was like spurs that goaded me on. So with
them nipping and me galloping, we came up to the surface of the water, where something happened that was
the cause of all my troubles. The fish and I were caught
up in some nets that some fishermen had thrown out, and
when they felt the fish in the nets they pulled so mightily,
and water began to flow into me just as mightily, so that
I couldn't hold out, and I started to drown. And I would
have drowned if the sailors had not pulled the booty on
board with their usual speed. What a God-awful taste! I
have never drunk anything that bad in my entire life. It
tasted like the archpriest's piss my wife made me drink
once, telling me it was good Ocaña wine.

With the fish on board and myself as well, the fishermen began to pull on the line and discovered the spool
(as the saying goes). They found me tangled up in the
rope and were astonished, and they said, "What sort of

fish is this? Its face looks like a man's. Is it the devil or a ghost? Let's pull on that rope and see what he has fastened to his foot."

The fishermen pulled so hard that their ship started to sink. When they saw the trouble they were in, they cut the rope, and at the same time they cut off Lazaro's hopes of ever becoming one of the landed gentry. They turned me upside down so I would empty out the water I had drunk and the wine, too. They saw that I wasn't dead (which was by no means the worst that could have happened to me), so they gave me a little wine, and I came back to life like a lamp with kerosene poured in. They asked me all kinds of questions, but I didn't answer a word until they gave me something to eat. When I got my breath back, the first thing I asked them about was the shackles that were tied to my foot. They told me that they had cut them to get out of the danger they had been in. Troy was lost and so were all of Lazaro's great desires: and right then his troubles, cares, and hardships began. There is nothing in the world worse than to have fancied yourself rich, on top of the world, and then to suddenly find yourself poor and at the bottom of the ladder.

I had built my castles on the water, and it had sunk them all. I told the fishermen what both of us lost when they had cut off my shackles. They were so angry that one of them nearly went mad. The shrewdest one said they should throw me back into the sea and wait for me there until I came up again. They all agreed with him, and even though I objected strongly, their minds were made up: they said that since I knew the way, it would be easy for me (as if I would be going to the pastry shop or the tavern!).

They were so blinded by their greed that they would

have thrown me out if my fortune (or misfortune) had not arranged for a ship to come up to us to help carry back the fish. They all kept quiet so that the others wouldn't find out about the treasure they had discovered. But they had to leave off their evil plan for the moment. They brought their boats to shore, and they threw me back with the fish to hide me, intending to hunt for me again when they could. Later, two of them picked me up and carried me to a little hut nearby. One man who didn't know the secret asked them what I was. They said I was a monster that had been caught with the tuna. When they had me inside that miserable pigsty, I begged them to give me some rags to cover my naked body so I could be presentable.

"You can do that," they said, "after you've settled your account with the hostess."

At the time I didn't understand their gibberish. The fame of the monster spread through the countryside, and many people came to the hut to see me. But the fishermen didn't want to show me; they said they were waiting for permission from the bishops and the Inquisition and that, until then, it was entirely out of the question. I was stupified. I didn't know what they were planning, and so I didn't know what to say or do. The same thing happened to me that happens to the cuckold: he is the last to find out. Those devils cooked up a scheme that Satan himself wouldn't have thought of. But that requires a new chapter and a new look.

IV. How They Took Lazaro through Spain

Opportunity makes the thief. And when the fishermen realized they had such a good opportunity, they grabbed it lock, stock, and barrel. When they saw that so many people were gathering around the new fish, they decided to win back what they had lost when they cut the rope from my foot. So they sent word to the ministers of the Inquisition, asking permission to show a fish with a man's face through all of Spain. And when they offered those gentlemen a present of the best fish they had caught, they were given that permission immediately. Meanwhile, our friend Lazaro was thanking God for having taken him out of the belly of the whale. (And that was a great miracle since my ability and knowledge were not very good, and I swam like a lead brick.)

Four of the fishermen grabbed hold of me, and they seemed more like executioners—the kind that crucified Christ—than men. They tied up my hands, and then they put a mossy wig and beard on me, and they didn't forget the mustache: I looked like a garden statue. They wrapped my feet in seaweed, and I saw that they had dressed me up like a stuffed and trussed trout. Then I began to groan and moan over my troubles, complaining to fate or fortune: Why are you always pursuing me? I have never seen or touched you, but if a man can tell the cause by the effects, I know from my experience with you that there is no siren, basilisk, viper, or lioness with her young more cruel than you are. By flattery and caresses you lift men up to the height of your riches and pleasures and then hurtle them into the abyss of all their misery and calamities, and their depths are as low as your favors were high.

One of those cutthroats heard my soliloquy, and with a rasping voice he said to me, "If you say another word, Mr. Tunafish, we'll salt you along with your friends, or we'll burn you as a monster. The Inquisition," he continued, "has told us to take you through the village and towns in Spain and to show you off to everyone as a wonder and monster of nature."

I swore to them that I was no tuna, monster, or anything out of the ordinary. I said that I was a man just like everyone else, and that if I had come out of the ocean it was because I had fallen into it along with the men who drowned while going to make war on Algiers. But they were deaf men, and even worse, because they didn't want to hear. When I saw that my begging was as useless as the soap they use to wash an ass's head, I became patient and waited for time—which cures everything—to cure my trouble, knowing it all came from suffering through that damned metamorphosis.

They put me in a barrel cut in half, made to look like a brigantine. Then they filled it with water that came up to my lips as I sat in it. I couldn't stand up because they had my feet tied with a rope, and one end of it came out between the mesh of that hairy mess of mine so that if I made so much as a peep, they would make me hop and sink like a frog and drink more water than a person with dropsy. I would keep my mouth closed until I felt whoever was pulling on the rope let it go slack. Then I would stick my head out like a turtle, and I learned by what happened to my own.

They showed me like this to everyone, and so many people came to see me (each one paying twenty coppers) that they made two hundred pieces of silver in one day. The more money they made the more they wanted, and they began to be very concerned about my health so they could prolong it. They held a summit conference and discussed whether or not they should take me out of the water at night: they were afraid that with all the wet and cold it might cut my life short, and they loved mine more than their own (because of all the profit they were getting from mine). They decided to keep me in the water all the time because they thought the force of habit would change my nature. So poor Lazaro was like a string of wet rice or the binding on a raft.

I leave to the dear reader's imagination what I went through in this situation: here I was, a captive in this free land, in chains because of the wickedness of those greedy puppeteers. The worst part about it, and what tormented me most, was that I had to pretend to be mute when I really wasn't. I wasn't even able to open my mouth because the instant I did my guard was so alert that without anyone being able to see him, he would fill me up with water, afraid that I would talk.

My meals were dunked bread that the people who came to see me threw in so they could watch me eat. So for the six months I spent in that cooler I didn't get another damned thing to eat: I was dying of hunger. I drank tub water, and since it wasn't very clean it was all the more nourishing—especially because its coldness gave me attacks of diarrhea that lasted me as long as that watery purgatory did.

V. How They Took Lazaro
to the Capital

Those torturers took me from city to town, from town to village, from village to farm, happier than a lark with their earnings. They made fun of poor Lazaro, and they would sing: "Hooray, hooray for the fish. He earns our keep while we loaf."

My "coffin" was placed on a cart, and three men went along with me: the mule driver, the man who pulled on the rope whenever I tried to say anything, and the one who told all about me. This last one would make a speech about the strange way they caught me, telling more lies than a tailor at Eastertime. When we were traveling and no one else was around, they let me talk, and that was the only courtesy they showed me. I asked them who the devil had put it in their heads to take me around like that, in a fish bowl. They answered that if they didn't do it I would die on the spot because, since I was a fish, I couldn't live out of water. When I saw how their minds were set on the idea, I decided to be a fish, and I finally convinced myself that I was one: after all, everyone else thought that's what I was, and that the seawater had changed me into one, and they say that the voice of the people is the voice of God. So from then on I was as silent as a man at mass. They took me to the capital, and there they really made a lot of money. Because the people there, being idlers, liked novelties.

Among all the people who came to see me there were two students. They studied the features of my face very carefully, and then, in a low tone, they said that they would swear on the Bible I was a man and not a fish. And they said if they were the authorities they would get at the naked truth by taking a leather strap to our naked shoulders. I was praying to God with all my heart and soul that they would do it, as long as they could get me out of there. I tried to help them by shouting, "You scholars are right." But I hardly had my mouth open when my guard pulled me under the water. Everyone's shouting when I ducked (or, rather, when they dunked me) stopped those good scholars from going on with their talk.

They threw bread to me, and I would bolt it down almost before it had a chance to get wet. They didn't give me half of what I could eat. I remembered the feasts I had in Toledo, how well I ate with my German friends, and that good wine I used to announce in the streets. I prayed to God to repeat the miracle of Cana of Galilee and not let me die at the hands of water—my worst enemy. I thought about what those students had said, which no one heard because of the noise. I realized that I was a man, and I never thought otherwise from then on, although my wife had told me many times that I was a beast, and the boys at Toledo used to say, "Mr. Lazaro, pull your hat down a little—we can see your horns."

All this, along with the sauce I was in, had made me doubt whether or not I really was a man. But after I heard those blessed earthly diviners, I had no more doubts about it, and I tried to escape from the hands of those Chaldeans.

Once, in the dead of night, I saw that my guards were fast asleep, and I tried to get loose. But the ropes around me were wet, and I couldn't. I thought about shouting, but I decided that that wouldn't work, since the first one who heard me would seal my mouth with a half-gallon of water. When I saw that way out cut off, I began to twist around impatiently in the slough, and I struggled and pushed so much that the cask turned over, and me along with it. All the water spilled out, and when I found myself freed I shouted for help.

The fishermen were terrified when they realized what I had done, and they quickly hit on a solution: they stopped up my mouth by stuffing it full of seaweed. And to muddle my shouts, they began to shout themselves, even louder, calling out, "Help, help, call the law!" And as they were doing all this, they filled the cask back up with water from a nearby well, with unbelievable speed. The innkeeper came running out with a battle-ax, and everyone else at the inn came out armed with iron pokers and sticks. All the neighbors came in, along with a constable and six deputies who happened to be passing by. The innkeeper asked the sailors what had happened, and they answered that thieves had tried to steal their fish. And like a madman he began shouting, "Get the thieves, get the thieves!" Some went to see if they had gotten out the door; others went to find out if they were escaping across the rooftops. And as for me, my custodians had put me back in my vat.

It happened that the water that spilled out all ran through a hole in the floor, onto the bed of a room downstairs where the daughter of the house was sleeping. Now this girl had been so moved to charity that she had brought a young priest in with her to spend the night in contemplation. They became so frightened when the deluge fell on the bed and all the people began shouting that they crawled out through a window as naked as Adam

6440.

and Eve, without even a fig leaf to cover their private parts. There was a full moon, and its brightness was so great that it could have competed with the sun. When the people saw them they shouted, "Get the thieves, catch the thieves!" The deputies and the constable ran after the girl and the priest and quickly caught up with them because they were barefoot and the stones on the ground made it difficult for them to run. And in one swoop they led them off to jail. Early next morning the fishermen left Madrid to go to Toledo, and they never did find out what God had done with that simple little maiden and the devout priest.

VI. How They Took Lazaro to Toledo

Man's efforts are vain, his knowledge is nil, and he has
no ability when God does not strengthen, teach, and
guide him. All my efforts only served to make my guards
more wary and careful. The outburst of the night before
made them very angry, and they beat me so much along
the road that they nearly left me for dead. They said,
"You damned fish—you were trying to get away. If we
weren't so kindhearted, we would kill you. You're like an
oak tree that won't give up its acorns unless it's beaten."

The fishermen took me into Toledo, pounded, cursed,
and dying of hunger. They found a place to stay, near the
square of Zocodover, at the house of a lady whose wines
I used to announce. They put me in a room downstairs,
and many people came to see me. One of them was my
Elvira, leading my daughter by the hand. When I saw
them I couldn't hold back two Nile Rivers of tears that
flowed from my eyes. I sighed and wept—but to myself
so the fishermen wouldn't deprive me of what I loved so
much and what I wanted to feast my eyes on. Although it
might have been better if those men who took away my
voice had taken away my sight, too, because when I
looked at my wife carefully I saw—I don't know if I
should say it—she looked like she was about to go into
labor. I sat there absolutely amazed, although I shouldn't
have been if I had thought about it because my lord the
archdeacon told me when I left that city to go to war that

he would treat her as if she were his very own. What really bothered me was that I couldn't convince myself that she was pregnant by me because I had been gone for more than a year.

When we were living together she used to say to me, "Lazaro, don't think I'm cheating on you, because if you do you're very wrong." And I was so satisfied that I avoided thinking anything bad about her the way the devil avoids holy water. I spent my life happy and content and not at all jealous (which is a madman's sickness). Time and again I have thought to myself that this business of children is all a matter of belief. Because how many men are there who love children they think are their own when the only thing they have in common is their name? And there are others who hate their children because they get the notion that their wives have put horns on their heads.

I began to count the days and months, and I found the road to my consolation closed off. Then I began to think that my wife might have dropsy. I didn't go on with this pious meditation very long because as soon as she left, two old women began to talk to each other: "What do you think of that archpriestess? She certainly doesn't need her husband around." "Who is the father?" asked the other. "Who?" answered the first, "Why, the archpriest. And he's such a good man that, to avoid the scandal that would spread if she gave birth in his house without a husband, he's going to marry her to that foreigner, Pierre, next Sunday, and that fellow will be just as understanding as my friend, Lazaro."

This was the last straw—the *non plus ultra*—of my understanding. My heart began to break out in a sweat in the water, and without being able to lift a hand I fainted in that hogsty. The water began to pour into me through every door and window, without any resistance. I looked like I was dead (although it was completely against my will, because I wanted to live as long as I could and as long as God would let me, in spite of those damned fishermen and my bad luck).

The fishermen were very upset, and they made everyone leave. Then they very quickly lifted my head out of the water. When they saw that I had no pulse and that I'd stopped breathing, they did, too. They started to moan over what they had lost (which was no small amount for them), and they took me out of the cask. Then they tried to make me vomit up all I had drunk, but that was useless because death had come in and closed the door behind. When they saw all their dreams gone up in smoke, they turned as ashen as lilies on the Sunday after Easter. They couldn't think of any way to abet or abate their trials and troubles. The Council of Three finally decreed that the following night they would take me to the river and throw me in with a stone tied around my neck so that what had caused my death would also be my grave.

VII. *What Happened to Lazaro on the Way to the Tagus River*

Never lose hope no matter how miserable you are, because when you least expect it God will open the doors and windows of His mercy and will show that nothing is impossible for Him, and that He has the knowledge, the ability, and the desire to change the plans of the wicked into healthful, beneficial remedies for those who trust in Him. Those brutal executioners decided that Death wasn't joking (it seldom does), so they put me in a sack, threw me across the back of a donkey like a wineskin—or rather a waterskin, since I was full of water up to my mouth—and started out along the road of Cuesta de Carmen. And they were more sorrowful than if they were going to bury the father who gave them life and the mother who bore them.

It was my good fortune that when they put me on the mule, I was belly side down. Since my head was hanging downward, I began to spew out water as if they had lifted the floodgates on a dam, or as if I were a drop hammer. I came to, and when I caught my breath I realized that I was out of the water and out of that blasted hairy mess. I didn't know where I was or where they were taking me. I only heard them saying, "For our own safety we'll have to find a very deep well so they won't discover him so soon." Then I saw the handwriting on the wall and guessed what was happening. I knew that

their bark could be no worse than their bite, and when I heard people approaching I called, "Help, help, for God's sake!"

The people I had noticed were the night watch, and they ran up when they heard my cries, their swords out and ready. They searched the sack, and they found poor Lazaro—a drenched haddock. Body and soul, they took us all off to jail on the spot: the fishermen were crying to see themselves imprisoned, and I was laughing to find myself free.

They put them in a cell and me in a bed. The next morning they took our statements. The fishermen confessed that they had carried me all over Spain, but they said that they had done it thinking I was a fish and that they had asked for the Inquisition's permission to do it. I told them the truth of the matter: how those fiends had tied me up so that I couldn't make a peep. They had the archpriest and my good Bridget come to testify as to whether or not I really was the Lazaro of Tormes I said I was. My wife came in first, and she looked me over very carefully, and then said it was true that I did look something like her good husband, but she didn't think I was him because even though I had been an animal, I was more like a drone than a fish, and more like a bullock than a tuna. After saying this she made a deep bow and left.

The attorney for those hangmen said I should be burned because I was undoubtedly a monster, and he was going to prove it.

I thought to myself: What if there really is an enchanter following me and changing me into anything he likes?

The judges told him to be quiet. Then the archpriest came in. He saw me looking as pale and wrinkled as an

old lady's belly, and he said he didn't recognize my face or my figure. I refreshed his memory about some past things (many of them secret) that had happened between us; I especially told him to think back on the night he came to my bed naked and said that he was afraid of a ghost in his bedroom, and then crawled into bed between my wife and me. So that I wouldn't go on with these reminders, he confessed that I really was his good friend and servant, Lazaro.

The trial ended with the testimony of the captain who had taken me with him from Toledo. He was one of those who escaped the storm in a skiff, and he confessed that I was, in fact, his servant Lazaro. The time and place the fishermen said they had fished me out supported that. The judges sentenced them to two hundred whippings apiece and the confiscation of their belongings: a third of it would be given to the King, a third to the prisoners, and a third to Lazaro. They found them with two thousand pieces of silver, two mules, and a cart, and after the costs and expenditures were paid I got two hundred pieces of silver. The sailors were plucked and skinned, and I was rich and happy because I had never in my life been the owner of so much money at one time.

I went to the house of a friend of mine, and after I had downed a few pitchers of wine to get rid of the bad taste of the water and was feeling mellow, I began to strut around like a count and to eat like a king; I was esteemed by my friends, feared by my enemies, and wooed by everyone. My past troubles seemed like a dream to me, my present luck was like a port of leisure, and my future hopes a paradise of delights. Hardships humiliate, prosperity makes a man haughty. For the time those two hundred silver pieces lasted, if the King had called me his cousin I would have taken it as an insult.

When we Spaniards get a silver coin, we're princes, and even if we don't have one we still have the vanity that goes with it. If you ask some shabby beggar who he is, he'll tell you at the very least that he is of noble blood and that his bad luck has him backed into a corner, and that's how this mad world is: it raises those who are on the bottom and lowers those who are on top. But even though it is that way, he won't give in to anyone, he puts only the highest value on himself, and he will die of hunger before he'll work. And if Spaniards do take a job or learn something, they have such contempt for it that either they won't work or, if they do, their work is so bad that you can hardly find a good craftsman anywhere in Spain.

I remember there was a cobbler in Salamanca, and whenever anyone brought him something to fix, he would deliver a soliloquy, complaining that fate had put him in such straits that he had to work in this lowly position when the good name of his family was so well known all over Spain. One day I asked one of his neighbors who that bragger's parents were. They told me his father was a grape stomper, and in winter a hogkiller, and that his mother was a belly washer (I mean the maid for a tripe merchant).

I bought a worn-out velvet suit and a ragged cast-off cape from Segovia. The sword I wore was so enormous that its tip would unpave the streets as I walked. I didn't want to go and see my wife when I got out of jail so that she would want to see me even more, and also to take revenge for the disdain for me that she was carrying around inside herself. I really thought that when she saw me so well-dressed she would repent and greet me with open arms. But obstinate she was, and obstinate she remained. I found her with a new baby and a new husband. When she saw me she shouted, "Get that damn

6445.

drenched fish—that plucked goose—out of my sight because, if you don't, I swear on my father's grave that I'll
get up and poke his eyes out!"

And I answered very coolly, "Not so fast, Mrs. Street-
walker. If you won't admit I'm your husband, then
you're not my wife either. Give me my daughter, and
we'll still be friends. I have enough of a fortune now," I
went on, "to marry her to a very honorable man."

I thought those two hundred pieces of silver would
turn out to be like the fifty silver coins of little Blessed
John who, every time he spent them, would find fifty
more in his purse. But since I was little Bedeviled
Lazaro, it didn't turn out that way with me, as you will
see in the next chapter.

The archpriest contested my demand. He said she
wasn't mine, and to prove it he showed me the baptismal
book, and when it was compared to the marriage
records, it was evident that the child had been born four
months after I knew my wife. Up to then I had felt as
spirited as a stallion, but I suddenly realized they had
made an ass of me: my daughter wasn't mine at all. I
shook the dust off my feet and washed my hands to show
my innocence and that I was leaving for good. I turned
my back on them, feeling as content as if I had never
known them. I went looking for my friends and told
them what had happened; they consoled me—which
wasn't hard for them to do.

I didn't want to go back to my job as a town crier
because my new velvet clothes had changed my self-
esteem. While I was taking a walk to the Visagra gate I
met an old woman, a friend of mine, at the gate of the
convent of San Juan de los Reyes. After she greeted me
she told me that my wife had softened when she'd found
out about all the money I had, especially now that that
Frenchman had chastened her.

I begged her to tell me what had happened. She said the archpriest and my wife had talked one day about whether it would be a good idea to take me back in and throw Frenchy out; and they discussed the pros and cons of it. But their discussion was not so secret that the bridegroom didn't hear it. He pretended he hadn't heard a thing, and the next morning he went to work at the olive grove. At noon, when his wife and mine brought his lunch out to him, he pulled off all her clothes, tied her to the trunk of a tree, and gave her more than a hundred lashes. And still not satisfied, he made all her clothes into a bundle, took off her jewelry, and walked away with it all, leaving her tied up, naked and bleeding. She would undoubtedly have died there if the archpriest hadn't sent someone looking for her.

The lady also told me she was absolutely sure that if I arranged for somebody to ask her, she would welcome me back, because she had heard my Elvira say, "Poor me, why didn't I take back my good Lazaro? He was as good as could be. He was never critical or particular, and I could do whatever I wanted."

This was the touch that turned me, and I was thinking of taking the good old woman's advice, but first I wanted to talk it over with my friends.

VIII. *How Lazaro Brought a Lawsuit against His Wife*

We men are like barnyard hens: if we want to do something good we shout it out and cackle about it; but if it's something bad, we don't want anybody to find out so they won't stop us from doing what we shouldn't. I went to see one of my friends, and I found three of them there together; because after I had come into money, they multiplied like flies. I told them what I wanted to do—go back to my wife and get away from wagging tongues because "Better certain evil than doubtful good." They painted a black picture to me and said I was spineless and that I didn't have a brain in my body because the woman I wanted to live with was a whore, a hussy, a trollop, a slut, and, finally, a devil's mule. (That's what they call a priest's mistress in Toledo.)

My friends said so many things to me and gave me so many arguments that I decided not to beg or even ask my wife. When my good friends (damned friends, anyway) saw that their arguments and advice had done their work, they went even further. They said they were advising me, because I was such a good friend, to remove the spots and the stains on my honor and to defend it, since it had fallen into such bad times, by suing the archpriest and my wife. They said it wouldn't cost so much as a penny since they were lawyers.

One of them was an attorney for lost causes, and he

offered me a thousand pieces of silver from the profits. The other one was more knowledgeable because he was a prostitutes' lawyer, and he told me that if he were in my shoes he wouldn't take less than two thousand. The third one assured me (and since he was a bumbailiff, he knew what he was talking about) that he had seen other lawsuits that were less clear, that had brought the people who began them an enormous amount of money. Furthermore, he thought that at the first confrontation that *Domine Baccalaureus* would fill my hands and anoint the lawyers' to make us withdraw the lawsuit, and that he would beg me to go back to my wife. So I would get more honor and profit from it than if I went back to her on my own.

My friends commended this business to me highly, luring me on with high hopes. I was taken in right then. I didn't know what to say to their sophist arguments, although it really seemed to me that it would be better to forgive and forget than to go to extremes, and that I should carry out the most difficult of God's commandments (the fourth one), which is to love your enemies— especially since my wife had never acted like an enemy to me. In fact, it was because of her that I had begun to rise in the world and become known by many people who would point at me and say, "There goes that nice fellow, Lazaro."

Because of my wife I was somebody. If the daughter that the archdeacon said wasn't mine, was or wasn't, only God, who looks into men's hearts, knows. It could be that he was fooled just the way I was. And it could happen that some of the people who are reading and laughing over my simpleness so hard they slobber on their beards might be raising the children of some ignorant priest. They might be working, sweating, and striving to leave the very ones rich who will impoverish their honor, and all the time they are so sure that if there is any woman in the world who is faithful, it's their wife. And even your name, dear reader—Lord Whitehall—might really come from Wittol.

But I don't want to destroy anyone's illusions. All these reflections still weren't enough, so I took out a lawsuit against the archpriest and my wife. Since there was ready money, they had them in jail inside of twenty-four hours: him in the archbishop's prison and her in the public one. The lawyers told me not to worry about the money that that business could cost me since it would all come out of that priest's hide. So, to make it even worse for the priest and to raise the costs, I gave whatever they asked me. They were walking around diligent, solicitous, and energetic. When they smelled my cash, they were like flies on honey: they didn't take a step in vain.

In less than a week the lawsuit had moved far ahead, and my pocketbook had lost as much ground. The evidence was gathered easily because the constables who arrested my wife and the archpriest caught them in the act and had taken them off to jail in their nightshirts, the way they found them. There were many witnesses who told the truth. My good lawyers and counselors and the court clerk saw how thin and weak my pocketbook was getting, and they began to falter. It reached the point where I had to spur them harder than a hired mule to get them to make a move.

The slowdown was so great that when the archpriest and his group heard about it, they started crowing and anointing the hands and feet of my representatives. They seemed like the weights on a clock that were going up just as fast as mine were coming down. They managed it so well that in two weeks the archpriest and my wife were out of jail on bond, and in less than one week more they condemned Lazaro with false witnesses so that he

had to apologize, pay the court costs, and be banished from Toledo forever.

I apologized the way I should have, since with only two hundred silver pieces I had taken a lawsuit out against a man who had that much money to burn. I gave them the shirt off my back to help pay the court costs, and I left the city in the raw.

There I was, rich for an instant, suing a dignitary of the Holy Church of Toledo, an undertaking fit only for a prince. I had been respected by my friends, feared by my enemies, in the position of a gentleman who wouldn't put up with a whisper of aspersion. And just as suddenly I found myself thrown out—not from any earthly paradise with figleaves to cover my private parts, but from the place I loved most and where I had gotten so much comfort and pleasure, using some rags I found in a rubbish heap to cover my nakedness.

I took refuge in the common consolation of all unfortunates. I thought that since I was at the bottom of the wheel of fortune I would be certain to go back up. I recall now what I once heard my master, the blind man (who was like a fox whenever he started to preach), say: Every man in the world rose and fell on the wheel of fortune; some followed the movement of the wheel, and others went against it. And there was this difference between them: those who followed the wheel's movement fell as quickly as they rose; and those who went against it, once they reached the top—even if they had to work hard at it—they stayed there longer than the others. According to this, I was going right with the grain—and so quickly that I was barely on top when I found myself in the abyss of misery.

I found myself a picaro—and a real one, since I had only been pretending up to then. And I could really say:

Naked was I born, naked am I now, nothing lost and nothing gained.

I started off toward Madrid, begging along the way since that was something I knew how to do very well. So there I was again, back at my trade. I told everyone about my troubles: some felt sorry, others laughed, and some gave me alms. Since I had no wife or children to support, with what they gave me I had more than enough to eat, and to drink, too. That year people had harvested so many grapes for wine that at nearly every door I went to they asked if I wanted anything to drink, because they didn't have any bread to give me. I never refused, and so sometimes I would down a good two gallons of wine before eating anything, and I'd be happier than a girl on the eve of a party.

Let me tell you what I really think: the picaresque life is the only life. There is nothing in the world like it. If rich men tried it, they would give up their estates for it, just the way the ancient philosophers gave up all they possessed to go over to that life. I say "go over" because the life of a philosopher and the life of a picaro is the same. The only difference is that philosophers gave up all they had for their love of that kind of life, and picaros find it without giving up anything. Philosophers abandoned their estates to contemplate natural and divine things, the movements of the heavens, with less distraction; picaros do it to sow all their wild oats. Philosophers threw their goods into the sea; picaros throw them in their stomachs. Philosophers despised those things as vain and transitory; while picaros don't care for them because they bring along cares and work—something that goes against their profession. So the picaresque life is more leisurely than the life of kings, emperors, and popes. I decided to travel this road because it was freer, less dangerous, and never sad.

IX.   How Lazaro Became a Baggage Carrier

There is no position, no science or art a man does not have to apply all his intelligence to if he wants to perfect his knowledge of it. Suppose a cobbler has been working at his job for thirty years. Tell him to make you a pair of shoes that are wide at the toe, high at the instep, with laces.

Will he make them? Before you get a pair the way you asked him, your feet will be shriveled. Ask a philosopher why a fly's stool comes out black when it's on a white object and white when it's on something black. He'll turn as red as a maiden who is caught doing it by candlelight, and he won't know what to answer. Or if he does answer this question, he won't be able to answer a hundred other tomfooleries.

Near the town of Illescas, I ran into a fellow who I knew was an archpicaro by the way he looked. I went up to him the way I would to an oracle to ask him how I should act in this new life of mine so I wouldn't be arrested. He said that if I wanted to keep free of the law I should combine Mary's idleness with Martha's work. In other words, if I was going to be a picaro I should also be a kitchenhelper, a brothel servant, a slaughterhouse boy, or a baggage carrier, which was a way of covering up for the picaresque life. Furthermore, he said that because he hadn't done this, even after the twenty years he'd been following his profession, they had just yesterday whipped him up one side and down the other for being a tramp.

I thanked him for the warning and took his advice. When I got to Madrid I bought a porter's strap and stood in the middle of the square, happier than a cat with gibblets. As luck would have it, the first person to put me to work was a maiden (God forgive my lie) about eighteen years old, but more primped up than a novice in a convent. She told me to follow her. She took me down so many streets that I thought she was getting paid for walking or was playing a trick on me. After a while we came to a house that I recognized as one of ill repute when I saw the side door, the patio, and the beastly old maids dancing there.

We went into her cell, and she asked me if I wanted her to pay me for my work before we left. I told her I would wait until we got to the place where I was taking the bundle. I loaded it on my back and started down the road to the Guadalajara gate. She told me to put it in a carriage to go to the Nagera fair. The load was light since it was mainly made up of mortars, cosmetics, and perfume bottles. On the way I found out that she had been in that profession for eight years.

"The first one to prick me," she said, "was the Father Rector at Seville, where I'm from, and he did it with such devotion that from that day to this I'm very devoted to them. He put me in the charge of a holy woman, and she provided me with everything I needed for more than six months. Then a captain took me from there. And since that time I've been led from pillar to post until here I am, like this. I wish to God I had never left that good father who treated me like a daughter and loved me like his sister. Anyway, I've had to work just to be able to eat."

At this time we came up to a carriage that was about to leave. I put the things I was carrying in it and asked her to pay me for my work. The chatterbox said she would be glad to, and she hauled off and hit me so hard she knocked me to the ground. Then she said, "Are you so stupid that you ask someone of my profession for money? Didn't I tell you before we left the brothel that I would give you satisfaction there for your work if you wanted?"

She jumped into the carriage like a nag and spurred the horses away, leaving me feeling the sting. So there I sat, like a jackass, not sure what had happened to me. I thought that if that job finished as well as it was starting out, I would be rich by the end of the year.

I hadn't even left there when another carriage arrived from Alcala de Henares. The people inside jumped down: they were all whores, students, and friars. One of them belonged to the Franciscan order, and he asked me if I would like to carry his bundle to his monastery. I told him I would be glad to because I saw that he certainly wouldn't trick me the way the whore had done. I loaded it onto my back, and it was so heavy I could barely carry it, but I thought of the payment I would get, and that gave me strength. When we reached the monastery I was very tired because it had been so far. The friar took his bundle and said, "May heaven reward you," and then he closed the door behind him.

I waited for him to come back out and pay me, but when I saw how long he was taking, I knocked on the door. The gatekeeper came out and asked me what I wanted. I told him I wanted to be paid for carrying the bundle I'd brought. He told me to go away, that they didn't pay anything there. As he closed the door he told me not to knock again because it was the hour for medi-

tations, and if I did he would whip me thoroughly. I stood there, stupified. A poor man—one of those who were standing inside the vestibule—said to me, "Brother, you might as well go away. These fathers never have any money. They live on what other people give them."

"They can live on whatever they want to, but they'll pay me or I'm not Lazaro of Tormes."

I began to knock again very angrily. The lay brother came out even angrier, and without saying so much as, How do you do? he knocked me to the ground like a ripe pear, and holding me down, he kicked me a good half-dozen times, then pounded me just as much, and left me flattened out as if the clocktower of Saragossa had fallen on top of me.

I lay there, stretched out, for more than a half-hour without being able to get up. I thought about my bad luck and that the strength of that irregular clergyman had been used so badly. He would have been better off serving under His Highness, the King, than living from alms for the poor—although they aren't even good for that since they're so lazy. The Emperor, Charles V, pointed this out when the General of the Franciscans offered him twenty-two-thousand friars, who wouldn't be over forty or under twenty-two years old, to fight in the war. The invincible Emperor answered that he didn't want them because he would have needed twenty-two-thousand pots of stew every day to keep them alive, inferring that they were more fit for eating than working.

God forgive me, but from that day to this I've hated those clergymen so much that whenever I see them they look to me like lazy drones or sieves that lift the meat out of the stew and leave the broth. I wanted to leave that work, but first I waited there that night, stretched out like a corpse waiting for his funeral.

X. *What Happened to Lazaro with an Old Bawd*

Feeling faint and dying from hunger, I went up the street very slowly, and as I passed by the Plaza of Cebada I ran into an old devout woman with fangs longer than a wild boar. She came up to me and asked if I wanted to carry a trunk to the house of a friend of hers, saying that it wasn't far away and that she would give me forty coppers. When I heard that, I praised God to hear such sweet words coming from such a foul-smelling mouth as hers: she would give me forty coppers! I told her I would, with pleasure—but my real pleasure was being able to grab onto those forty coppers rather than to carry anything, since I was more in a condition to be carried than to carry. I loaded the trunk on my back, but it was so big and heavy I could barely lift it. The good old woman told me to handle it carefully because inside were some perfume bottles that she prized highly. I told her not to worry because I would walk very slowly. (And even if I had wanted to I couldn't have done anything else: I was so hungry I could barely waddle.)

We reached the house we were taking the chest to. They were very happy to get it, especially a young maiden, plump and dimpled (I was wishing that after I'd eaten a good meal and was in bed, the lice there looked like her): she smiled happily and said she wanted the trunk in her dressing room. I took it there: the old lady

gave her the key and told her to keep it until she got back from Segovia. She said she was going there to visit a relative of hers, and she thought she would be back in four days. She gave the girl a hug before she left and whispered a few words in her ear that turned the maiden as red as a rose. And although I thought that was nice, I would have thought it was nicer if I had had plenty to eat. She said good-by to everyone in the house, and asked the girl's father and mother to forgive her for being so bold. They told her she was welcome there anytime. She gave me forty coppers and whispered in my ear to come back to her house the next morning and I would earn forty more.

I went away, happier than a bride in June. I spent thirty coppers on supper, and kept ten to pay for a room. I thought about the power of money. As soon as that old woman gave me the forty coppers I found myself lighter than the wind, more valiant than Roland, and stronger than Hercules. Oh, money, it is not without reason that most men consider you their God. You are the cause of all good, and the root of all evil. You are the inventor of all the arts and the one who keeps them excellent. Because of you some maidens remain pure and other maidens give up their purity. Finally, there is no difficulty in the world difficult for you, no hidden place that you do not penetrate, no mountain you do not level, no humble hill you do not raise up.

The next morning I went to the old lady's house the way she asked me. She told me to go back with her and pick up the trunk she had left the day before. She told the people at the house that she had come back for it because when she was about a mile from Madrid, on the way to Segovia, she had met her relative who had had the same idea she did and was coming to visit her, and that she had to have it now because there were clean linens in it that she needed for her relative's room. The plumpish girl gave her back the key, kissing and hugging her more eagerly than the first time; and after she had whispered to her again, they helped me load the trunk on my back, and it seemed to me lighter than the day before because my belly was fuller.

As I went down the stairs I stumbled over something that the Devil must have put there. I tripped and fell with the baggage, and as I rolled down to the bottom of the stairs where the parents of the innocent girl were waiting, I broke both my nose and my ribs. With the knocks that damned chest got, it opened up, and inside there appeared a dashing young man with sword and dagger at his side. He was dressed in traveling clothes, without a cloak. His trousers and jacket were of green satin, and in his hat he wore a feather of the same color. He had on red garters with pearl-white stockings and white sandals. He stood up very elegantly, and making a deep bow he walked right out the door. Everyone stood there agape at the sudden vision, and they looked at each other like wooden puppets.

When they came out of their trance, they quickly called two of their sons and told them what had happened. With a great outcry the sons grabbed their swords, and shouted, "Kill him, kill him!" They ran out looking for that dandy, but since he had left in a hurry, they weren't able to catch up with him.

The parents had stayed behind in the house, and they closed the door and went to take revenge on the bawd. But she had heard the noise and knew what the cause of it was, and she went out a back door with the eternal bride-to-be right behind her. So the parents found themselves totally taken in. They came back down to take

176

their revenge out on me, and I was all crippled up, unable to move. If it hadn't been for that, I would have been right behind that fellow who had caused all my damage. The brothers came in sweating and panting, vowing and swearing that since they hadn't caught that wretch, they would kill their sister and the go-between. But when they were told they had gotten away by the back door, there was swearing and cursing everywhere.

One of them said, "If only the Devil himself were here right now with all his hellish throng: I would polish them off like flies. Come on, you devils, come on! But what am I calling you for? I know that where you are, you're so afraid of my temper you wouldn't dare show yourselves here. If I'd seen that coward, I would only have had to breathe hard on him, and he would have blown so far away you'd never hear of him again."

The other one said, "If I had caught up with him, I wouldn't have left a piece of him bigger than his ear. But if he's to be found anywhere in this world—or even if he's not—he won't escape my hands. I'll get him even if he hides in the center of the earth."

They kept on with these boasts and other empty threats, and poor Lazaro was expecting all those heavy clouds to unload on him. But he was more afraid of the ten or twelve little boys there than of those braggers. Everyone, old and young, attacked me in a fury: some kicked me, others hit me with their fists; some pulled my hair, others boxed my ears. My fear hadn't been in vain because the girls stuck long penny needles into me, and that made me cry out at the top of my lungs. The family slaves pinched me until I saw stars.

Some of them said, "Let's kill him."

Others said, "Better yet, let's throw him in the privy."

The clamor was so great it sounded like they were

179

pulverizing chaff, or that they were hammers in a fulling mill that weren't letting up. When they saw that I was out of breath, they stopped beating me, but they didn't stop threatening me. Since the father was more mature, or more rotten, he told them to leave me alone, and he said that if I would tell the truth about who had robbed him of his honor, they wouldn't hurt me any more. I couldn't do what he asked because I didn't know who the fellow was: I had never even seen him before he'd come out of the casket. Since I didn't say anything, they started in again. And there I was groaning, crying over my bad luck, sighing, and cursing my misfortune since it was always finding new ways to persecute me. I was finally able to tell them to stop and I would tell them the facts of the matter. They did, and I told them to the letter what had happened, but they wouldn't believe the truth.

Seeing that the storm wasn't letting up, I decided to outwit them if I could, and so I promised to show them the villain. They stopped hammering on me and offered me wonders. They asked me what his name was and where he lived. I told them I didn't know his name, much less that of the street he lived on, but if they wanted to carry me (it was impossible for me to go on foot because of the way they had beaten me), I would show them his house. They were delighted, and they gave me a little wine, so that I recovered my spirits a bit. Then they gathered all their weapons, and two of them picked me up under the arms like a French lady and carried me through the streets of Madrid.

The people who saw me said, "They're taking that man to jail."

And others said, "No, it's to the hospital."

And none of them were right. I was confused and

stunned. I didn't know what to do or what to say. Because if I cried for help, they would complain about me to the law, and I was more afraid of that than death. It was impossible for me to run away, not only because of the beating they had given me, but because I was surrounded by the father, sons, and relatives—eight or nine of them had gotten together for the enterprise. They were walking along, like Saint George, armed to the teeth.

We crossed streets and passed by alleys without my knowing where I was or where I was taking them. We reached the Sol Gate, and I saw a gallant young fellow coming up one of the streets that led to it, prancing on tiptoe, his cape under his arm, with a huge glove in one hand and a carnation in the other, swinging his arms like he was the first cousin of the Duke of Infantado. He was moving his hands and swaying back and forth. I recognized him immediately: it was my master, the squire, who had stolen my clothes in Murcia. I don't doubt for a minute but that some saint put him there for me (because there wasn't one left in the litany that I hadn't called on). When I saw opportunity knocking, I grabbed it by the head and decided to kill two birds with one stone—taking vengeance on that bragger and freeing myself from those hangmen.

So I said to them, "Look! That libertine who stole your honor is coming this way, and he's changed his clothes."

They were blind with rage, and without further ado they asked me which one he was. I pointed him out. They fell on him, and grabbing him by the collar, they threw him to the ground and kicked, trampled, and clouted him. One of the boys, a brother of the girl, wanted to run him through with his sword, but his father stopped him and called the law officers over, and they put shackles on the squire. When I saw all the turmoil and everyone busy, I made myself scarce and hid as well as I could.

My good squire had recognized me, and thinking that those were relatives of mine demanding my clothes back, he said, "Let me go, let me go! I'll pay you enough for two suits of clothes!"

But they stopped up his mouth with their fists. Bleeding, his head pounded in, and beaten to a pulp, they took him off to jail while I left Madrid, damning my job and whoever had invented it.

*XI.   How Lazaro Left for His Homeland
       and What Happened to Him
       on the Way*

I wanted to be on my way, but my strength wasn't equal
to my intentions, and so I stayed in Madrid for a few
days. I didn't get along badly there because I used a pair
of crutches—since I couldn't walk without them—and I
begged from door to door and from convent to convent
until I had enough strength to set out. I was quick to do
it because of what I heard a beggar tell who was sitting
in the sun with some others, picking off fleas.

It was the story of the trunk I've just told about, but
the beggar added that the man they put in jail, thinking
he was the one who had been inside the chest, had
proved it wasn't him. Because at the time it had all happened he was in his room; and none of his neighbors had
ever seen him wearing any other clothes than the ones he
had on when they arrested him. But even at that, they
had still paraded him through the streets for being a
vagabond, and had banished him from Madrid. The beggar also told how that man and the maiden's relatives
were looking for a baggage carrier, who had contrived
the whole business, and they swore that the first one who
found him would run him through until he looked like a
sieve.

When I heard that, I was all eyes, and I put a patch

185

over one of them. Then I shaved off my beard like a mock priest, and the way I looked then, I was sure that not even the mother who bore me would have recognized me. I left Madrid, intending to go to Tejares to see whether fortune would disown me if I went back to the mold. I passed by the Escorial, a building that reflects the greatness of the monarch who was having it built (it wasn't finished yet) and so much so that it can be counted among the wonders of the world, although you can't say it is a very pleasant place to have it built at, since the land is barren and mountainous. But the summer air is so nice that all you have to do is sit in the shade and you won't be bothered by the heat or the cold, and the air is very healthy.

Less than three miles from there I met a band of gypsies who had set up camp in an old country house. When they saw me from a distance they thought I was one of them because my clothes seemed to promise no less; but when I got close they saw they were mistaken. They shunned me a little because, as I saw, they were holding a conference or debate on thievery. They told me that wasn't the road to Salamanca but to Valladolid. Since my business didn't force me to go to one place instead of any other, I told them that if that's the way it was, I wanted to see that city before I went back to my own town.

One of the oldest men there asked me where I was from, and when I told him Tejares, he invited me to eat with them because we were almost neighbors: he was from Salamanca. I accepted, and afterwards they asked me to tell about myself and my life. I did (they didn't have to ask me twice), with the fewest and shortest words that such great things allowed. When I came to the part about the barrel and what happened to me at the innkeeper's place in Madrid, they burst into laughter, especially a man and woman gypsy who nearly split their sides. I began to feel ashamed, and my face turned red.

The gypsy who was my neighbor saw me blushing, and he said, "Don't be ashamed, brother. These people aren't laughing at you; your life is more deserving of admiration than laughter. And since you have told us so much about yourself, it is only right that we should repay you the same way. We will put our trust in you just as you have trusted us. And if the people here will allow me, I will tell you the reason for their laughter."

Everyone told him to go ahead because they knew he was discreet and experienced enough not to let things go too far.

"For your information, then," he continued, "those people who are laughing over there are the maiden and the priest who jumped *in puribus* when the deluge from your barrel nearly flooded them. If they want to they can tell you how the turns of fortune have brought them to their present state."

The brand new gypsy girl asked them to let her do it, capturing the benevolence of the illustrious audience, and so, with a sonorous, peaceful, and grave voice, she told her story.

"The day I left, or leaped (to be more accurate), from my father's house and they took me off to prison, they put me in a room that was darker than it was clean and that reeked more than it was decorated. Father Urbez, who is here and won't let me lie, was put in jail until I told them he was a priest. Then they immediately gave him over to the bishop, who scolded him severely for having let himself be overcome by a drop in the ocean and for having caused such a scandal. But when he promised to be more careful and watch himself so that

not even the ground would know of his comings and goings, they let him loose and told him not to say mass for a month.

"I stayed in the warden's charge, and since he was a young, handsome fellow and I was not a bad-looking girl, he took special care of me. For me, jail was a palace—a garden of pleasures. My parents were indignant at my looseness but did what they could so I could get loose. But it was useless: the warden arranged things so I wouldn't escape his hands. Meanwhile the priest, who is here with us, was walking around the prison like an Irish setter, trying to get to talk to me. He was able to do it by means of a third party who was first in the bawdry business. She dressed him up like one of her maids, in a skirt and blouse, then she put a muffler over his beard, as if he had a toothache. At this interview my escape was planned.

"The next night there was a party at the house of Count Miranda, and some gypsies were going to dance at the end of it. Canil (that's the name of Reverend Urbez now) arranged for them to help him with his plans. The gypsies did everything so well that, because of their cleverness, we got the liberty we wanted and their company, too—the best on earth. The afternoon before the party I smiled at the warden more than a cat at a tripe stand, and I made more promises than a sailor in a storm. Feeling favored by them, he answered with just as many and begged me to ask him for anything and he would give it, as long as it wasn't to lose sight of me. I thanked him very much and told him that if I lost sight of him that would be the worst thing that could happen to me. Seeing that I had struck home, I begged him— since he could do it—to take me to the party that night. He thought it would be difficult, but not to go back on

189

his promise and because the little blind archer had wounded him with an arrow, he gave his word.

"The chief constable was in love with me, too, and he had ordered all the guards, and even the warden, to take care of me and not to move me anywhere. To keep it secret, the warden dressed me up like a page in a damask green suit, trimmed in gold. The cloak was velvet of the same color, lined with yellow satin; the brimmed cap had feathers and a little diamond band. The neck was scalloped lace, the stockings were straw-colored with large, embroidered garters, the shoes were white with a perforated design, and there was a gilded sword and dagger like those made by Ayresvola.

"We came to the hall where there were large numbers of ladies and gentlemen: the men were gallant and jovial, the ladies were elegant and beautiful, and many kept their faces covered with shawls and capes. Canil was dressed like a braggadocio, and when he saw me he came up to my side, so that I was standing between him and the warden.

"The festivities began, and I saw things I won't tell about since they're beside the point. The gypsies came out to dance and do tumbling tricks. Two of them began to have words about their tumbling; one word led to another, and the first one called the other a liar. The one who had been called a liar brought his knife down on the other one's head, and so much blood began pouring out you would have thought they had killed an ox. The people there, who thought it was a joke until then, began to run around, shouting, 'Help, help!' Some law officers ran over, and everyone reached for his sword. I pulled out my own, and when I saw it in my hand I trembled at the sight of it. They grabbed the guilty man, and a man who had been put there for that purpose by the gypsies said the warden was there and would take care of him. The chief constable called the warden over to put the murderer in his hands. The warden wanted to take me with him, but he was afraid I might be recognized, and he told me to go over to a corner he pointed out and not to move from there until he came back. When I saw that that crab louse had let go of me I took hold of Father Canil's hand. He was still by my side, and we were in the street like a shot. There we found one of these gentlemen who took us to his camp.

"When the wounded man (whom everyone believed was dead) thought we must have escaped, he got to his feet and said, 'Gentlemen, the joke is over. I'm not hurt, and we did this to brighten up the party.'

"He took off his cap, and inside was an ox bladder on top of a good steel helmet. It had been filled with blood and had burst open when the knife struck it. Everyone began to laugh at the joke except the warden, who didn't like it at all. He went back to the place where he had told me to wait, and when he didn't find me there he started looking for me. He asked an old gypsy woman if she had seen a page of such and such a description, and since she was in on our game she told him she had and that she had heard him say as he was leaving, holding a man's hand, 'Let's go hide in the convent of San Felipe.'

"He quickly went after me, but it did no good because he went east and we were running to the west.

"Before we left Madrid we exchanged my clothes for these, and they gave me two hundred pieces of silver besides. I sold the diamond band for four hundred gold pieces. And when we got here I gave these gentlemen two hundred, as Canil had promised them. That's the story of how I was set free, and if Mr. Lazaro wants anything else, let him ask. We will do for him whatever the gentleman desires."

I thanked her for the courtesy, and as best I could I

took my leave of them all. The good old man walked with me for a few miles. As we were walking along I asked him if those people were all gypsies born in Egypt. He told me there wasn't a damned one from Egypt in Spain: all of them there were really priests, friars, nuns, or thieves who had escaped from jail or from their convents. But the biggest scoundrels of all were the ones who had left their monasteries, exchanging the contemplative life for the active one. The old man went back to his camp, while I rode to Valladolid on the shank's mare.

XII. What Happened to Lazaro in an Inn Three Miles outside of Valladolid

What thoughts I had all along the road about my good gypsies: their way of life, their customs, the way they behaved. It really amazed me that the law let such thieves go around so freely, since everyone knows that their life involves nothing but stealing. Theirs is an asylum—a shelter for thieves, a congregation of apostates, and a school for evil. I was especially astonished that friars would leave a life of rumination to follow the one of ruination and fatigue of the gypsies. I wouldn't have believed what the gypsy told me if he hadn't shown me a gypsy man and woman a mile from the camp, behind the walls of a shelter: he was broad-shouldered, and she was plump. He wasn't sunburned, and she wasn't tanned by harsh weather. One of them was singing a verse from the psalms of David, and the other was answering with another verse. The good old man told me that they were a friar and a nun who had come to his congregation not more than a week ago, wanting to profess a more austere life.

I came to an inn three miles from Valladolid, and I saw the old lady from Madrid, along with the young maiden of yore, sitting in the doorway. A gallant young fellow came out to call them in to eat. They didn't recognize me because of my good disguise: my patch still over one eye and my clothes worn in the roguish style. But I knew I was the Lazaro who had come out of the tomb that had been so harsh on me. I went up to them to see if they would give me anything. But they couldn't because they didn't have anything for themselves. The young man who served as their steward was so generous that, for himself, his sweetheart, and the old bawd, he'd had a tiny bit of pork liver prepared with a sauce. I could have shoveled down everything on the plate in less than two mouthfuls. The bread was as black as the tablecloth, and that looked like a penitent's tunic or a rag for cleaning stoves.

"Eat, my dove," the gentleman said. "This meal is fit for a prince."

The go-between ate without a word so as not to lose any time and because she saw there wasn't enough for all of them. They began to clean up the plate with such gusto that they removed the finish. When the poor, sad meal was over—and it had made them more hungry than full—the gentle lover made excuses by saying the inn didn't have much food.

When I saw they didn't have anything for me, I asked the innkeeper what there was to eat. He told me, "It depends how much you want to pay." He wanted to give me a few chitterlings. I asked him if he had anything else. He offered me a quarter of kid that the lover hadn't wanted because it was too expensive. I wanted to impress them, so I told him to give it to me. I sat down with it at the end of the table, and their stares were a sight to behold. With each mouthful I swallowed six eyes, because those of the lover, the girl, and the bawd were fastened on what I was eating.

"What's going on?" asked the maiden. "That poor

man is eating a quarter of kid, and there was nothing for us but a poor piece of fried liver."

The young fellow answered that he had asked the innkeeper for some partridges, capons or hens, and that he had told him he didn't have anything else to offer. I knew the truth of the matter—that he had put them on that diet because he didn't want to pay or couldn't, but I decided to eat and keep quiet. The kid was like a magnet. Without warning, I found all three of them hovering over my plate.

The brazen-faced little bitch picked up a piece and said, "With your permission, brother." But before she had it, she had the piece in her mouth.

The old woman said, "Don't steal his meal from this poor sinner."

"I'm not stealing it," she answered. "I intend to pay him for it very well."

And in the same breath she began to eat so fast and furiously that it looked like she hadn't eaten in six days. The old woman took a bite to see how it tasted.

"Is it really that good?" said the young man. And he filled his mouth with an enormous piece. When I saw that they were going too far, I picked up everything on the plate and stuck it in my mouth. It was so big that it couldn't go down or up.

While I was in this struggle, two armed men came riding up to the door of the inn, wearing vests and helmets and carrying shields. Each of them had one musket at his side and another on the saddle. They dismounted and gave their mules to a foot servant. They asked the innkeeper if there was anything to eat. He told them he had a good supply of food, and if they liked they could go into the hall while he was preparing it. The old woman had gone over to the door when she heard the noise, and she came back with her hands over her face, bowing as much as a novice monk. She spoke with a wee, tiny voice and was laboriously twisting back and forth like she was going into labor.

As softly and well as she could, she said, "We're lost. Clara's brothers (Clara was the maiden's name) are outside."

The girl began to pull and tear at her hair, hitting herself so hard it was like she was possessed. The young man was courageous, and he consoled her, telling her not to worry, that he could handle everything. I was all ears, with my mouth full of kid, and when I heard that those braggers were there I thought I was going to die of fear. And I would have, too, but since my gullet was closed off, my soul didn't find the door standing open, and it went back down.

The two Cids came in, and as soon as they saw their sister and the bawd they shouted, "Here they are! At last we have them. Now they'll die!"

I was so frightened by their shouts that I fell to the floor, and when I hit I ejected the goat that was choking me. The two women got behind the young man like chicks under a hen's wing running from a hawk. Brave and graceful, he pulled out his sword and went at the brothers so furiously that their fright turned them into statues. The words froze in their mouths, and the swords in their sheaths. The young man asked them what they wanted or what they were looking for, and as he was talking he grabbed one of them and took away his sword. Then he pointed this sword at his eyes, while he held his own sword at the other one's eyes. At every movement he made with the swords, they trembled like leaves. When the old woman and the sister saw the two Rolands so subdued, they went up and disarmed them. The inn-

197

keeper came in at the noise we were all making (I had gotten up and had one of them by the beard).

It all seemed to me like the gentle bulls in my town: boys, when they see them, run away; but they gradually get more and more daring, and when they see they aren't as fierce as they look, they lose all their fear and go right up and throw all kinds of garbage on them. When I saw that those scarecrows weren't as ferocious as they looked, I plucked up my courage and attacked them more bravely than my earlier terror had allowed.

"What's this?" asked the innkeeper. "Who dares to cause such an uproar in my house?"

The women, the gentleman, and I began shouting that they were thieves who had been following us to rob us. When the innkeeper saw them without any weapons, and at our mercy, he said, "Thieves in my house!"

He grabbed hold of them and helped us put them in a cellar, not listening to one word of their protests. Their servant came back from feeding the mules, and he asked where his masters were: the innkeeper put him in with them. He took their bags, their saddle cushions, and their portmanteaus and locked them up, and he gave us the weapons as if they belonged to him. He didn't charge us for the food so that we would sign a lawsuit he had drawn up against them. He said he was a minister of the Inquisition, and as a law officer in that district, he was condemning the three of them to the galleys for the rest of their lives, and to be whipped two hundred times around the inn. They appealed to the Chancery of Valladolid, and the good innkeeper and three of his servants took them there.

When the poor fellows thought they were before the judges, they found themselves before the Inquisitors, because the sly innkeeper had put down on the record some words they had spoken against the officials of the Holy Inquisition (an unpardonable crime). They put the brothers in dark jail cells, and they couldn't write their father or ask anyone to help them the way they had thought they could.

And there we will leave them, well guarded, to get back to our innkeeper, because we met him on the road. He told us that the Inquisitors had commanded him to have the witnesses who had signed the lawsuit appear before them. But, as a friend, he was advising us to go into hiding. The young maiden gave him a ring from her finger, begging him to arrange things so we wouldn't have to appear. He promised he would. But the thief said this to make us leave, so that if they wanted to hear witnesses they wouldn't discover his chicanery (and it wasn't his first).

In two weeks Valladolid was the scene of an *auto de fe*, and I saw the three poor devils come out with other penitents, with gags in their mouths, as blasphemers who had dared speak against the ministers of the Holy Inquisition—a group of people as saintly and perfect as the justice they deal out. All three of them were wearing pointed hats and sanbenitos, and written on them were their crimes and the sentences they had been given. I was sorry to see that poor foot servant paying for something he hadn't done. But I didn't feel as much pity for the other two because they'd had so little on me. The innkeeper's sentence was carried out, with the addition of three hundred lashes apiece, so they were given five hundred and sent to the galleys where their fierce bravado melted away.

I sought out my fortune. Many times, on the street of Magdalena, I ran into my two women friends. But they never recognized me or were aware that I knew them.

After a few days I saw the missionary-minded young maiden in the prisoners' cells where she earned enough to maintain her affair and herself. The old woman carried on her business in that city.

XIII.   *How Lazaro Was a Squire for*
Seven Women at One Time

I reached Valladolid with six silver pieces in my purse because the people who saw me looking so skinny and pale gave me money with open hands, and I didn't take it with closed ones. I went straight to the clothing store, and for four silver coins and a twenty-copper piece I bought a long baize cloak, worn out, torn and unraveled, that had belonged to a Portuguese. With that, and a high, wide-brimmed hat like a Franciscan monk's that I bought for half a silver piece, and with a cane in my hand, I took a stroll around.

People who saw me mocked me. Everyone had a different name for me. Some of them called me a tavern philosopher. Others said, "There goes Saint Peter, all dressed up for his feast day."

And still others: "Oh, Mr. Portugee, would you like some polish for your boots?"

And somebody even said I must be a quack doctor's ghost. I closed my ears like a shopkeeper and walked right past.

After I had gone down a few streets I came upon a woman dressed in a full skirt, with very elegant shoes. She also had on a silk veil that came down to her bosom and had her hand on a little boy's head. She asked me if I knew of any squires around there. I answered that I was the only one I knew of and that if she liked she could use me as her own. It was all arranged in the twinkling of an eye. She promised me sixty coppers for my meals and wages. I took the job and offered her my arm. I threw away the cane because I didn't need it anymore, and I was only using it to appear sickly and move people to pity. She sent the child home, telling him to have the maid set the table and get dinner ready. For more than two hours she took me from pillar to post, up one street and down another.

The lady told me that when she got to the first house we were going to stop at, I was to go up to the house first and ask for the master or mistress of the house, and say, "My lady, Juana Perez (that was her name), is here and would like to pay her respects."

She also told me that whenever I was with her and she stopped anywhere, I was always to take off my hat. I told her I knew what a servant's duties were, and I would carry them out.

I really wanted to see my new mistress's face, but she kept her veil over it, and I couldn't. She told me she wouldn't be able to keep me by herself but that she would arrange for some ladies who were neighbors of hers to use me, and between them they would give me the money she had promised. And meanwhile, until they all agreed—which wouldn't take long—she would give me her share. She asked me if I had a place to sleep. I told her I didn't.

"I'll get you one," she said. "My husband is a tailor, and you can sleep with his apprentices. You couldn't find a better-paying job in the whole city," she continued, "because in three days you'll have six ladies, and each of them will give you ten coppers."

I was nearly dumbstruck to see the pomposity of that woman who appeared to be, at the very least, the wife of

203

a privileged gentleman or of some wealthy citizen. I was also astonished to see that I would have to serve seven mistresses to earn seventy poor coppers a day. But I thought that anything was better than nothing, and it wasn't hard work. That was something I fled from like the Devil, because I was always more for eating cabbage and garlic without working than for working to eat capons and hens.

When we came to her house, she gave me the veil and the shoes to give to the maid, and I saw what I was longing for. The young woman didn't look bad at all to me: she was a sprightly brunette, with a nice figure. The only thing I didn't like was that her face gleamed like a glazed earthen pot.

She gave me the ten coppers and told me to come back two times every day—at eight in the morning and three in the afternoon—to see if she wanted to go out. I went to a pastry shop, and with a ten-copper piece of pie I put an end to my day's wages. I spent the rest of the day like a chameleon because I had spent the money I'd begged along the road. I didn't dare go begging anymore because if my mistress heard about it she would eat me alive.

I went to her house at three o'clock; she told me she didn't want to go out, but she warned me that from then on she wouldn't pay me on the days she didn't go out, and that if she only went out once a day she would give me five coppers and no more. But she said that since she was giving me a place to sleep, she expected to be served before all the others, and she wanted me to call myself *her* servant. For the sort of bed it was, she deserved that and even more. She made me sleep with the apprentices on a large table without a damned thing to cover us but a worn-out blanket.

I spent two days on the miserable food that I could

afford with ten coppers. Then the wife of a tanner joined the fraternity, and she haggled over the ten coppers for more than an hour. Finally, after five days, I had seven mistresses, and my wages were seventy coppers. I began to eat splendidly: the wine I drank wasn't the worst, but it wasn't the best either (I didn't want to overreach my hand and have it lopped off). The five other women were the wife of a constable, a gardener's wife, the niece (or so she said) of a chaplain in the Discalced order, a good-looking, sprightly girl, and a tripe merchant. This last woman I liked best because whenever she gave me the ten coppers she invited me to have some tripe soup, and before I left her house I would have guzzled down three or four bowlsful.

So I was living as content as could be. The last mistress was a devout woman: I had more to do with her than with the others because all she ever did was visit with friars, and when she was alone with them she was in her glory. Her house was like a beehive: some coming, others going, and they all came with their sleeves stuffed with things for her. For me, so I would be a faithful secret-ary, they brought some pieces of meat from their meals, which they put in their sleeves. I have never in my life seen a more hypocritical woman than she was. When she walked down the street she never took her eyes off the ground; her rosary was always in her hand, and she would always be praying on it in the streets. Every woman who knew her begged her to pray to God for them since her prayers were so acceptable to Him. She told them she was a great sinner (and that was no lie), but she was lying with the truth.

Each of my mistresses had her own special time for me to come. When one of them said she didn't want to go out, I went to the next one's house, until I finished my rounds. They told me what time to come back for them and without fail, because if I (sinner that I am) was even a little bit late, the lady would insult me in front of everyone she visited, and she would threaten me, saying that if I kept being so careless she would get another squire who was more diligent, careful, and punctual. Anyone hearing her shout and threaten me so haughtily undoubtedly thought she was paying me two pieces of silver every day and a salary of three hundred silver pieces a year besides. When my mistresses walked down the street each one looked like the wife of the judge over all Castile, or at least, of a judge of the Chancery.

One day it happened that the chaplain's niece and the constable's wife met in a church, and both of them wanted to go home at the same time. The quarrel about which one I would take home first was so loud that it was as though we were in jail. They grabbed hold of me and pulled—one at one side and one at the other—so fiercely that they tore my cloak to shreds. And there I stood, stark naked, because I didn't have a damned thing under it but some ragged underwear that looked like a fish net. The people who saw the fish hook peeping out from the torn underwear laughed their heads off. The church was like a tavern: some were making fun of poor Lazaro; others were listening to the two women dig up their grandparents. I was in such a hurry to gather up the pieces of my cloak that had fallen in their ripeness that I didn't get a chance to listen to what they were saying. I only heard the widow say, "Where does this whore get all her pride? Yesterday she was a water girl, and today she wears taffeta dresses at the expense of the souls in purgatory."

The other woman answered, "This one, the old gossip, got her black frocks at bargain prices from those who pay with a *Deo Gratias*, or a 'be charitable in God's name.' And if I was a water girl yesterday, she's a hot-air merchant today."

The people there separated the women because they had begun to pull each other's hair. I finished picking up the pieces of my poor cloak, and I asked a devout woman there for two pins. Then I fixed it as well as I could and covered up my private parts.

I left them quarreling and went to the tailor's wife's house. She had told me to be there at eleven because she had to go to dinner at a friend's house. When she saw how ragged I looked, she shouted at me, "Do you think you're going to earn my money and escort me like a picaro? I could have another squire with stylish trousers, breeches, a cape and hat, for less than I pay you. And you're always getting drunk on what I give you."

What do you mean, getting drunk? I thought to myself. With seventy coppers that I make a day, at most? And many days my mistresses don't even leave their houses just so that they won't have to pay me a cent. The tailor's wife had them stitch together the pieces of my cloak, and they were in such a hurry that they put some of the pieces on top that belonged on the bottom. And that's the way I went with her.

XIV. Where Lazaro Tells What Happened to Him at a Dinner

We went flying along like a friar who has been invited out to dinner because the lady was afraid there wouldn't be enough left for her. We reached her friend's house, and inside were other women who had been invited, too. They asked my mistress if I would be able to guard the door; she told them I could. They said to me, "Stay here, brother. Today you'll eat like a king."

Many gallant young men came, each one pulling something out of his pocket: this one a partridge, that one a hen; one took out a rabbit, another one a couple of pigeons; this one a little mutton, that one a piece of loin; and someone brought out sausage or blackpudding. One of them even took out a pie worth a silver piece, wrapped up in his handkerchief. They gave it to the cook, and in the meantime they were frolicking around with the ladies, romping with them like donkeys in a new field of rye. It isn't right for me to tell what happened there or for the reader to even imagine it.

After these rituals there came the victuals. The ladies ate the *Aves*, and the young men drank the *ite misa est*. Everything left on the table the ladies wrapped in their handkerchiefs and put in their pockets. Then the men pulled the dessert out of theirs: some, apples; others, cheese; some, olives; and one of them, who was the cock of the walk and the one who was fooling with the tailor's wife, brought out a half-pound of candied fruit. I really liked that way of keeping your meal so close, in case you need it. And I decided right then that I would put three or four pockets on the first pair of pants God would give me, and one of them would be of good leather, sewn up well enough to pour soup into. Because if those gentlemen who were so rich and important brought everything in their pockets and the ladies carried things that were cooked in theirs, I—who was only a whore's squire—could do it, too.

We servants went to eat, and there wasn't a damned thing left for us but soup and bread sops, and I was amazed to see that those ladies hadn't stuck that up their sleeves. We had barely begun when we heard a tremendous uproar in the hall where our masters were: they were referring to their mothers and discussing what sort of men their fathers had been. They left off talking and started swinging, and since variety is necessary in everything, there was hitting, slapping, pinching, kicking, and biting. They were grabbing one another's hair and pulling it out; they pounded each other so much you would think they were village boys in a religious procession. As far as I could find out, the quarrel broke out because some of the men didn't want to give or pay those women anything: they said that what the women had eaten was enough.

It happened that some law officers were coming up the street, and they heard the noise and knocked on the door and called out, "Open up, in the name of the law!"

When they heard this, some of the people inside ran one way, and others another way. Some left behind their cloaks, and others their swords; one left her shoes, another her veil. So they all disappeared, and each one hid as best he could. I had no reason to run away, so I stood there, and since I was the doorman, I opened the door so they wouldn't accuse me of resisting the law. The first officer who came in grabbed me by the collar and said I was under arrest. When they had me in their hands, they locked the door and went looking for the people who had been making all the noise. There was no bedroom, dressing room, basement, wine cellar, attic, or privy they didn't look in.

Since the officers didn't find anyone, they took my statement. I confessed from A to Z about everyone at the gathering and what they had done. The officers were amazed, since there were as many as I'd said, that not one of them had turned up. To tell the truth, I was amazed, too, because there had been twelve men and six women. Simple as I was, I told them (and I really believed it) that I thought all the people who had been there and made that noise were goblins. They laughed at me, and the constable asked his men who had been to the wine cellar if they'd looked everywhere carefully. They said they had, but not satisfied with this, he made them light a torch, and when they went in the door they saw a cask rolling around. The officers were terrified, and they started to run away, crying, "For God's sake, that fellow was right; there are nothing but spooks here!"

The constable was shrewder, and he stopped the officers, saying he wasn't afraid of the Devil himself. Then he went over to the cask and took off the lid, and inside he found a man and a woman. I don't want to tell how he found them so I won't offend the pure ears of the wholesome, high-minded reader. I will only say that the violence of their movements had made the cask roll around and was the cause of their misfortune and of showing in public what they were doing in private.

The officers pulled them out: he looked like Cupid

211

with his arrow, and she like Venus with her quiver. Both of them were as naked as the day they were born because, when the officers had knocked, they were in bed, kissing the holy relics, and with the alarm they didn't have a chance to pick up their clothes. And, to hide, they had climbed into that empty cask, where they continued their devout exercise.

Everyone stood there, agape at the beauty of these two. Then they threw two cloaks over them and put them in the custody of two officers, and they started looking for the others. The constable discovered a large earthen jug filled with oil, and inside he found a man fully dressed and up to his chest in the oil. As soon as they saw him he tried to jump out, but he didn't do it so agilely that the jug and he both didn't tip over. The oil flew out and covered the officers from head to foot, staining them without any respect. They stood there cursing the job and the whore who taught it to them. The oiled man saw that instead of grabbing him they were avoiding him like the plague, and he began to run away.

The constable shouted, "Stop him! Stop him!" But they all made room for him to go past. He went out a back door, pissing oil. What he wrung from his clothes he used to light the lamp of Our Lady of Afflictions for more than a month.

The law officers stood there, bathed in oil, and cursing whoever had brought them to the place. And so was I, because they said I was the pander and they were going to tar and feather me. They went out like fritters from the frying pan, leaving a trail wherever they walked. They were so irate that they swore to God and to the four holy Gospels that they would hang everyone they found. We prisoners trembled. They went over to the storeroom to look for the others. They went in, and from the top of a door a bag of flour was poured down on them, blinding them all.

They shouted, "Stop, in the name of the law!"

If they tried to open their eyes, they were immediately closed up with flour and water. The men holding us let go so they could help the constable who was yelling like a madman. They had hardly gotten inside when their eyes were covered with flour and water, too. They were wandering around like they were playing blindman's bluff, bumping into and clouting each other so much they broke their jaws and teeth.

When we saw that the officers were done in, we threw ourselves on them, and they attacked each other so wildly that they fell, exhausted, to the floor while blows and kicks rained and hailed down on top of them. Finally, they didn't shout or move any more than dead men. If one of them tried to open his mouth, it was immediately filled with flour and stuffed like a capon at a poultry farm. We bound their hands and feet and carried them along like hogs to the wine cellar. We threw them in the oil like fish to be fried, and they squirmed around like pigs in a mire. Then we locked up the doors, and we all went home.

The owner of that one had been in the country, and when he came back he found the doors locked and that no one answered when he called. A niece of his had loaned out his house for that feast, and she had gone back to her father's, afraid of what her uncle would do. The man had the doors unlocked, and when he saw his house sown with flour and anointed with oil, he flew into a rage and began shouting like a drunkard. He went to the wine cellar and found his oil spilled all over and the law officers wallowing in it. He was so angry to see his home devastated that he picked up a cudgel and hammered away on the constable and the officers, leaving them half dead. He called his neighbors over, and they helped drag them out to the street, and there boys threw mud, garbage, and filth on the officers and the constable. They were so full of flour no one recognized them. When they came to and found themselves in the street, free, they took to their heels. Then people could very well have said, "Stop the name of the law—it's running away!"

They left behind their cloaks, swords, and daggers and didn't dare go back for them so that no one would find out what had happened.

The owner of the house kept everything that was left behind as compensation for the damage that had been done. When I came out, ready to leave, I found a cloak that wasn't at all bad, and I took it and left mine there. I thanked God I had come out ahead this time (something new for me), since I was always getting the short end of things. I went to the house of the tailor's wife. I found the house in an uproar, and the tailor, her husband, was thrashing her with a stick for having come back alone without her veil or shoes and for running down the street with more than a hundred boys after her. I got there at just the right time because, as soon as the tailor saw me, he left his wife and sailed into me with a blow that finished off the few teeth I still had. Then he kicked me ten or twelve times in the belly, and that made me throw up what little I had eaten.

"You damned pimp!" he cried. "You mean you're not ashamed to come back to my house? I'll give you enough payment to settle every score—past and present."

He called his servants, and they brought a blanket and tossed me in it to their own pleasure, which was my grief. They left me for dead and laid me out on a bench like that. It was nighttime when I recovered my senses, and I tried to get up and walk. But I fell to the ground and broke an arm. The next morning I made my way to the door of a church, little by little, and there I begged with a pitiful voice from the people going in.

XV. *How Lazaro Became a Hermit*

Stretched out at the door of the church and reviewing my past life, I thought over the misery I had gone through from the day I began to serve the blind man down to the present. And I came to the conclusion that even if a man always rises early, that doesn't make dawn come any earlier, and if you work hard, that won't necessarily make you rich. And there's a saying that goes like this: "The early riser fails where God's help succeeds." I put myself in His hands so that the end would be better than the beginning and the middle had been.

A venerable, white-bearded hermit was next to me with his staff and a rosary in his hand, and at the end of the rosary hung a skull the size of a rabbit's.

When the good Father saw me in such misery he began to console me with kind, soft words, and he asked me where I was from and what had happened to bring me to such a pitiful state. I told him very briefly the long process of my bitter pilgrimage. He was astonished by what I said and showed his pity on me by inviting me to his hermitage. I accepted the invitation, and as well as I could (which wasn't painlessly) I reached the oratory with him, a few miles from there, in the side of a hill. Attached to it was a little house with a bedroom and a bed. In the patio was a cistern with fresh water, and it was used to water a garden—neater and better cared for than it was large.

very weighty witnesses for that because I looked more like a robber than an honest man. I immediately ran out of the hermitage to see if anyone was around who could be a witness to the old man's death. I looked everywhere and saw a flock of sheep nearby. I quickly (although painfully because of the beating I had gotten in the tailor skirmish) went toward it. I found six or seven shepherds and four or five shepherdesses resting in the shade of some willows, next to a shining, clear spring. The men were playing instruments and the women were singing. Some were capering, others were dancing. One of the men was holding a woman's hand, another was resting with his head on a woman's lap. And they were spending the heat of the day wooing each other with sweet words.

I ran up to them, terrified, and begged them to come with me right away because the old hermit was dying. Some of them came along while others stayed behind to watch over the sheep. They went into the hermitage and asked the good hermit if he was approaching death. He said, "Yes" (but that was a lie because he wasn't going anywhere: it was death that was approaching him, and against his will). When I saw that he was still in his rut about saying yes, I asked him if he wanted those shepherds to be witnesses for his last will and testament. He answered, "Yes."

I asked him if he was leaving me as his sole and lawful heir. He said, "Yes." I went on, asking if he acknowledged and confessed that everything he possessed or might possess he was leaving to me for services and other things he had received from me. Again he said, "Yes."

I was wishing that would be the last noise he'd make, but I saw that he still had a little breath left in him, and, so that he wouldn't do me any harm with it, I went on with my questions and had one of the shepherds write

down everything he said. The shepherd wrote on a wall with a piece of coal since we didn't have an inkwell or a pen.

I asked him if he wanted that shepherd to sign for him since he was in no position to do it himself, and he died, saying, "Yes, yes, yes."

We went ahead and buried him: we dug a grave in his garden (and did it all very quickly because I was afraid he might come back to life). I invited the shepherds to have something to eat; they didn't want to because it was time to feed their sheep. They went away, giving me their condolences.

I locked the door of the hermitage and walked all around the inside. I found a huge jug of good wine, another one full of oil, and two crocks of honey. He had two sides of bacon, a good quantity of jerked beef, and some dried fruit. I liked all of this very much, but it wasn't what I was looking for. I found his chests full of linens, and in the corner of one of them was a woman's dress. This surprised me, but what surprised me even more was that such a well-provided man wouldn't have any money. I went to the grave to ask him where he had put it.

It seemed to me that after I had asked him he answered: "You stupid fellow. Do you think that living out here in the country the way I do, at the mercy of thieves and bandits, I would keep it in a coffer where I'd be in danger of losing what I loved more than my own life?"

It was as if I had really heard this inspiration from his mouth, and it made me look around in every corner. But when I didn't find anything, I thought: If I were going to hide money here so no one else could find it, where would I put it? And I said to myself: In that altar. I went over to it and took the frontpiece of the altar off the pedestal, which was made of mud and clay. On one side I saw a crack that a silver coin could fit into. My blood started humming, and my heart began to flutter. I picked up a spade, and in less than two clouts I had half the altar on the ground, and I discovered the relics that were buried there. I found a jar full of coins. I counted them, and there were six hundred silver pieces. I was so over-joyed at the discovery that I thought I would die. I took the money out of there and dug a hole outside the her-mitage where I buried it so that if they turned me out of there I would have what I loved most outside.

When this was done I put on the hermit's garb and went into town to tell the prior of the brotherhood what had happened. But first I didn't forget to put the altar back the way it had been before. I found all the members of the brotherhood that the hermitage depended on to-gether there. The hermitage was dedicated to Saint Lazarus, and I thought that was a good sign for me. The members saw that I was already gray-haired and of an exemplary appearance, which is the most important part of positions like this. There was, however, one difficulty, and that was that I didn't have a beard. I had sheared it off such a short time before that it hadn't yet sprung back. But even with this, seeing by the shepherds' story that the dead man had left me as his heir, they turned the hermitage over to me.

About this business of beards, I remember what a friar told me once: In his order, and even in the most re-formed orders, they wouldn't make anyone a Superior unless he had a good beard. So it happened that some of them who were very capable of being in that position were excluded, and others who were woolly were given the position (as if good administration depended on hair and not on mature, capable understanding).

226

They warned me to live with the virtuous character and good reputation my predecessor had had, which was so great that everyone thought him a saint. I promised them I would live like a Hercules. They advised me to beg for alms only on Tuesdays and Saturdays because if I did it any other day the friars would punish me. I promised to do whatever they ordered me, and I especially didn't want to make enemies of them because I had previously experienced the taste of their hands. I began to beg for alms from door to door, with a low, humble, devout tone, the way I had learned in the blind man's school. I didn't do this because I was in need, but because it's the beggar's character that the more they have the more they ask for and the more pleasure they get from doing it. The people who heard me calling, "Alms for the candles of Saint Lazarus," and didn't recognize my voice, came out their doors and were astonished when they saw me. They asked me where Father Anselmo was (that was the name of the good old fellow). I told them he had died.

Some said, "May he rest in peace, he was such a good man."

Others said, "His soul is in the glory of God."

And some, "God bless the man whose life was like his: he ate nothing warm for six years."

And others, "He lived on bread and water."

Some of the foolish pious women got down on their knees and called on the name of Father Anselmo. One asked me what I had done with his garb. I told her I was wearing it. She took out some scissors, and without saying what she wanted she began to cut a piece from the first part she found, which was the crotch. When I saw her going after that part, I started to shout because I thought she was trying to castrate me.

228

When she saw how upset I was, she said, "Don't worry, brother. I want some relics from that blessed man, and I'll pay you for the damage to your robe."

"Oh," some said, "before six months are up they are certain to canonize him because he's performed so many miracles."

So many people came to see his grave that the house was always full, so I had to move the grave out to a shelter in front of the hermitage. From then on I didn't beg alms for the candles of Saint Lazarus, but for the blessed Father Anselmo. I have never understood this business of begging alms to light the candles of saints. But I don't want to continue on this note because it will sound bad. I wasn't at all interested in going to the city because I had everything I wanted at the hermitage. But, so no one could say I was rich and that's why I didn't go out begging alms, I went the next day, and there something happened to me that you'll find out if you read:

XVI. *How Lazaro Decided to Marry Again*

Good fortune has more value than horse or mule; for an unlucky man a sow will bear mongrels. Many times we see men rise from the dust of the earth, and without knowing how, they find themselves rich, honored, feared, and held in esteem. If you ask: Is this man wise? They'll tell you: Like a mule. Is he discreet? Like an ass. Does he have any good qualities? Those of a dunce. Well, how did he become so wealthy? They'll answer: It was the work of fortune.

Other people, on the contrary, who are discreet, wise, prudent, with many good qualities, capable of ruling a kingdom, find themselves beaten down, cast aside, poor, and made into a rag for the whole world. If you ask why, they'll tell you misfortune is always following them.

And I think it was misfortune that was always pursuing and persecuting me, giving the world a sample and example of what it could do. Because since the world was made there has never been a man attacked so much by this damned fortune as I was.

I was going down a street, begging alms for Saint Lazarus as usual, because in the city I didn't beg for the blessed Anselmo—that was only for the naive and ignorant who came to touch the rosary at his grave, where they said many miracles took place. I went up to a door, and giving my usual cry I heard some people call me from a stairway, "Why don't you come up, Father?

Come on, come on, what are you doing, staying down there?"

I started to climb the stairs, which were a little dark, and halfway up some women clasped me about the neck; others held onto my hands and stuck theirs in my pockets. And since we were in the dark, when one of the women reached for my pocket she hit upon my locket.

She gave a cry, and said, "What's this?"

I answered, "A little bird that will come out if you touch it."

They all asked why they hadn't seen me for a week. When we reached the top of the stairs they saw me in the light from the windows, and they stood there looking at each other like wooden puppets. Then they burst out laughing and laughed so hard I wondered if they would ever stop. None of them could talk. The first to speak was a little boy who said, "That isn't Daddy."

After those bursts of laughter had subsided a little, the women (there were four of them) asked me what saint I was begging alms for. I told them for Saint Lazarus.

"Why are you begging for him?" they asked. "Isn't Father Anselmo feeling well?"

"Well?" I answered. "He doesn't feel bad at all because a week ago he died."

When they heard that, they burst into tears, and if the laughter had been loud before, their wailing was even louder. Some of them screamed, others pulled their hair, and with all of them carrying on together, their music was as grating as a choir of hoarse nuns.

One of them said, "What will I do. Oh, me! Here I am without a husband, without protection, without consolation. Where will I go? Who will help me? What bitter news! What a misfortune!"

Another was lamenting with these words: "Oh, my

son-in-law and my lord! How could you leave without saying good-by? Oh, my little grandchildren, now you are orphans, abandoned! Where is your good father?"

The children were carrying the soprano of that unharmonious music. They were all crying and shouting, and there was nothing but weeping and wailing. When the water of that great deluge let up a little they asked me how and what he had died from. I told them about it and about the will he had made, leaving me as his lawful heir and successor. And then it all started. The tears turned into rage, their wails into curses, and their sighs into threats.

"You're a thief, and you killed him to rob him, but you won't get away with it," said the youngest girl. "That hermit was my husband, and these three children are his, and if you don't give us all his property, we'll have you hanged. And if the law doesn't do it there are swords and daggers to kill you a thousand times if you had a thousand lives."

I told them there were reliable witnesses there when he'd made his will.

"That's a pack of lies," they said. "Because the day you say he died, he was here, and he told us he didn't have any company."

When I realized that he hadn't given his will to a notary, and that those women were threatening me, along with the experience I'd had with the law and with lawsuits, I decided to be courteous to them. I wanted to try to get hold of what I would lose if it came into the hands of the law. Besides, the new widow's tears had touched my heart. So I told them to calm down, they wouldn't lose anything with me; that if I had accepted the inheritance, it was only because I didn't know the dead man was married—in fact, I had never heard of hermits being married.

Putting aside all their sadness and melancholy, they began to laugh, saying that it was easy to see that I was new and inexperienced in that position since I didn't know that when people talked about solitary hermits they didn't mean they had to give up the company of women. In fact, there wasn't one who didn't have at least one woman to spend some time with after he was through contemplating, and together they would engage in active exercises—so sometimes he would imitate Martha and other times Mary. Because they were people who had a better understanding of the will of God they knew that He doesn't want man to be alone. So, like obedient sons, they have one or two women they maintain, even if it is by alms.

"And this one was especially obedient because he maintained four: this poor widow, me (her mother), these two (her sisters), and these three children who are his sons (or, at least, he considered them his)."

Then the woman they called his wife said she didn't want them to call her the widow of that rotten old carcass who hadn't remembered her the day he died, and that she would swear those children weren't his, and from then on she was renouncing the marriage contract.

"What is that marriage contract?" I asked.

The mother said, "The marriage contract I drew up when my daughter married that ungrateful wretch was this. . . . But before I tell that, I'll have to give you the background.

"I was living in a village called Duennas, twenty miles from here. I was left with these three daughters from three different fathers who were, as near as I can figure out, a monk, an abbot, and a priest (I have always been devoted to the Church). I came to this city to live, to get away from all the gossiping that always goes on in small towns. Everyone called me the ecclesiastical widow because, unfortunately, all three men had died. And even though others came to take their place, they were only mediocre men of lower positions, and not being content with the sheep, they went after the young lambs.

"Well, when I saw the obvious danger we were in and that what we earned wouldn't make us rich, I called a halt and set up my camp here. And with the fame of the three girls, they swarmed here like bees to honey. And the ones I favored most of all were the clergy because they were silent, rich, family men, and understanding. Among them, the Father of Saint Lazarus came here to beg alms. And when he saw this girl, she went to his heart, and in his saintliness and simplicity he asked me to give her to him as his wife.

"So I did, under the following conditions and articles:

"First, he would have to maintain our household, and what we could earn ourselves would go for our clothes and our savings.

"Second, because he was a little decrepit, if my daughter should at any time take on an ecclesiastical assistant, he would be as quiet as if he were at mass.

"Third, that all the children she would have, he would have to take as his own and promise them what he did or might possess. And if my daughter didn't have any children, he would make her his sole and lawful heir.

"Fourth, that he would not come into our house when he saw a jug, a pot, or any other vessel in the window because that was a signal that there wasn't any place for him.

"Fifth, that when he was in the house and someone else came, he would have to hide where we told him until the other person left.

"Sixth and last, that twice a week he would have to bring us some friend or acquaintance who would provide us with a great feast.

"These are the articles of the marriage contract," she continued, "that that poor wretch and my daughter swore to. The marriage took place without their having to go to a priest because he said it wasn't necessary. The most important part, he said, was for there to be mutual agreement about their wishes and intentions."

I was astonished at what that second Celestina* was telling me and at the marriage contract she had used to marry her daughter. I was confused: I didn't know what to say. But they lit up the road to my desire because the young widow grabbed me around the neck and said, "If that poor fellow had had the face of this angel, I would really have loved him."

And with that she kissed me. After that kiss something started up in me—I don't know what it was—and I began to burn inside. I told her that if she wanted to stop being a widow and take me as her own, I would keep not only the contract of the old man but any other articles she wanted to add. They were happy with that and said they only wanted me to give them everything in the hermitage for safekeeping. I promised to do that, but I intended to hold back the money in case I ever needed it.

The marriage ceremony was to take place the next morning, and that afternoon they sent a cart to take away everything but the nails that held the place together. They didn't overlook the altarcloth or the saint's clothing. I was so bedazzled that if they had asked me for the phoenix or the waters from the river Styx, I

---

* The unforgettable and infamous old bawd of the Spanish masterpiece *La Celestina* (ca. 1492)—TRANSLATOR.

would have given it to them. The only thing they left me was a poor piece of sackcloth to lie on like a dog. When that lady—my future wife—who had come with the cart saw that there wasn't any money she was angry. Because the old man had told her that he had some, but he didn't say where. She asked me if I knew where the treasure was. I told her I didn't. Being astute, she took me by the hand so we could go looking for it. She led me to every corner and crevice in the hermitage, including the base of the altar. And when she saw that it had recently been fixed, she became very suspicious.

She hugged and kissed me and said, "My life, tell me where that money is so we can have a happy wedding with it."

I still denied that I knew anything about any money. She took my hand again and led me outside to walk around the hermitage, watching my face all the time. When we got to the place where I had hidden it, my eyes darted there. She called her mother and told her to look under a stone I had put on top of it. She found it, and I found my death.

She feigned a smile and said, "Look. With this we'll have a wonderful life."

She caressed me over and over again, and then, since it was getting late, they went back to the city, telling me to come to their house in the morning and we would have the happiest wedding there had ever been. I hope to God it's full of roses and not thorns, I said to myself.

All that night I was caught between the hope that those women wouldn't trick me and the fear that they would, although I thought it was impossible for there to be any trickery in a woman who had such a good face. I was expecting to enjoy that little pigeon, so the night seemed like a year to me.

2 3 7

It wasn't yet dawn when I closed up my hermitage and went to get married (as if that were nothing), not remembering that I already was. I arrived just as they were getting up. They welcomed me so joyfully that I really thought I was fortunate, and with all my fears gone, I began to act right at home. We ate so well and the food was so good that I thought I was in paradise. They had invited six or seven lady friends of theirs in to eat. After dinner we danced, and although I didn't know how, they made me do it. To see me dancing with my hermit's garb on was a sight.

When evening came, after a good supper and even better drinking, they took me into a nicely decorated room where there was a good bed. They told me to get into it. While my wife was undressing, a maid pulled off my shoes and stockings and told me to take off my shirt because, for the ceremonies that would take place, I had to be completely naked. I obeyed her. Then all the women came into my room with my wife behind them, dressed in a shift, and one of the women was carrying the train.

The first thing they made me do was kiss her arse, saying that was the first ceremony. After this, four of them grabbed me—two by the feet and two by the arms—and with great care they tied four ropes to me and fastened the ends to the four bedposts. I was like a Saint Andrew on the Cross. They all began to laugh when they saw my jack-in-the-box, and they threw a jar of cold water on it. I gave out a terrible shriek, but they told me to be quiet, or else. They took a huge pot of hot water and stuck my head in it. I was burning up, and the worst part was that if I tried to shout they whipped me. So I decided to let them do what they wanted. They sheared off my beard, my hair, my eyebrows and eyelashes.

"Be patient," they said. "The ceremonies will be over soon, and you will enjoy what you desire so much."

I begged them to let me go because my appetite had gone away.

They cut away the hair from my crotch, and one of them who was the boldest took out a knife and said to the others, "Hold him down tight, and I'll cut off his plums so he'll never again feel tempted to get married. This hermit thought everything we told him was the gospel truth. Why, it wasn't even the epistle. He trusted women, and now he'll see what the payment is."

When I saw my precious stones in danger, I pulled so hard that I broke a rope and one of the bedposts. I grabbed my jewels with one hand and clutched them so that even if they had cut off my fingers, they couldn't have gotten to them. So they wouldn't break the bed completely apart, they untied me and wrapped me in a sheet. Then they gave me such a blanketing that they left me half dead.

"These, my dear sir," they said, "are the ceremonies our wedding begins with. If you want to come back tomorrow, we'll finish the rest."

The four of them picked me up and carried me far away from their house. They put me down in the middle of a street. And when morning came, boys began to chase and beat me, so that, to get away from their hands, I ran into a church next to the high altar where they were saying mass. When the priests saw that figure, which must have looked like the devil they paint at Saint Michael's feet, they began to run away, and I was right behind them, trying to get away from the boys.

The people in the church were shouting. Some said, "Look! There goes the devil!" Others said, "Look at the madman!"

I was shouting, too, but that I wasn't a devil or a madman; I was only a poor fellow who looked like that because of my sins. At this, they all quieted down. The priests went back to their mass, and the sacristan gave me a cover from a tomb to wrap myself in. I went over to a corner and thought about the reverses of fortune and that no matter where you go bad luck is there. So I decided to stay in that church for the rest of my life. And if past misfortunes were any indication, my life wouldn't be a long one. Besides, I wanted to save the priests the trouble of going somewhere else to get me when I was dead.

This, dear reader, is all of the Second Part of the life of Lazarillo. I have neither added nor subtracted anything from what I heard my great-grandmother tell. If you enjoyed it, wait for the Third Part: you will find it no less enjoyable.

Bibliography

Ayala, Francisco. "El 'Lazarillo': Nuevo examen de algunos aspectos." *Cuadernos Américos* 150 (1967): 209–35.

Bataillon, Marcel. *El sentido del Lazarillo de Tormes.* Paris-Toulouse: Librarie des Editions Espagnoles, 1954.

———. *Novedad y fecundidad del Lazarillo de Tormes.* Translated by Luis Cortés Vázquez. Madrid: Ediciones Anaya, 1968.

Boehmer, Eduard. "Juan de Luna." *Zeitschrift für vergleichende Literaturgeschichte* 15, no. 6 (1904): 423–30.

Caso González, José. *La vida de Lazarillo de Tormes. Boletín de la Real Academia Española.* Anejo 17. (Critical edition, with a preface and notes.) Madrid, 1967.

Castillo, Homero. "El comportamiento de Lázaro de Tormes." *Hispania* 33, no. 4 (1950): 304–10.

Castro, Américo. *El pensamiento de Cervantes. Revista de filología española.* Anejo 6. Madrid, 1925.

———. *Hacia Cervantes.* Madrid: Taurus Ediciones, 1957.

Chandler, Frank Wadleigh. *The Literature of Roguery.* 2 vols. Boston and New York: Houghton, Mifflin and Co., 1907.

———. *Romances of Roguery.* New York: Burt Franklin, 1961.

Chaytor, H. J. *La vida de Lazarillo de Tormes.* (Introduction and notes in English.) Manchester, England: University Press, 1922.

Cossío, José María de. "Las continuaciones del Lazarillo de Tormes." *Revista de filología española* 25, no. 3 (1941): 514–23.

De Haan, Fonger. *An Outline of the History of the Novela Picaresca in Spain.* The Hague and New York: Martinus Nijhoff, 1903.

Díaz-Plaja, Guillermo. *Lazarillo de Tormes: Vida del Buscon don Pablos.* (Preliminary study.) Mexico: Editorial Porrua, 1965.

Gilman, Stephen. "The Death of Lazarillo." *PMLA* 81, no. 3 (1966): 149–66.

González Palencia, Angel. *Del "Lazarillo" a Quevedo.* Madrid, 1946.

Guillén, Claudio. "La disposición temporal del *Lazarillo de Tormes." Hispanic Review* 25, no. 4 (1957): 264–79.

———. *Lazarillo de Tormes and El Abencerraje.* (Introduction and notes in English.) New York: Dell Publishing Co., 1966.

Hesse, Everett W., and Williams, Harry F. *La vida de Lazarillo de Tormes.* (Introduction in English by Américo Castro.) Madison, Wisconsin: University of Wisconsin Press, 1961.

Jones, R. O. *La vida de Lazarillo de Tormes.* (Introduction and notes in English.) Manchester, England: University Press, 1963.

Laurenti, Joseph L. *Estudio crítico de la Segunda Parte de la Vida de Lazarillo de Tormes de Juan de Luna.* Mexico: Ediciones de Andrea, 1965.

Lázaro Carreter, Fernando. "Construcción y sentido del *Lazarillo de Tormes." Ábaco: Estudios sobre literatura española* 1 (1969): 45–134.

Luna, Juan de. *La Segunda Parte de la Vida de Lazarillo de Tormes.* (Introduction and notes in English by Elmer Richard Sims.) Austin, Texas: University of Texas, 1928.

Piper, Anson C. "The 'Breadly Paradise' of Lazarillo de Tormes." *Hispania* 44, no. 2 (1961): 269–71.

Rico, Francisco. "Problemas del 'Lazarillo.'" *Boletín de la Real Academia Española* 46 (1966): 277–96.

Rudder, Robert S. "La segunda parte de 'Lazarillo de Tormes': La originalidad de Juan de Luna." *Estudios filológicos* 6 (1970): 87–112.

Tarr, F. Courtney. "Literary and Artistic Unity in the *Lazarillo de Tormes.*" *PMLA* 42, no. 2 (1927): 404–21.

Wardropper, Bruce. "El trastorno de la moral en el *Lazarillo.*" *Nueva Revista de Filología Hispánica* 15 (1961): 441–47.

Willis, Raymond S. "Lazarillo and the Pardoner: The Artistic Necessity of the Fifth Tractado." *Hispanic Review* 27, no. 3 (1959): 267–79.